STEEL
BOAT
BUILDING

STEEL
BOAT
BUILDING
From plans to bare hull

▽

Volume 1

Thomas E. Colvin

INTERNATIONAL MARINE
PUBLISHING COMPANY
Camden, Maine

©1985 by International Marine Publishing Company

Typeset by The Key Word, Inc., Belchertown, Massachusetts
Printed and bound by Fairfield Graphics, Fairfield, Pennsylvania

Second printing 1986

Published by International Marine Publishing Company
21 Elm Street, Camden, Maine 04843
(207) 236-4342

Library of Congress Cataloging in Publication Data

Colvin, Thomas E.
   Steel boatbuilding.

   Includes index.
   1. Steel boats.   2. Boatbuilding   I. Title.
VM321.C68 1985   623.8'207   84-48520
ISBN 0-87742-189-7 (v. 1)
ISBN 0-87742-203-6 (v. 2)

$\bigtriangledown$

CONTENTS

$\bigtriangledown$

PREFACE

I have prepared this work with the hope that it will become a useful reference for those designing, building, repairing, and maintaining steel vessels, whether they be used for yachting or commercial purposes. The scope of the book has been limited to vessels of 25 to 79 feet in length. Although it is indeed possible to construct in steel a vessel smaller than 25 feet, rather specific hull forms and techniques are involved. For vessels longer than 79 feet, various agencies—the American Bureau of Shipping, Lloyd's, Bureau Veritas, and others—promulgate rules and regulations that are normally followed, and techniques of construction more akin to shipbuilding are used, for which there are many standard texts.

The chapters are arranged in a logical sequence from planning to completion, having due regard to differences in hull shape and displacement. The distinct differences as well as the similarities among flat-bottom, V-bottom, multi-chine, and round-bottom constructions are covered, and the effect of size upon each is discussed. Skills necessary for construction in steel and the ways to acquire these skills are discussed in a positive way, to encourage those involved in building steel vessels to depend on their own abilities.

With the increasing popularity of steel construction, builders and owners must realize that a steel vessel has a long life and low maintenance *if* it is properly thought out and built. Steel must be understood from its making to its end use. If these caveats are ignored, then nothing but monstrosities will result. A properly designed and built metal structure is functional, light, and strong. If it encompasses all of these, it will also be beautiful. This is not to imply that styling cannot also be added, but in many cases this will be gilding the lily.

This book does not replace *Boatbuilding With Steel* by Gilbert C. Klingel (International Marine Publishing Co., 1973), a book to which I contributed a chapter on building with aluminum. It does, however, go into greater detail for the builder and owner. The professional and amateur alike will, I hope, find their needs well served.

$$\triangledown$$

INTRODUCTION
How to Use This Book

In ship and boat building there are numerous exceptions to any presumed logic; therefore, the reading of *Steel Boatbuilding* may commence wherever the reader's interest lies, always bearing in mind that each chapter, while it stands alone, is *always* related to the whole. I would suggest that the first-time builder of a steel vessel make a general perusal of the entire text in the order it was written, and then follow with a thorough study of individual chapters as the need to know becomes imperative. To clutter one's mind with too many facts at one time is often discouraging, unless those facts can be related to a specific application.

If you are anxious to start with the actual sequence of construction, then I would suggest that the best place to begin is Chapter 9, where I commence the construction of a pinky schooner. Chapter 15 completes the steelwork on the Pinky, and Volume 2 gives the additional information—including launching procedures—needed to make the vessel ready for sea. Chapters 1 through 8 of Volume 1 are general chapters that a builder will need to read eventually in order to understand the "what" and the "why" of what follows.

Volume 2 is also a reference for those who are already sailing steel vessels, or are contemplating alterations to a steel vessel, or plan to purchase a hull and do the remainder of the work themselves. One might suppose that such people have no need to know what is in Volume 1, but that is not so; lofting and template making as described in Chapter 7 of this volume will be needed for much of the joinerwork, sparmaking, and rigging, and the information given in Chapter 2 about materials will aid in selecting the correct alloys for a particular application. The list of suppliers in Chapter 3 may save hours of time that might otherwise be spent in finishing the vessel. Major alterations to a hull can be as extensive as building an entire vessel.

The decision to expand the scope of *Steel Boatbuilding* into two volumes was based on my desire, as well as that of my editor and publisher, to offer a work that is as complete and specific as possible and will not leave the builder/owner dangling in a void of omission. As an inveterate reader of labels, I have the need to know specifics as well as generalities, and so should you. It has never been my intention, however, to write a "how-to-do-it" type of book, so elemental and detailed that the builder's every motion is described. My intention is and has been to guide an individual through the construction of a steel vessel, and to explain, within reason, the whys and wherefores, always leaving him the option of doing it his own way. You and I realize that there are only three ways of doing anything—the right way, the wrong way, and my way!

The Pinky whose construction begins in Chapter 9 is a working vessel that was designed for a specific purpose; it is not a yacht, but it could be one. The complete plans are included in the text as illustrations. If one wishes to build this vessel and is content to work from the small-scale plans that appear in the book, there is no reason not to do so, since my office plans to a larger scale are exactly the same. I personally think that working with small-scale drawings to avoid paying the royalty to a designer is foolish, because the builder then forfeits the right to free consultation by mail, as will any subsequent owner of the vessel. I will not entertain any correspondence concerning the Pinky or any other design if that correspondence is not part of my normal office interaction with clients. Since I live aboard my vessel and am more often than not outside United States waters, a large volume of correspondence would be too time-consuming for me, and the postage would be costly. The usual procedure in writing books on boatbuilding and designing is to fragment the material so that no single design is set forth in its entirety. I have found that such texts are often difficult not only for the layman but also for the professional, because there is no way to relate the information within a specific context, but only in generalities.

What it all boils down to is this: *If* you plan to go to sea in a vessel you build or have built, you need to know as much as possible about her construction, her limitations if any, and how to care for her properly; otherwise, needless anxiety and expense can result.

Thomas E. Colvin
aboard the junk *K'ung Fu-Tse*
May 1985

1
▽

PLANS
FOR
STEEL VESSELS

The history of boatbuilding and designing is a fascinating subject as well as a useful one, since vessel designs and construction techniques today benefit from what was learned by trial and error yesterday. To say that progress has always been made would be erroneous, however, for it seems that each generation discards many lessons as having been handed down from rather ignorant forefathers who "did not have the advantages of our modern technology," and we spend much of our lives reinventing what those before us knew and practiced instinctively. It seems appropriate, then, to begin this book with a backward glance at the skills and methods of our predecessors.

The ancient and perhaps primitive builder was also the designer in that the eventual shape of the hull evolved directly from his mental picture of what was necessary to meet specific requirements. We cannot say for sure that he did not construct a model, but we do know that the use of models as decorative objects certainly preceded their use as an aid to design. More recently, from the need to delineate the shape of the model, drafting methods were devised, and these permit present-day designers to dispense with models altogether when defining the shape of the hull. Designing solely by models, however, cannot be discarded as decadent or obsolete. In my own lifetime, I have known builders who could neither read nor write, yet could carve a model of a proposed vessel and then, without benefit of refined offsets, build it full size, preserving its form and proportions. Others had mastered one of several techniques for taking off the half-breadths from a model, enabling them to prepare a table of offsets to be used for the construction of the vessel. What these men lacked in drafting skills was compensated by an acute visual sense of proportion and form.

Modeling by a skilled craftsman is a very accurate method of designing the hull of a vessel, and it has the advantage of producing a three-dimensional form that can be judged from an infinite number of angles. Results of modifications are instantly visible. In the not-too-distant past there were many designers who worked this way, and many of their vessels became famous. The models most commonly used for this purpose were known as half-models. They were made up from a number of planks of wood, known as "lifts," which were pegged together prior to carving. Frame or mold lines were marked on the back of the model, and when the model was completed, the pegs were removed and the frame lines were traced across the top face of each lift and measured. This produced the half-breadth for that horizontal plane; once corrected for scale, these half-breadths could be used to loft the sections full size. A lines drawing could also result by laying down each lift on paper and scribing its outline, giving the plan view of the lift or level line. The whole model pegged back together gave the profile and the ticking-off of the lift spacing. The body plan was drawn from the half-breadths. Most of the better builders developed lines drawings, for this permitted calculations for displacement and other hydrostatic data. (It should be noted that the lifts seldom represented actual waterlines; they were merely lines parallel to the keel or rabbet.)

While an accurate half-model represented a number of hours of labor that might otherwise have been spent in actual construction, almost without exception this time was more than compensated during the actual construction and ordering of material. When additional offsets were needed for buttocks and diagonals to further define a frame shape on the mold loft floor, they were measured directly from the body plan after this was drawn, projected, and faired longitudinally on the floor. The buttocks and diagonals were not always transferred back to the original lines drawing, however—hence the frequent discrepancy between "as drawn" and "as built."

Another use of the half-model involved cutting it across at the various sections, then measuring these sections at the lifts to obtain the required offsets for each station. When traced, these produced a body plan at the same scale as the model. No profile or plan view drawings were produced, but the body plan permitted the designer at least to establish cargo hold and between-decks arrangements, taking much of the "by guess and by golly" out of building. With this method, too, customs house tonnage could be manipulated to the advantage of the owner. Once the model had been treated in this way, though, about all it was good for was the firebox, since the storage of the numerous pieces was troublesome.

A third method was to take the sections off the model directly. This could be accomplished in several ways, the most popular being lead strips molded to contour or a vertically sited pantograph. The latter method would permit the sectional outline to be reproduced directly on paper or another medium.

A half-model usually represented the inside of the planking, which varied in thickness from the garboards to the sheer strake, especially in the larger vessels. The modeler was often also the builder, and working directly with the frames and not the skin saved time and labor when lofting.

Today, the preparation of a vessel's lines is done by direct drafting, which is fast and accurate for most hull forms. The half-model is still used, however, to lay out plating for metal vessels and planking for wooden vessels, since there is no easy method of expanding the entire shell of a vessel with drafting methods. These models are glued together rather than pegged. Models are also frequently used for precise material take-off when the vessel is to be built in a remote area where freight costs and delivery of materials have a greater impact on completion than they would in industrial centers. A builder often requires a working model in order to plan hawse pipes, anchor pockets, davits, and catheads, and also certain complex cargo-handling arrangements such as ramps, heavy (jumbo) lift booms, new net handling gear, and other details. This is less expensive than a full-size mockup or a "by guess and by golly" attack of the actual item. A first-time builder will find it advantageous to construct a frame-and-plate model using a modelmaker's balsa sheets for the plates, or urethane foam cut to the shape of each transverse section and glued together and faired longitudinally. The length of each section equals a frame space (see Figure 1). This gives a three-dimensional form in small scale that duplicates the full-size vessel.

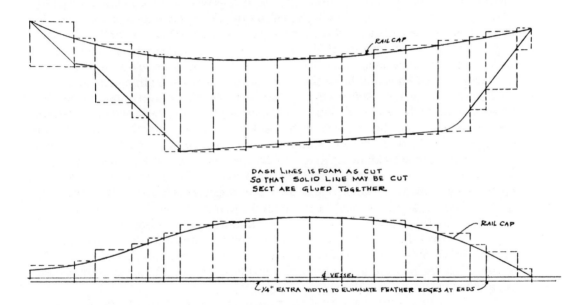

Figure 1. *A model made from urethane foam cut to the section shapes.*

THE PLANS PACKAGE

The plans for vessels constructed in metal are always drawn to the inside of all shell plating, the underside of all decks, and the underside of the keel—in other words, they are drawn to the molded lines of the vessel. The dimensions given in the table of offsets are therefore true dimensions, and there is no allowance for the shell thickness.

Offsets are given in feet, inches, and eighths of an inch (F-I-E) and, if they are "returned" (that is, corrected after fairing on the mold loft), a "+" is sometimes added to indicate that the loftsman should add ¹⁄₁₆ inch to the offset indicated (F-I-E+). Except in rare instances, other measurements are given in inches and fractions of an inch when less than 24 inches, and in feet, inches, and fractions of an inch thereafter. The zero is always included when the measurement is a foot plus a fraction of an inch, such as 6'–0¾".

The metric system is by far the easiest, fastest, and most accurate method of dimensioning, and is used in most boatbuilding countries. Some plans contain both systems. However, we in the United States, I suppose, will continue with the old system until absolutely forced to change.

The designer has an obligation to furnish enough detailed drawings so that the builder can properly construct the vessel full size. The number of drawings necessary will vary according to the complexity of the vessel's structure, rig, machinery, and outfit. The scale to which the plans are drawn will also have a direct bearing on the total number of drawings required, as will the vessel's intended use— that is, yacht, cargo, fishing, passenger, sail, motor, or a combination of several of the above. It is *not* the designer's duty to draw every nut and bolt, nor to endlessly detail a structure. He must depend on "ordinary practice" and the common sense of the builder. On the other hand, this does not license him just to draw up a few sketches and meaningless lines and hope that the builder will do everything correctly.

There is little if any difference in detail between plans drawn for the general professional and the amateur—either of whom may be using the designer's plans for the first time—since the facilities of the backyard builder, though limited, may be equal to or better than those of some one-man-shop professionals. Plans are not meant to teach boatbuilding but to tell the builder how a particular vessel should be constructed. For this reason, I have incorporated in this book many details not customarily shown on stock plans. Just the same, a designer selling plans to backyard builders should consider the limited equipment available to them, and not offer designs that require an investment of hundreds of thousands of dollars for bending and roll-forming machines, machine shops, and foundries to build one vessel. (This is not an idle statement, since such plans do exist and are offered to the amateur builder. If I have done my work well, this book will enable you to recognize such plans when you see them.)

Plans furnished by the designer are drawn to various scales to fit his office's standard sheets, if a standard size has been established. The common scales are 1 inch, ¾ inch, ½ inch, ⅜ inch and ¼ inch equaling one foot. Down to a scale of ⅜ inch equals 1 foot (¹⁄₃₂ of the full-size vessel), it is possible to read the scale to the nearest ⅛ inch in the full-size vessel. To save wear on the eyes, however, most designers prefer to prepare their lines and working drawings to a scale of ½ inch equals one foot or larger. My own practice in small craft design is to keep the drawings within a 40-inch length; thus, I will use ¾ inch equals 1 foot for vessels 53 feet or less, and ½ inch equals 1 foot for larger vessels up to 80 feet. As a builder I prefer the ¾-inch drawings, since ¹⁄₁₆ inch will equal 1 inch full size, affording a quick scale by which to check a dimension in the yard. Sail plans and outboard profiles are normally drawn to half the size of the lines plan. Details may be drawn at any scale, but usually double that of the drawing. For maximum clarity, it is often necessary to draw a detail at half or full size.

When the drawings are prepared to a scale of ¾ inch or larger, most of the details will appear with sufficient clarity on any section to that scale, and extra detailing will be minimal. If enlarged details of a particular item are needed, there is usually space to show it either on that drawing, or referenced to another drawing where space is available. When drawn to a smaller scale, plans will need to include more detail drawings to amplify the standard set. Some designers have one or more standard sheets that take care of most of the details they normally use. In any case, the thoughtful designer will avoid cluttering up a sheet with so much detail or writing that the basic drawing becomes obscured.

To construct a metal yacht you would need the following plans:

1) Sail and Spars (Outboard Profile)
2) Lines and Offsets
3) Construction Plan
4) Construction Sections
5) Interior Arrangement

Piping, wiring, and machinery installation drawings are not customary in yacht designs, especially stock plans, because *any* change in type and number of fixtures would require a modification of the drawing, as would a different engine or any change in interior arrangement. Arrangement plans are really only intended to offer guidance, and you will rarely see identical interiors in custom and semicustom sister ships. In custom design work these plans may be furnished. As a builder, however, I think they are a waste of time, because you have to get down inside the actual hull before you can determine the best method of running wiring, piping, and other systems properly.

Commercial vessels subject to a classification society such as the U.S. Coast Guard, the Board of Trade (Great Britain), or one of the numerous other bodies around the world having similar functions, or carrying not more than 150 passengers, will need the following plans in addition to those required for yachts:

6) Midship Scantling Section
7) Arrangement of Decks
8) Machinery Installation
9) Electrical Installation
10) Fuel Tanks
11) Piping System
12) Hull Penetrations and Shell Connections

Vessels carrying more than 150 passengers or over 100 gross tons will also need:

13) Curves of Form (Hydrostatic Curves)

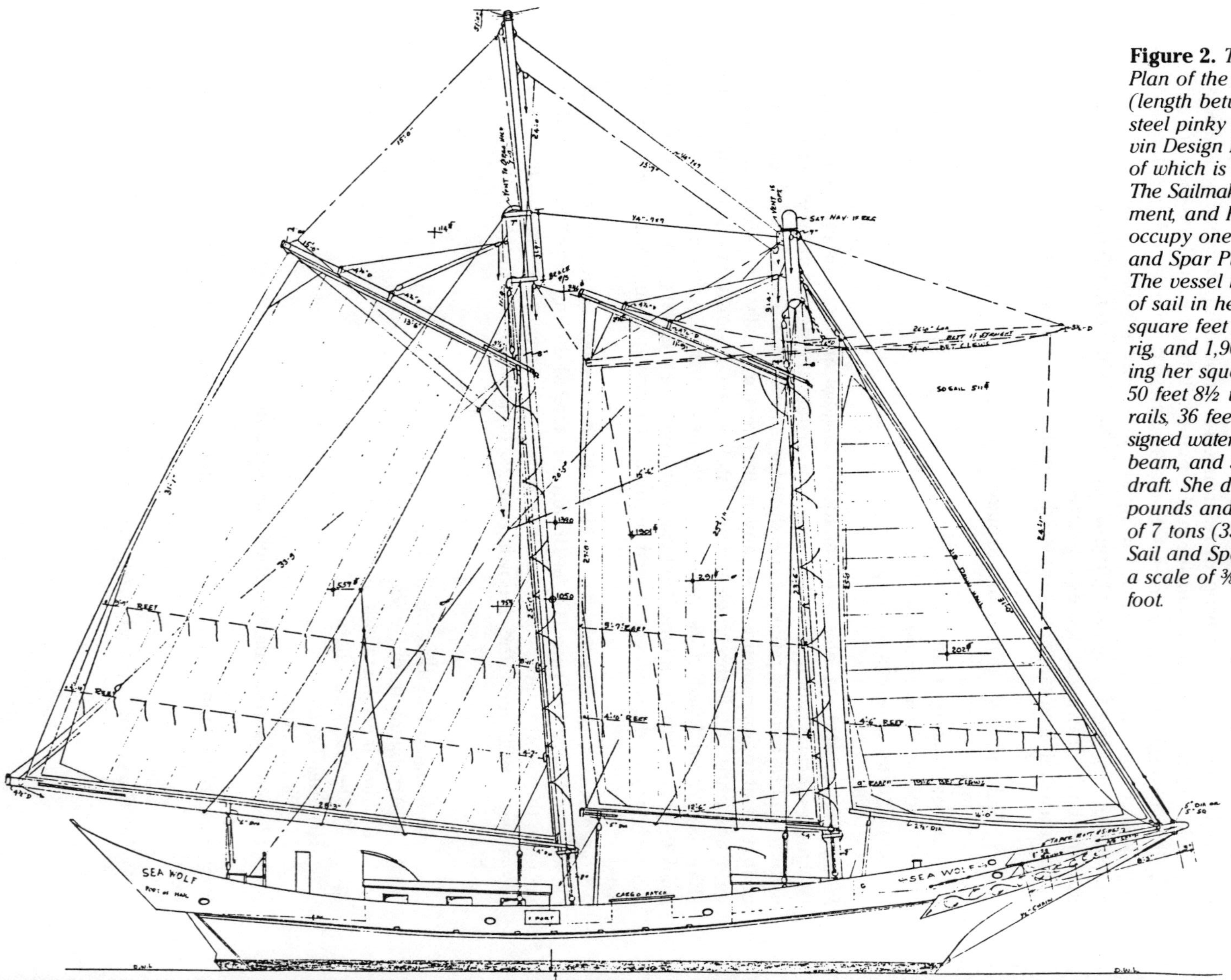

Figure 2. *The Sail and Spar Plan of the 42-foot 7½-inch (length between perpendiculars) steel pinky cargo schooner, Colvin Design No. 169, the building of which is described in this text. The Sailmaker, Sparmaker, Equipment, and Rigger's Notes, which occupy one corner of the Sail and Spar Plan, are also shown. The vessel has 1,050 square feet of sail in her three lowers, 1,390 square feet in her fore-and-aft rig, and 1,901 square feet including her squaresail. She measures 50 feet 8½ inches long over the rails, 36 feet 1 inch on her designed waterline, 12 feet in molded beam, and 5 feet 9 inches in draft. She displaces 38,000 pounds and has a hold capacity of 7 tons (350 cubic feet). The Sail and Spar Plan was drawn to a scale of ⅜ inch equals one foot.*

SAIL MAKERS NOTES:

1. SAILS TO BE TRIPLE STITCHED 13⁹ VIVATEX OR 7.75 #3 DACRON.
2. SAILS TO HAVE HAND SEWEN BOLT ROPES ALL AROUND ~ JIB WILL HAVE A ROPE LUFF.
3. DIMENSIONS ARE PIN TO PIN FULLY STRETCHED ~ MAST HOOPS ARE 11" DIA IF USED OR LACING AS SHOWN - OWNERS OPTION.
4. N8 BATTENS IN ANY SAIL
5. CLOTHS ARE FALSE SEAMED IF VIVATEX OR 18' WIDE DACRON CLOTH TO BE USED
6. TOP SAILS TO BE 5⁹ DACRON
7. SQ. SAIL TO BE 6#3 DACRON.
8. REEFS ARE TO BE IN BANDS & NETTLES FITTED
9. GROMMETS AT EACH SEAM ON FOOT & HEAD.

SPAR MAKERS NOTES:

1. MASTS MAY BE OF WOOD, ALU. ALLOY OR STEEL TUBING - BOOMS & GAFFS ARE WOOD OR ALU. ALLOY.
2. MAIN MAST - IS 40'5" ABV D.WL & 43'9"LOA~ 8" SCH 40 ALU. ALLOY PIPE (6061-T6), 9"DIA DOUG FIR, OR 8" STEEL TUBE 10 GA WALL THICKNESS
3. MAIN TOP MAST - 14'0" LOA - 4" SCH 40 ALU. ALLOY PIPE OR 4¾" DIA. DOUG FIR.
4. MAIN BOOM - 29'7" LOA TO MAST - DEDUCT FOR CLAPPER ~ DOUG FIR
5. MAIN GAFF - 14'3" LOA TO MAST - DEDUCT FOR CLAPPER - DOUG FIR
6. FORE MAST - 39'5" ABV D.WL - LOA IS LESS AS PER MAST STEP
7. FORE BOOM - 13'2" LOA TO MAST - DEDUCT FOR CLAPPER ~ D. FIR.
8. FORE GAFF - 12'4" LOA TO MAST - DEDUCT FOR CLAPPER ~ D. FIR.
9. JIB CLUB - 7'0" LOA ~ DOUG. FIR.
10. BOWSPRIT - 8"x 8" x 18'6 STEEL TUBE OR 8"DIA STEEL TUBE 10.G MIN 7GA MAX
11. YARD - 6" STEEL TUBE - 11 GA - TAPERED
12. WISKER - 5'0" LOA. 1½" SCH. 80. PIPE ~ END CLIPS 1"x 1¼" F.BAR
13. THUMBS - EYES - ET. & ALU. FT (ALU. SPARS) STEEL FT (STEEL SPARS): GALV. STEEL EYE BANDS ON WOOD SPARS
14. JAWS DETAILED ON DWG 35-B

EQUIPMENT:

1. 2-55# CMC - FISHERMAN TYPE - BOWERS. ANCHOR
2. 1-35# CMC - FISHERMAN TYPE - KEDGE ANCHOR
3. 50 FATHOMS 5/16" GRADE 40 ARCO CHAIN - STBD - WORKING BOWER
   45 FATHOMS 5/16" GRADE 40 ARCO CHAIN - PORT ~ CORAL - SPARE BOWER
   5 FATHOMS 5/16" GRADE 40 ARCO CHAIN - PORT + ¾" NYLON - BANKS ‡
4. LIFE JACKETS FOR EA. BERTH + 2 EXTRA
5. MARINASPEC TRI COLOR LIGHT - ON MAIN TOP MAST - M-7001.
6. ANCHOR LIGHT (OIL)
7. 6" FOG BELL ~ MECH. FOG HORN
8. BILGE PUMP (MANUEL) 2" SUCTION & DISCHARGE (EDSON)
9. SESTRAL 5" SPHERICAL COMPASS FOR STEEL HULLS
10. 12' BOAT HOOK ~ GALV HOOK
11. 4½" SOUNDING LEAD & MARKED LINE (10. FATH)
12. 300,000 C.P. PORTABLE LIGHT. ~ 2 OUTLETS.
13. 6 MOORING LINES - ¾" NYLON - 8 FATH EA - WITH A 20" EYE SPLICED IN ONE END.
    3 WARPS ~ 50 FATH EACH ~ ¾" NYLON - SPLICE ON EACH END
14. AWNINGS & SAIL COVERS TO SUIT OWNER REQ
15. NAME & PORT OF HAIL ~ EA SIDE OF STERN & NAME ON EA. SIDE OF BOW.
16. 9' BOTT. LENGTH DORY - 3'11" BEAM 18" DEPTH ~ WOOD
17. 2-DRY CHEM FIRE EXT (SAILING VESSELS)
18. ANY & ALL OTHER EQUIPMENT REQ BY USCG OR FLAG OF REGISTER & REQ FOR SEA KEEPING ABILITY & SAFETY
19. LUNENBURG RATCHET GYPSY WIND LASS SIZE #1 FOR CHAIN ~ 2 WILDCATS
20. " " " " " SIZE #1 FOR ROPE ~ 2 WARPING HEADS

RIGGERS NOTES

1. STANDING RIGGING TO BE 7x7 GALV. IMPVD PLOW STEEL ~ SHROUDS & JIBSTAY ⅜"DIA. HEAD STAY 5/16" DIA ~ TRIATIC & SPRING STAY ¼" DIA
2. ALL TERMINALS TO BE NICOPRESS SPLICING SLEAVES OVER THE PROPER SIZE SOLID THIMBLE WHEN REQ.
3. EYES OVER MASTS TO BE WORMED, PARCLED & SERVED
4. SHROUDS ARE PASSED OVER AS PAIRS FROM 1 CONT. WIRE ON EA. SIDE & ARE MARRIED WITH A "NICO PRESS" SLEAVE
5. DEADEYES FROM A. DAUPHINE & SONS - LUNENBURG N.S.
6. TURNBUCKLES ARE JAW & JAW - GALV. BARREL TYPE WITH LOCKING NUTS
7. BOB STAY IS ½" GALV. CHAIN - BOWSPRIT SHROUDS ARE ⅜" GALV CHAIN
8. LAZY JACKS ARE 5/16" (3)STRAND DACRON & MAY BE SET UP BOTH P/S.
9. TOPPING LIFTS ARE ⅜" (3)STRAND DACRON.
10. HALYARDS FOR LOWERS & THEIR SHEETS IS ½"(3) STRAND DACRON
11. TOPSAIL SHEETS, HALYARDS, AND SQUARE SAIL LIFTS, BRACES, & SHEETS ⅜"(3)STRAND DACRON ~ OUT HAULS, IN HAULS, & CLEW LINES 5/16"(3)STRAND DACRON
12. JIB DOWNHAUL ~ 5/16" DACRON.
13. PIN RAILS P/S FORE & MAIN RIGGING.
14. FORE & MAIN SHROUDS ARE RATTLED DOWN.
15. JIB MAY BE RIGGED BUGEYE STYLE ~ OWNERS OPTION.

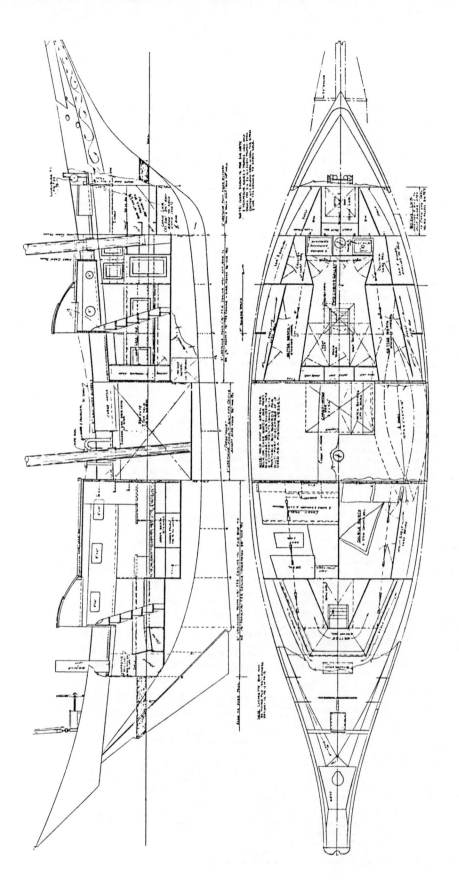

Figure 3. *Interior Arrangement Plan of the Pinky, Colvin Design No. 169. The Pinky's other plans are presented as needed in the chapters that follow, and the Sail and Spar Plan and Interior Arrangement Plan appear again where rigging and interior joinerwork are discussed in Volume 2 of this text.*

If the drawings are to a large enough scale, then plans 6, 7, 8, 10, and 12 may suffice without the extra drawings. Plans 9 and 11 are often furnished by the builder according to his own standards, or he will have subcontractors, in which case they will provide the required drawings.

Yachts do not have to be built to the approval of any particular body, but it is not uncommon to have them built under the inspection and approval of Lloyds, the American Bureau of Shipping, or the U.S. Coast Guard. This practice adds an expense that most owners avoid without any detriment to their craft, since a good builder usually equals or exceeds the requirements of the classification societies in regard to workmanship, quality of material, and strength of structure. It would be foolish for any builder to ignore entirely the research from which the rules were promulgated, but to follow them blindly would be more foolish still. Blind adherence prevents new development and may cause a builder to include features that are not only impractical or virtually impossible, but also against all common sense and seamanlike intuition.

None of the various regulatory bodies designs or takes responsibility for the performance of vessels built to its rules or under its supervision. These groups formulate rules, guides, standards, and other criteria for the design and construction of vessels, which, if followed, will (for certain types of vessels) assure the designer, builder, and owner of obtaining adequate strength and quality of materials. These rules *do not* substitute for the independent judgment of the designer or builder. I mention this because many owners suffer from the delusion that certification obtains perfection in all things (and for this reason, vessels built to classification society rules may bring a higher resale value in Europe). Much of what is considered proper (modern, scientific, or state-of-the-art) in hull form is the result of tonnage laws, tax laws, and racing rules, none of which necessarily improve either hydrostatic performance or structural symmetry. On the contrary, rules often encourage grotesque hull forms and revolting structures. The scantlings required by the regulatory bodies are often needlessly heavy, and totally impossible for a vessel that differs markedly from the model on which the rules were formulated—for example, with respect to length, breadth, and depth. When the intended vessel differs from the model, it will be classified as an "unusual model" or one of "novel construction," which simply means that if it has been used before, and if it was successful, and if it works in this particular instance, the regulating body will give provisional approval. It is well always to remember that a builder may build 100 vessels and still be referred to as a builder, but if he builds one bad vessel, he will be referred to as a lousy builder. His reputation, more than a set of certification rules, will guarantee quality.

Depending on the vessel, several other plans may be required, such as a Spar Plan for hollow wooden spars; Rig Details for cargo booms, outriggers, davits, equipment masts, and the like; and the Expanded Shell Plating Plan (for round-bottom designs), which is made from direct measurements taken off a plating half-model. The main purpose of this drawing is to indicate the maximum width of plates that can be used without deformations. The expense of making the model and drawing prompts many designers to pass the task on to the builder. For single and multi-chine vessels an Expanded Shell Plating Plan is unnecessary, but many builders will draw one for their own use if it is not furnished by the designer, since it does not require a half-model. You should not automatically reject any design that excludes this drawing; a designer's warehouse book may indicate plate sizes not available to the builder, and an Expanded Shell Plating Plan based on these sizes would be of little use. This drawing has the advantage of making certain that plate edges are well clear of frames and bulkheads, that seams are eliminated inside tanks that cannot readily be welded, that valves and through hulls are clear of structures, and that other miscellaneous complications are avoided (see Chapter 12).

Written Specifications

Written specifications in essence provide a wordy description of all items shown on the plans, as well as those not shown. Some people set great store by them. Having written hundreds of pages of specifications, I have come to feel that the plans should show enough detail to make them unnecessary. This is especially true in regard to stock plans and the backyard builder. The specifications for a stock design may have been written 10 or 20 years ago, so that the items specified either no longer exist, come in a different size, or are now manufactured by another company. Then, too, the backyard builder may not have access to the companies that manufacture a specific item. We all know about the government's specifications for an Allen wrench that cost $900 as per specifications but might have cost only nine cents at the local hardware store. Local junkyards and hardware stores are often the best sources of fittings, and you can actually see, touch, and even partially assemble what you need, rather than search through catalogs. Written specifications can effectively tie the builder's hands when he could do a better job a little differently and for less cost.

Important items should be specified in the construction contract, but the simpler this document is, the better. If an owner cannot trust the builder, or dislikes him, he had better find another builder. (Naturally, the home builder will not have this problem.) I have yet to see any contract or specifications that would make a good builder out of a bad one or an honest one out of a crook. Occasionally, a resident inspector represents the owner, or the owner or architect furnishes the basic materials and most of the equipment and hardware. In such cases the builder in essence furnishes only his yard and labor force, becoming little more than a laborer. He must then require very detailed written specifications so that he can coordinate delivery of material as needed to maintain uninterrupted construction progress. He has *no control* over the progress of construction when he is at the mercy of the suppliers, owner, and architect.

Other Considerations

Hydrostatic curves of form are not supplied for yachts, for which only one waterline is usually calculated. The yacht designer may do some rather extensive calculations for his own reference, but there is no need for a builder or owner to have access to any information of this type other than what the designer supplies in the title block of the drawing. For cargo and certain other types of commercial vessels, the designer furnishes a booklet or drawing showing the hull characteristics at various drafts, and cross curves of stability for various angles of heel and loading.

The proper design approach for any vessel should reflect the construction material and its method of fabrication, always taking into account the tools available and the physical limitations imposed when a human body must fit into an area and perform the necessary work. The designer's ability to conceive a hull that will function properly or even superbly is not in question from a builder's point of view; rather, the builder cares about his ability to *think* in the material in which the vessel is constructed. Lacking this ability, he can design a structure that is not only costly but almost impossible to build. Each material is its own testing ground; what is acceptable in wood is not in steel, nor should steel building practices necessarily be copied in aluminum. In selecting plans from which to build, one should hold suspect those that claim the vessel can be built in any material. A vessel intended to be built in steel may also be built in aluminum alloy; however, a vessel designed for aluminum construction can rarely be built in steel. Figure 4 gives an example of the transition from wood to iron to steel construction in the stem of a vessel. It is not uncommon to see this transition carried to the absurd by designers using, say, a 12-inch stem bar

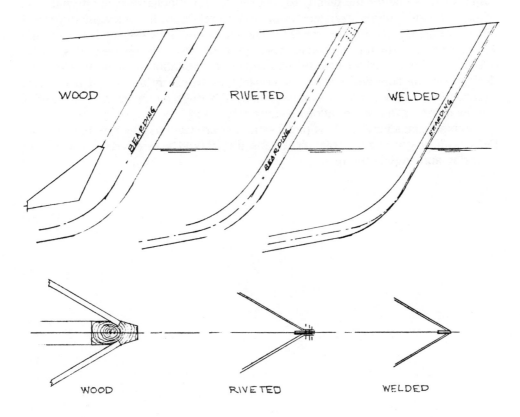

Figure 4. *The transition from wood to iron to steel in the stem of a vessel. The sketches are not to scale.*

with the shell plating landing 3 inches aft of the face. In wood, plenty of material was needed to cover the hood ends of the planking and to provide sufficient anchorage for the plank fastenings. In riveted construction, the shell plates were knuckled and the plates riveted through the stem. In welding, there is no need for any more exterior face than the minimum required for proper welding. Similarly, the depth of the stem should not be greater than absolutely necessary, for a normal human must be able to position himself not only to see but also to work (weld) the inner joint. The generally accepted minimum space required for welding is 18 inches in a 60-degree arc of the area to be welded. This allows for the electrode plus the hand holding it; extra space is needed for the welder's head, which is protected by a shield.

Stock plans are available from the designer's office and, in some instances, through his agents. There is no standard cost for plans, nor is there a standard number of drawings furnished. You will often find five or six well-detailed drawings more complete than 20 miscellaneous drawings that require hours of interpretation and juggling to use; thus, you should never purchase plans based on their numbers alone. Occasionally, a designer includes miscellaneous drawings with the basic plans, such as one for the dinghy to be used on a particular design, alternate sail plans, alternate interior arrangement plans, or a reference list of manufacturers of major equipment items. The designer should furnish two sets of plans for the vessel—one to use during construction, and one for the owner's files. Many designers, without further charge, also include consultation by mail or telephone during construction, and furnish small sketches to clarify an item if necessary. Sketches do not extend to complete new drawings, such as a new interior arrangement, or major alterations to an existing one.

Complete plans for a working pinky schooner are used to illustrate this volume. Besides offering an example of typical plans, they should be referred to as necessary to clarify and amplify the text.

2

$\triangledown$

MATERIALS

HISTORICAL DEVELOPMENT

The use of *iron* in ship construction began in England in the latter part of the 18th century; however, the first major use was not until 1818, when the river barge *Vulcan* was built. Although not totally constructed of iron, she represented the first real attempt to make extensive use of the material. It may seem strange now, but at the time, people resisted using iron because it would not float; it stood to reason that a vessel built of iron would not be buoyant. Nevertheless, by 1831 there were iron shipbuilders on the Thames, Mersey, and Clyde rivers, and along the east coast of Scotland. By 1860, the English had developed composite construction using iron frames, beams, knees, and keelsons with wood planking and copper-sheathed bottoms. These vessels were less expensive to build and operate than all-iron vessels, especially if they were to be used primarily in the tropics.

The use of iron in the United States was limited at the time to riverboats propelled by steam. Americans had a virtually unlimited supply of wood suitable for shipbuilding, and the success of American wooden clippers and packets further strengthened the reluctance to change. Under these circumstances, iron's advantages went unheeded: industry in general, and shipbuilding in particular, make changes only when forced to for economic reasons, and never to make a better product. The large six-masted schooner *Edward B. Winslow*, of 3,424 gross tons, launched in 1908 from the Percy & Small yard in Bath, Maine, is an example of the size wooden vessels attained. Even as late as World War I, extensive construction of large wooden steam and sailing ships continued under the sponsorship of the War Shipping Board. At 3,500 tons dead weight (for the steamships), these wooden vessels were floating lumberyards. The bilge ceiling was often 12 inches thick, while the hold ceiling was 8 inches and that along the sides of the vessel as much as 10 inches; the planking was rather light, at about 5 inches. By this time, England, Europe, and the Scandinavian countries had long since recognized the superiority of metal construction and the serious limitations of wood, particularly in trying to splice end connections of timbers and strength members, as well as in the cargo-reducing bulk of heavy timbers necessary to achieve adequate strength. Lower insurance rates offered to owners of iron and steel vessels gave them an even greater competitive advantage over the American wooden hulls.

First used for shipbuilding in 1859, *steel* (puddled or cast) was at first inferior to iron in all respects except strength; it was hard and brittle, and the manufacturing process was unreliable. The Bessemer process, introduced in 1863, was costly at first, and what it yielded was not much better than the then-available puddled steel. By 1873, however, both the Bessemer and the Siemens processes were employed, and reliable, good-quality steel became available. The processes were then much the same, but by 1875 the Siemens process had undergone vast improvements, to such an extent that little further improvement took place up to World War I.

Steel replaced iron not so that vessels could be built stronger, but rather because the strength and better mechanical properties of steel permitted smaller and lighter scantlings, which, in turn, reduced the structural weight and increased the volume, thereby increasing the earning capacity of the vessels. The strength and stiffness of steel and iron structures were about the same in the early years, while a 20-percent saving in weight favored steel only slightly. Today, with the extensive alloying of steel and with all-welded structures, a saving of about 50 percent over iron can be achieved.

TERMINOLOGY

You don't need to become a metallurgist in order to build in steel and iron, any more than you need to be a timber farmer and lumberjack in order to build in wood. The more familiar you are with the subject, however, the easier it is to understand the limitations of the materials. To start, it is enough to establish a common vocabulary so that you can communicate coherently with manufacturers. Here, then, is the fundamental terminology of iron and steel:

Pig Iron is produced from iron ores by heating with a flux in a blast furnace, and is then graded by appearance. The darkest is grey iron No. 1, and the lighter irons are Nos. 2, 3, 4 (foundry), 4 (forge), mottled, and white. The mottled and No. 4 (forge) are used in the manufacture of wrought iron, and the remaining numbers are used for cast iron.

Cast Iron is produced by melting down and purifying pig iron. While having a compressive strength of about 80,000 pounds per square inch, it is weak in both tension and shear, and its ductility is poor; however, these properties are influenced by the amount of silicon, phosphorus and manganese present. Grey cast iron is used in small castings requiring not much strength but good appearance. White and light grey cast iron are used for the larger castings.

Malleable Cast Iron is much less brittle and is made of ordinary iron casting heated in contact with iron oxide. A special process allows a further refinement to permit its use in castings that require moderate tensile strength (cleats), pressure tests (valves), or both.

Wrought Iron is almost pure iron in which the carbon has been removed by heating the cast iron to white with a basic slag, which both oxidizes and removes the major impurities. This is called "puddling." The puddled iron is then hammered and rolled, after which it is cut up, piled, reheated, and rolled again. This process is again repeated for the best quality. The amount of work iron receives during the hammering and rolling has a greater influence on the mechanical qualities of the iron than does the presence of impurities; impurities are, for the most part, merely entangled in the iron mass, not alloyed with it, so variations in their amount have little effect on iron's behavior under stress. Impurities are not removed by the hammering and rolling.

Wrought iron is extremely ductile, malleable, and readily weldable; however, it cannot be more than superficially hardened by quenching, and its tensile strength is less than steel's. Its strength is greatest in the direction of rolling, and the more it is rolled, the greater its longitudinal strength. A fine, close-grained, uniform, fibrous structure without any appearance of crystallization, blue-grey in color, indicates toughness. First-class wrought iron has a tensile strength of about 40,000 psi with the grain and 36,000 psi across the grain. For the highest quality, 44,000 psi with the grain is possible. Pure Swedish soft iron is considered the best. Iron in shipbuilding posed a problem, since bends of more than 90 degrees could not be made across the grain; however, its slow rate of corrosion has given many iron vessels a useful life of well over 100 years. Today, wrought iron plates are virtually impossible to obtain.

Steel, in the manufacturing process, is a liquid mass of variable composition. When its composition is correct, it is poured into a mold to form the ingots from which plates and bars will later be rolled. The foreign elements in steel differ from the impurities found in iron in that they are well defined in quantity and so thoroughly mixed that they form a dense, homogenous alloy; the slag and light impurities found in iron are absent because they float on the top of the molten metal. In contrast to iron, the mechanical treatment (rolling and hammering) of steel has little effect on its mechanical properties in spite of changing its molecular arrangement. Iron has a fiber that hammering and rolling improve, but steel lacks a definite fiber, so the physical qualities are practically constant regardless of the direction in which stress is applied.

There are two distinct processes for producing mild steel: the *open hearth*, or *Siemens-Martin*, and the *Bessemer*. Making steel by the open-hearth process confers the advantage of absolute control over the important foreign elements; this not only assures a uniform composition, but also allows variation of elements to obtain different mechanical qualities in the finished steel.

The steelmaking process, regardless of method, is further subdivided into the making of *acid steel* and *basic steel*. Acid steel is made from hematite pig iron, which has about 3.3 percent carbon, 2.0 percent silicon, 1.0 percent manganese, a trace of copper, and very small amounts of sulfur and phosphorus. Mild steel consists of pure iron with about 0.20 percent carbon and 0.50 percent manganese. Thus, to convert the hematite pig iron into steel, you need only deprive it of most of its carbon, about half of its manganese, and all of the other impurities. This is done by melting the hematite pig iron together with some scrap steel, and then adding some hematite iron ore (pure oxide of iron), which supplies oxygen and causes an increase in temperature as it combines with the manganese, silicon, and carbon of the pig. When oxygen and carbon combine, they form a gas; silicon and manganese combine to form a slag. This slag absorbs a quantity of iron and floats to the surface, where it protects the steel from the oxidizing and cooling effects of air. The oxygen released from the hematite ore does not combine with the carbon of the pig until it has carried away all the manganese and silicon. A further supply of ore is added at that time, to adjust the remaining carbon to the exact amount desired. All the carbon cannot be burned out, however, or you would then have oxide of iron (burned iron), and the resulting steel would be crumbly if worked at high heat.

Phosphorus and sulfur are unwanted impurities, since the former causes brittleness when cold, and the latter, brittleness at red heat. The acid process does not eliminate them. If they occur in the original raw material, they will also be present in the finished product, which is the reason for using hematite pig iron, as it is almost free of these two elements.

Although the acid process cannot eliminate phosphorus, the basic process can. In principle, you simply introduce into the blast furnace an alkali, such as lime, which has a strong affinity for phosphorus; the alkali removes the phosphorus. Unfortunately, the acid process furnace lining is composed mostly of acid silicate, and when lime attacks this, the lining will soon disappear. Therefore, when the pig contains a lot of phosphorus, an alkaline rather than acid lining is used in the furnace to permit the addition of lime. Basic steel results.

The Bessemer process differs from the open-hearth acid-steel process in the method of purifying the molten pig. First, the molten pig iron is poured into the converter, a large globular vessel lined with fire brick. Oxygen is then introduced through the bottom of the converter to burn off the carbon, manganese, and silicon, forming air in the process. As the air rises through the molten pig, it decomposes and forms the gases nitrogen and oxygen. Oxygen decomposes the manganese, silicon, and carbon, raising the temperature of the cooler pig. Since oxygen burns out these elements, ferromanganese is added next, as it contains both carbon and manganese. The steel is then poured off from the converter. The whole process takes less than one-quarter of an hour.

The Bessemer process makes it difficult to determine when all the carbon is burned off—a major disadvantage. Since the converter is closed, you can tell when the carbon is gone only by the color of the flame coming from the neck of the converter. If you carry decarbonization too far, the resulting steel will be burned, and if you don't carry it far enough, there will be an excess of carbon. In this process, the pour must be made as soon as the air is shut off, as the steel would otherwise cool too much to pour into the ingot molds.

Carbon transforms pure iron into steel, and the higher the carbon content, the harder and stronger the steel. The softest steel is chemically almost the same as pure iron, having less than 0.10 percent carbon and a tensile strength of about 40,000 psi, and stretching (elongating) more than 30 percent of its length before breaking. It is therefore considered very ductile. Razor steel, by contrast, has a carbon content of 1.40 percent, is very brittle, and is neither weldable nor ductile, although it has a tensile strength of 200,000 psi. This comparison points to an implicit trade-off. You might at first think that steel's percentage of elongation (ductility) should matter less than its tensile strength. True, steel that yields easily will sacrifice some strength. On the other hand, without the ability to elongate, it could not withstand the abuse of handling while forming or, for that matter, the shocks imparted in the stranding of a vessel.

You might compare soft steel to taffy: like taffy, it has a slight elongation when lightly pulled in one direction, but when the strain is released it returns to its original shape. The *elasticity* is perfect because the amount of stretch is within the *elastic limit*. If you pulled the steel again with sufficient force to visibly change its shape, you would reach the steel's *yield point*, beyond which it might continue changing shape even without the application of additional force, but would certainly not recover its original shape. With the addition of still more pressure, the material would finally part into two pieces, the measure of force required being termed the *ultimate strength* of the material.

Contrary to what you might intuitively suppose, then, it is more important to know the elastic limit than the ultimate strength of your material. When you substitute peanut brittle for taffy, you have a material that is initially very strong but not ductile, and which, when stretched, will not recover but will instead break immediately. For all practical purposes, the yield point and the ultimate strength of peanut brittle coincide. The same goes for a high-tensile, low-ductility steel.

Steel, or any other material, can be repeatedly strained below its elastic limit without permanent damage, but when the stresses approach the elastic limit and are repeated with enough frequency, the material will *fatigue* and fail. How many times will it take—10 times, 1,000 times, or 10,000,000 times? The closer the stress comes to the elastic limit, the fewer the repetitions needed to cause failure. It could be once a second for 10 seconds or once a year for 10 years, but rest assured that, when a material is stressed repeatedly, failure due to fatigue will eventually occur. Chapter 5 will briefly cover longitudinal and transverse strength considerations.

CUSTOMIZING THE MANUFACTURERS' STANDARD SHAPES

The ideal steel structure for any vessel is strong, light, easy to erect, easy to maintain, and economical. Sadly, some builders ignore long-term maintenance by not taking care to eliminate pockets that will not drain, by not chipping or grinding rough edges from flame cutting, and by leaving sharp edges that will not hold paint. Furthermore, builders often do an inadequate cleaning job prior to painting, and apply too little paint. This causes headaches for the owner, who should be able to expect years of troublefree use of a vessel as far as interior maintenance of the hull is concerned. I am not just talking about the contract builder here. The builder is always distinct from the owner, even though he may be both by turns, for he cannot be both at one and the same time. "I am building a vessel for my own use"— these are the words of a builder. Later the same person may say, "I built this vessel for my own use"—but these are the words of an owner. We cannot assume that because the present owner was once the builder, he will necessarily feel completely satisfied with his vessel. Boatbuilding involves much tedious labor, and when you are bored, you tend to give the work at hand "a lick and a promise" and go on to the more interesting jobs—only to rue that decision years later after having to spend tenfold hours to rectify what should have been done properly in the first place.

Such "shortcuts" result, in part at least, because the builder has to manufacture special shapes for frames, beams, railcaps, and other parts, which are not manufactured by the mills but are needed in the vessel. To get the shapes he needs, he may weld up several standard shapes, in the process leaving numerous crevices, inclusions, and other irregularities, and opening the door to rust and premature failure. Alternatively, he may flange plates in order to avoid such irregularities. When available as part of the yard equipment, flanging offers the most versatile way of fabricating exactly what you need; however, if flange work must be sent to a job shop, the added costs outweigh the advantages of being able to develop the infinite variety of sections that you may wish to use. Flanged plates are a bit easier to paint than welded shapes, and welding up the required shapes is also a time-consuming and often costly task. You can often minimize it, however, by splitting standard I-beams and channels. The savings in welding labor and weight of structure you can gain this way will more than offset cutting costs if the strength of the resulting shape equals or exceeds that of a welded piece and if the weight is about the same. An advantage of splitting I-beams and channels thoughtfully is that you can have exactly what you need for several items from one piece of steel: the floors can use the full depth of the beam or channel; frames may use one-half the depth; brackets, knees, or any other item that may be required can be cut from the same or another piece; and all will have the same flange width.

Structural requirements for marine members are unique in that the depth of the sections is the most important dimension for strength. The thickness of the webs and the width of their flanges, while less important, also definitely contribute to making the vessel a series of girders, as does the plating, which becomes an integral part of the whole when it is welded to the shell, deck, or bulkheads to give it the necessary stiffness. Knowing the relative importance of each part makes a difference. At all times the weight of a vessel's structure must be kept to a minimum, while the strength must be kept at the maximum, since each extra pound or ton of weight reduces the cargo capacity of that vessel, not to mention possibly raising its center of gravity and doing many other irritating things.

Table 1 indicates the common sizes of I-beams and channels that may be split to form T's and L's. These same sections, of course, can be cut in an infinite number of ways to yield other combinations of sections.

Figure 5 shows the most common alternatives for sections. The full-depth sections are used for web frames, girders, stringers, and keelsons. In general, transverse frames are made from L's or flat bars (FB), while web frames and girders are made from T's. Hull longitudinals and stringers may be T's, L's, or flat bars (in my order of preference). The local steel supplier normally stocks or has access to a large variety of standard shapes that are not listed in the table. Suffice it to say that the stock list varies considerably throughout the United States.

TABLE 1. Common Sizes of I-Beams and Channels, with the Sizes of the T's and L's They May Be Split to Form

Shape		Thickness in inches	
I-Beam (inches x inches x lbs/ft)	*Corresponding T* (inches x inches x lbs/ft)	*Flange*	*Web*
6" x 1⅞" x 4.4	3" x 1⅞" x 2.2	.171	.114
7" x 2⅛" x 5.5	3½" x 2⅛" x 2.75	.180	.126
8" x 2¼" x 6.5	4" x 2¼" x 3.25	.189	.135
10" x 2¾" x 9.0	5" x 2¾" x 4.5	.206	.155
12" x 3" x 11.8	6" x 3" x 5.9	.225	.175
6" x 4" x 8.5	3" x 4" x 4.25	.194	.170
8" x 4" x 10.0	4" x 4" x 5.0	.204	.180
10" x 4" x 11.5	5" x 4" x 5.75	.204	.180
12" x 4" x 14.0	6" x 4" x 7.0	.224	.200
Channel	*Corresponding L*	*Flange*	*Web*
10" x 1⅛" x 6.5	5" x 1⅛" x 3.25	.406	.150
10" x 1½" x 8.4	5" x 1½" x 4.2	.250	.170
12" x 1½" x 10.6	6" x 1½" x 5.3	.313	.190
5" x 1⅞" x 9.0	2½" x 1⅞" x 4.5	.320	.325
6" x 1⅞" x 8.2	3" x 1⅞" x 4.2	.343	.200
7" x 2¼" x 12.25	3½" x 2¼" x 6.13	.366	.314
8" x 2¼" x 11.5	4" x 2¼" x 5.75	.390	.220

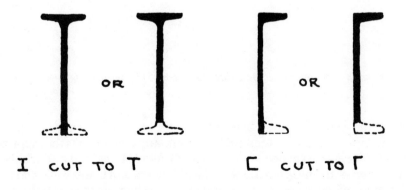

Figure 5. *The most common approaches to cutting I-beams and channels to make other sections.*

GENERAL CONSIDERATIONS

Table 2 indicates sheet and plate thicknesses and weights per square foot used in vessels up to 80 feet long. The generally accepted minimum sheet thickness that you will find practical to use in the construction of a vessel's hull is 11 gauge when corrosion, warpage, and welding production are prime considerations. Ten gauge is even easier and faster to work with than 11 gauge; thus, a majority of builders consider this the most desirable minimum. You *can* construct small steel hulls with 16-gauge material, using the Manual Metal Arc welding process; however, the welding goes very slowly, as the maximum electrode size is $\frac{3}{32}$ inch for welding the heavier framing members to the shell, and $\frac{1}{16}$ inch for the butt welds in the shell itself. The extensive framing needed when using lighter than 11-gauge sheet will more than offset the saving in shell weight; therefore, it will usually be better to use heavier plates and less framing.

TABLE 2. Sheet and Plate Thicknesses and Weights

	Sheets*			Plates	
gauge	*thickness (inches)*	*weight (lbs/ft²)*		*thickness (inches)*	*weight (lbs/ft²)*
16	.0598	2.50		$\frac{3}{16}$	7.65
14	.0747	3.125		$\frac{1}{4}$	10.20
12	.1046	4.375		$\frac{5}{16}$	12.75
11	.1196	5.00		$\frac{3}{8}$	15.30
$\frac{1}{8}$"	.1250	5.10		$\frac{7}{16}$	17.85
10	.1345	5.625		$\frac{1}{2}$	20.40
8	.1644	6.875		$\frac{9}{16}$	22.95
7	.1875	7.50		$\frac{5}{8}$	25.50
				$\frac{11}{16}$	28.05
				$\frac{3}{4}$	30.60
				$\frac{13}{16}$	33.15
				$\frac{7}{8}$	35.70
				1	40.80

Note: sheets are usually referred to by gauge number, and plates are designated by weight.

Much of the steel presently available to the builder is imported and comes dimensioned in the metric system. Table 3 lists metric conversions that approximate the standard sheets and plates available in the United States, and also tabulates the nearest millimeter to any given fraction. Metric sheets and plates will seldom have a direct U.S. equivalent; the builder should therefore substitute the nearest equivalent, whether slightly higher or lower than the one specified in the design, with due regard for the advantage of increasing or decreasing the structural weight and for the effect a dimensional change will have on the strength of the vessel. For example, 6.0-millimeter plate is about $\frac{1}{64}$ inch (.64 pound per square foot) thinner and 6.5-millimeter plate is about $\frac{1}{128}$ inch (.32 pound per square foot) thicker than $\frac{1}{4}$-inch plate. The conversion factor is millimeters $\times$ .0937 = decimal inches; 1 millimeter = 1.61 pounds of steel per sqare foot.

TABLE 3. Approximate Metric Equivalents for Standard U.S. Sheet and Plate Sizes

Metric Thickness (mm)	U.S. Equivalent	Thickness (inches)	Metric Equivalent (mm)
sheet			
1.50	16 gauge	$\frac{1}{64}$	.40
1.90	14 gauge	$\frac{1}{32}$	.80
2.70	12 gauge	$\frac{1}{16}$	1.60
3.00	11 gauge	$\frac{3}{32}$	2.40
3.20	$\frac{1}{8}$"	$\frac{5}{32}$	3.95
3.40	10 gauge	$\frac{7}{32}$	5.55
4.20	8 gauge	$\frac{9}{32}$	7.20
4.75	7 gauge	$\frac{11}{32}$	8.75
plate		$\frac{13}{32}$	10.25
4.75	$\frac{3}{16}$"	$\frac{15}{32}$	11.75
6.40	$\frac{1}{4}$"	$\frac{17}{32}$	13.50
7.90	$\frac{5}{16}$"	$\frac{19}{32}$	15.00
9.50	$\frac{3}{8}$"	$\frac{21}{32}$	16.75
11.25	$\frac{7}{16}$"	$\frac{23}{32}$	18.25
13.00	$\frac{1}{2}$"	$\frac{25}{32}$	19.75
14.25	$\frac{9}{16}$"	$\frac{27}{32}$	21.50
16.00	$\frac{5}{8}$"	$\frac{29}{32}$	23.00
17.50	$\frac{11}{16}$"	$\frac{31}{32}$	24.50
19.00	$\frac{3}{4}$"		
20.50	$\frac{13}{16}$"		
22.25	$\frac{7}{8}$"		
25.40	1.0"		

For welding purposes, the American Welding Society classifies steel into six groups, four of which are commonly used in boatbuilding: carbon steels, high-strength low-alloy steels, chromium-molybdenum steels, and precoated steels. Also, the carbon content of the various steels within each overall group determines specific subgroups into which they are further classified, as follows:

Low-carbon steel: having a maximum of 0.15 percent carbon; available in plates, shapes, sheets, and strips; excellent weldability.

Mild steel: having a carbon content of 0.15 to 0.30 percent; available in plates, shapes, sheets, and bars; good weldability.

Medium-carbon steel: having a carbon content of 0.30 to 0.50 percent; used in machine tools and parts; only fair weldability; usually requires pre- and post-heat treatment and the use of low-hydrogen welding methods.

High-carbon steel: having a carbon content of 0.50 to 1.00 percent; used for springs, dies, and railroad rails; weldability is poor. Low-hydrogen welding, pre- and post-heat treatment are required.

Strength is added to steels by additional alloying, and some alloys also increase resistance to corrosion, suitability for high and low temperature applications, and other special properties. Steels of 0.28 percent carbon are available, and still qualify as mild steel; however, for shell plating it is best to demand, and be assured, that the steel used is below 0.23 percent, which is the highest carbon content allowed by the American Bureau of Shipping (ABS) for plates under ½ inch. Table 4 lists the steels customarily used in boatbuilding, along with their chemical and mechanical compositions.

TABLE 4A. Chemical Compositions of Common Shipbuilding Steels (as percentages)

	A242*	A373	A36	ABS/A	ABS/B	A440*	A441*	Commercial and Merchants Grade
Carbon	.09	.28	.28	.23**	.21**	.28**	.21	.15**
Manganese	.38	.5-.9	.6-.9	.25 x Carbon	.8-1.1	1.1 (1.6 for plate thicker than ½")	.85 (1.25 for plate thicker than ½")	.25-.4
Phosphorus	.09							.04
Sulfur	.033							.05
Silicon	.48				.35	.30	.30	
Copper	.41	.20***	.20***			.20	.20	
Chromium	.84							
Nickel	.28							

TABLE 4B. Mechanical Properties of Common Shipbuilding Steels

	A242	A373	A36	ABS/A	ABS/B	A440	A441	Commercial and Merchants Grade
yield point (thousands of psi)	50	32	36	34	34	50	50	32
tensile strength (thousands of psi)	70	58-75	60-80	58-71	58-71	75	70	50-60
elasticity (as a percentage, related to a 2-inch piece)	22	21	20					
elasticity (as a percentage, related to an 8-inch piece)	19	24	23	21	21	18	18	21
cold bend (as diameter of mandrel around which a 180-degree bend can be accomplished)	1t (i.e., the required diameter equals the thickness of the piece)	½t (i.e., one-half the thickness of the piece)	½t			1t	1t	flat
corrosion rate (relative to that of mild steel)	4-6 (i.e., A242 corrodes at ¼ to ⅙ the rate of mild steel)	1-2***	1-2***	1	1	2	2	
endurance limit (thousands of psi)	35	28	28			39	42	

* A242, A440, A441 are proprietary steels with chemical variations. The popular trade name for A242 is Corten, made by the United States Steel Corporation.

** Maximum permitted.

*** May be specified, and will affect the corrosion resistance.

Each grade of steel can be welded with one or more processes, and each process may utilize one or more suitable electrodes, shielded either with a flux coating or an inert gas. Selection of the electrode depends on the welding process used, the similarities in chemical composition of the metals being joined, and the conditions under which the welding is to be done. The different types of welding machines will be covered in Chapter 3.

Figure 6 is a series of drawings showing the various types of joints used in ship- and boatbuilding, and their efficiencies. These reflect the standards used by the Colvin Manufacturing Corporation and the Colvin Shipbuilding Company. They do not conform in all instances to the American Welding Society standards, except in symbols, nor do they conform to the American Bureau of Shipping or other regulatory bodies in their limitations. The stated efficiencies are based on tests conducted by my yard to determine suitable safety factors for seagoing vessels. These types of welds are used in marine construction regardless of whether the vessel is produced by a one-time backyard builder or a full-time building yard. Many other welds are possible in each category—C, T, B, lap, plug, etc. However, they are used only in very special cases, at which time they are detailed or a special note is offered on the drawing, describing the type of weld to be made. Heavy weldments must be detailed, and designers usually incorporate these on their drawings, since there are quite definite procedures to follow when welding thicker than 1-inch plate (40.8 pounds per square foot) to minimize stress and at the same time obtain maximum strength.

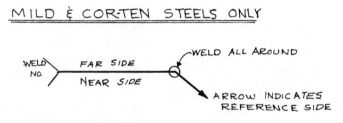

Figure 6. *The various types of joints used in the building of steel vessels are shown on the following pages. The efficiencies of the joints, as determined in tests conducted by the author's shipyard, are also indicated. The sketch above is a key to the drawings.*

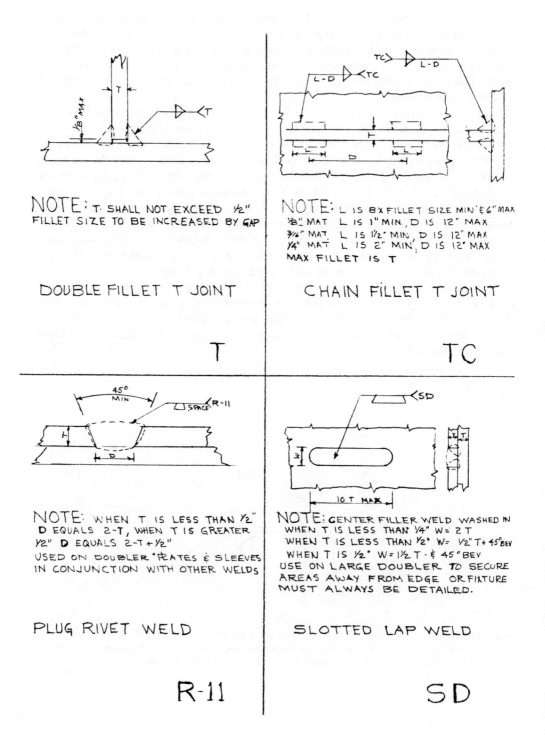

NOTE: T SHALL NOT EXCEED ½"
FILLET SIZE TO BE INCREASED BY GAP

DOUBLE FILLET T JOINT

T

NOTE: L IS 8 X FILLET SIZE MIN & 6" MAX
⅛" MAT L IS 1" MIN, D IS 12" MAX
³/₁₆" MAT L IS 1½" MIN, D IS 12" MAX
¼" MAT L IS 2" MIN, D IS 12" MAX
MAX FILLET IS T

CHAIN FILLET T JOINT

TC

NOTE: WHEN T IS LESS THAN ½"
D EQUALS 2-T, WHEN T IS GREATER
½" D EQUALS 2-T + ½"
USED ON DOUBLER PLATES & SLEEVES
IN CONJUNCTION WITH OTHER WELDS

PLUG RIVET WELD

R-11

NOTE: CENTER FILLER WELD WASHED IN
WHEN T IS LESS THAN ¼" W= 2 T
WHEN T IS LESS THAN ½" W= ½" T + 45° BEV
WHEN T IS ½" W= 1½ T - & 45° BEV
USE ON LARGE DOUBLER TO SECURE
AREAS AWAY FROM EDGE OR FIXTURE
MUST ALWAYS BE DETAILED.

SLOTTED LAP WELD

SD

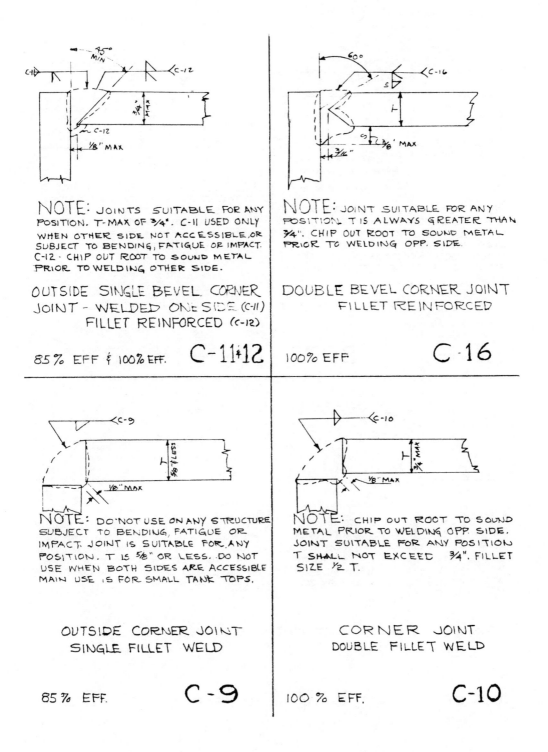

NOTE: JOINTS SUITABLE FOR ANY POSITION. T-MAX OF 3/4". C-11 USED ONLY WHEN OTHER SIDE NOT ACCESSIBLE, OR SUBJECT TO BENDING, FATIGUE OR IMPACT. C-12 - CHIP OUT ROOT TO SOUND METAL PRIOR TO WELDING OTHER SIDE.

OUTSIDE SINGLE BEVEL CORNER JOINT - WELDED ONE SIDE (C-11) FILLET REINFORCED (C-12)

85% EFF $ 100% EFF. C-11$12

NOTE: JOINT SUITABLE FOR ANY POSITION. T IS ALWAYS GREATER THAN 3/4". CHIP OUT ROOT TO SOUND METAL PRIOR TO WELDING OPP. SIDE.

DOUBLE BEVEL CORNER JOINT FILLET REINFORCED

100% EFF C-16

NOTE: DO NOT USE ON ANY STRUCTURE SUBJECT TO BENDING, FATIGUE OR IMPACT. JOINT IS SUITABLE FOR ANY POSITION. T IS 5/8" OR LESS. DO NOT USE WHEN BOTH SIDES ARE ACCESSIBLE MAIN USE IS FOR SMALL TANK TOPS.

OUTSIDE CORNER JOINT SINGLE FILLET WELD

85% EFF. C-9

NOTE: CHIP OUT ROOT TO SOUND METAL PRIOR TO WELDING OPP. SIDE. JOINT SUITABLE FOR ANY POSITION T SHALL NOT EXCEED 3/4". FILLET SIZE 1/2 T.

CORNER JOINT DOUBLE FILLET WELD

100% EFF. C-10

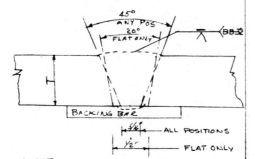

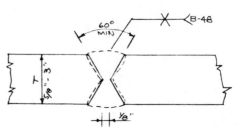

NOTE: JOINT SUITABLE FOR ANY POSITION EXCEPT AS NOTED. T 3/4 IS NORMALLY MORE THAN 3/4" & T 1/2 IS OVER 1 1/2" - AVOID THIS WELD IF BOTH SIDES ARE ACCESSIBLE. USE 1/8" DIA RODS TO FUSE ROOT TO BACKING BAR

SINGLE V GROOVE BUTT JOINT
WELDED ONE SIDE ON BACKING

100% EFF   BB-32

NOTE: CHIP OUT ROOT TO SOUND METAL PRIOR TO WELDING OPP SIDE JOINT SUITABLE FOR ANY POSITION. WHEN POSSIBLE ALTERNATE PASSES FROM IN & OUT SIDE TO REDUCE STRESS. MAIN USE - KEEL BOTT & STEMS

DOUBLE V GROOVE BUTT JOINT
WELDED BOTH SIDES

100% EFF.   B-48

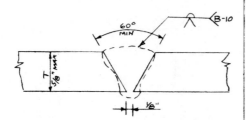

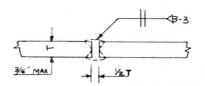

NOTE: CHIP OUT ROOT TO SOUND METAL PRIOR TO WELDING OPP SIDE. JOINT SUITABLE FOR ANY POSITION. T SHALL NOT EXCEED 5/8" ROOT WELD IS ALWAYS ON THE INSIDE OF ALL SHELL PLTG. OUTSIDE MAY BE GROUND FLUSH

SINGLE V GROOVE BUTT JOINT
WELDED BOTH SIDES

100% EFF   B-10

NOTE: CHIP OUT ROOT TO SOUND METAL PRIOR TO WELDING OPP SIDE. JOINT SUITABLE FOR ANY POSITION. JOINT IS USED ONLY ON PLTG & MAY BE GROUND SMOOTH ON ONE SIDE ONLY

SQUARE GROOVE BUTT JOINT
WELDED BOTH SIDES

100% EFF   B-3

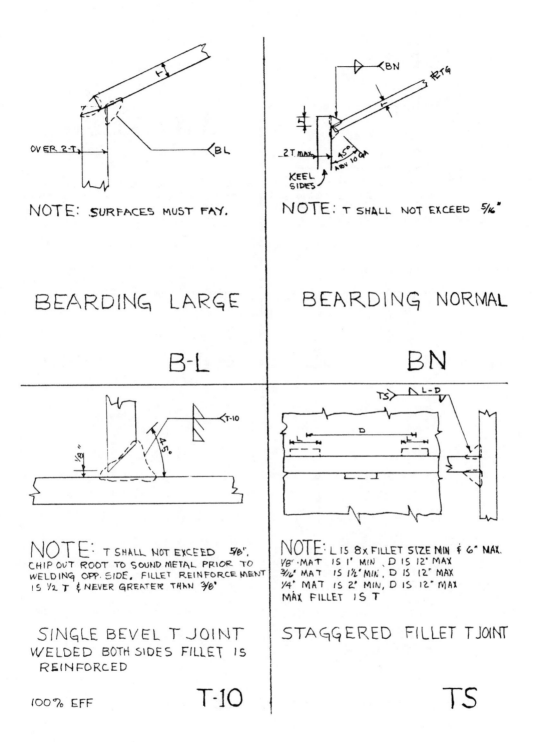

OVER 2·T

NOTE: SURFACES MUST FAY.

BEARDING LARGE

B-L

BN

2T MAX.

45°

ABV 10 GA

KEEL SIDES

NOTE: T SHALL NOT EXCEED 5/16"

BEARDING NORMAL

BN

1/8"

45°

T-10

NOTE: T SHALL NOT EXCEED 5/16". CHIP OUT ROOT TO SOUND METAL PRIOR TO WELDING OPP. SIDE. FILLET REINFORCEMENT IS 1/2 T & NEVER GREATER THAN 3/8"

SINGLE BEVEL T JOINT
WELDED BOTH SIDES FILLET IS
  REINFORCED

100% EFF   T-10

TS   L-D

D

NOTE: L IS 8x FILLET SIZE MIN & 6" MAX.
1/8" MAT IS 1" MIN. D IS 12" MAX
3/16" MAT IS 1½" MIN. D IS 12" MAX
1/4" MAT IS 2" MIN. D IS 12" MAX
MAX FILLET IS T

STAGGERED FILLET T JOINT

TS

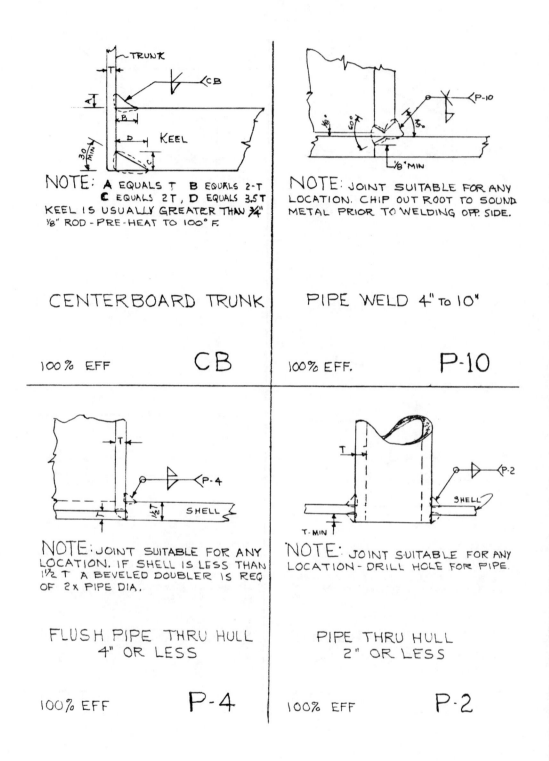

NOTE: A EQUALS T B EQUALS 2-T
C EQUALS 2T , D EQUALS 3.5T
KEEL IS USUALLY GREATER THAN ¾"
⅛" ROD - PRE-HEAT TO 100° F.

NOTE: JOINT SUITABLE FOR ANY
LOCATION. CHIP OUT ROOT TO SOUND
METAL PRIOR TO WELDING OPP. SIDE.

CENTERBOARD TRUNK

PIPE WELD 4" TO 10"

100% EFF   CB

100% EFF.   P-10

NOTE: JOINT SUITABLE FOR ANY
LOCATION. IF SHELL IS LESS THAN
1½ T A BEVELED DOUBLER IS REQ
OF 2 x PIPE DIA.

NOTE: JOINT SUITABLE FOR ANY
LOCATION - DRILL HOLE FOR PIPE.

FLUSH PIPE THRU HULL
4" OR LESS

PIPE THRU HULL
2" OR LESS

100% EFF   P-4

100% EFF   P-2

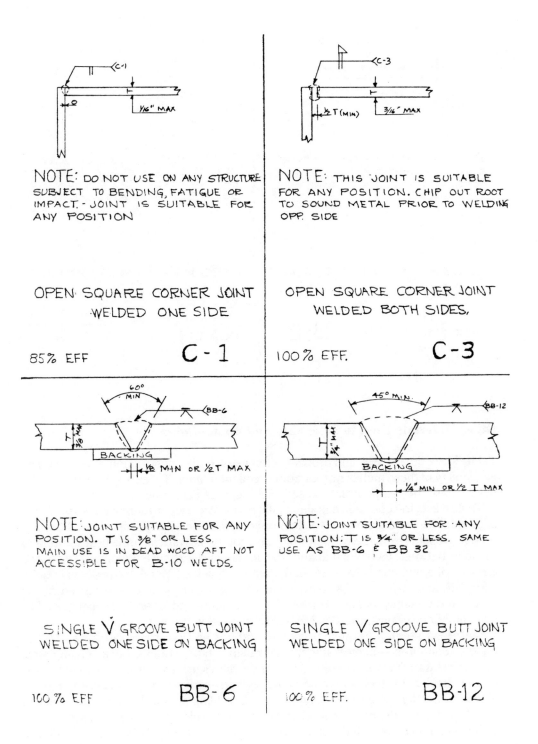

NOTE: DO NOT USE ON ANY STRUCTURE SUBJECT TO BENDING, FATIGUE OR IMPACT. JOINT IS SUITABLE FOR ANY POSITION

OPEN SQUARE CORNER JOINT WELDED ONE SIDE

85% EFF   C-1

NOTE: THIS JOINT IS SUITABLE FOR ANY POSITION. CHIP OUT ROOT TO SOUND METAL PRIOR TO WELDING OPP. SIDE

OPEN SQUARE CORNER JOINT WELDED BOTH SIDES.

100% EFF.   C-3

NOTE: JOINT SUITABLE FOR ANY POSITION. T IS 3/8" OR LESS. MAIN USE IS IN DEAD WOOD AFT NOT ACCESSIBLE FOR B-10 WELDS.

SINGLE V GROOVE BUTT JOINT WELDED ONE SIDE ON BACKING

100% EFF   BB-6

NOTE: JOINT SUITABLE FOR ANY POSITION. T IS 3/4" OR LESS. SAME USE AS BB-6 & BB 32

SINGLE V GROOVE BUTT JOINT WELDED ONE SIDE ON BACKING

100% EFF.   BB-12

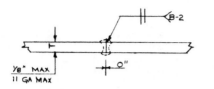

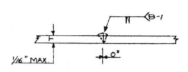

NOTE: JOINT IS SUITABLE FOR ANY POSITION.~ FOR SHELL PLTG. A GROUND 'V ON EXT. WHEN POSSIBLE.

NOTE: DO NOT USE ON ANY STRUCTURE SUBJECT TO BENDING FATIGUE OR IMPACT ~ JOINT IS SUITABLE FOR ANY POSITION

SQUARE GROOVE BUTT JOINT WELDED BOTH SIDES

SQUARE GROOVE BUTT JOINT WELDED ONE SIDE

100% EFF.   B-2

85% EFF.   B-1.

Other Materials Used in Steel Ship and Boatbuilding

Table 5 lists the brasses and bronzes often used in the construction of vessels. The weldability of these metals ranges from excellent to poor. These metals are not to be used where the temperature exceeds 500 degrees Fahrenheit.

Table 6 lists the common aluminum alloys that are used in marine construction. It is possible to weld aluminum to steel only by the use of a transition bar. Bars are readily available from the various aluminum companies and offer the best solution to the joint between the steel hull and the aluminum deckhouse. When only a limited amount of aluminum is to be welded, then the Shielded Metal Arc process is quite adequate and requires a DC power source. For small parts, Gas Tungsten Arc is better and certainly cleaner. For heavier weldments and where a frequent need to weld aluminum exists, the Gas Metal Arc method is the best.

Stainless steel is frequently used for fittings and hardware fabricated by the builder. Such items include stanchions, railings, bitts, chocks, tangs, chainplates, pintles, cleats, cavels, davits, etc. Some of the alloys used are readily welded to low-carbon steel, mild steel, and most of the high-strength, low-alloy steels. In order to eliminate brittleness and cracking of welds, welding should be done with special stainless steel rods, not the steel rods used for welding the mild steel hull. The welding can be done with the Shielded Metal Arc process if a DC source is available.

TABLE 5. Brasses and Bronzes Used in Shipbuilding

Symbol	Common Name	Common Use
A	Admiralty Metal	Tubes for feedwater heaters, condensers, evaporators, etc.
B-c	Commercial Brass	Name plates, trim, handrail fittings, etc., when corrosion resistance and strength are not important.
B-r	Commercial Brass	Shims, liners, label plates, trim, etc., when corrosion resistance and strength are not important.
BE	Ornamental Bronze	Electrical fixtures, instruments and other castings.
G	Gun Metal (c)	Valves and pipe fittings of 100 lbs. pressure and over, gears, and other castings, when strength and resistance to corrosion are required.
H	Journal Bronze (c)	Slippers, bushings, and other bearing surfaces.
M	Valve Bronze (c)	Valves, pipe fittings, hose couplings, and fittings of less than 100 lbs. pressure; also, flanges for copper pipe and other brazed fittings.
Mn-c	Manganese Bronze	Propeller hubs and blades, worm gears, wheels, and other parts that require great strength and resistance to corrosion.
Mn-r	Manganese Bronze	Bolts, studs, valve stems, and other parts that require great strength and resistance to corrosion.
CN-c	Monel Metal (c)	Valves and other fittings used at high temperatures that require strength and resistance to corrosion.
CN-r	Monel Metal (r)	Bolts, pump rods, valve stems, etc., used at high temperatures, that require strength and resistance to corrosion.
N-c	Naval Brass (c) or Tobin Bronze	Handwheels and other misc. parts with a quality between B-c and G.
N-r	Naval Brass (r)	Nuts, bolts, screws, forgings, valve stems, and other parts that require strength and resistance to corrosion.
P-c	Phosphor-bronze (c)	Parts requiring medium strength, when exposed to salt water.
P-r	Phosphor-bronze (r)	Valve stems, pump rods, springs, and other parts exposed to salt water.
S-c	Screwed Brass (c)	Screwed pipe fittings.
S	Scrap Brass	Misc. castings

Cast=c; rolled=r. The chemical composition of these brasses and bronzes includes copper, zinc, tin, lead, iron, manganese, phosphorus, and nickel in varying amounts, according to type. Those that are cast have tensile strengths of about 22,000 psi for journal bronze to 65,000 psi for manganese bronze and monel metal. The rolled bronzes have strengths of 50,000 psi to 90,000 psi.

TABLE 6. Aluminum Alloys Used in Shipbuilding

Alloy	Temper	Available	Use
5052	H112, H32	sheet, plate, tube, shapes, rod, bar	tanks, fan blades, ladders, and hulls of small craft
5083	H116, H111	sheet, plate, tube, shapes, rod, bar	high-strength welded structure below 150 °F
5086	H116, H111	sheet, plate, tube, shapes, rod, bar	best for hull plating
5454	H112, H111	sheet, plate, rod, shapes, bar	for welded structures up to 400 °F: stacks, vents, etc.
5456	H116, H111	sheet, plate, rod, shapes, bar	hull plating, framing, etc.
6061	T6	sheet, plate, tube, tread plate, pipe, rod, bar, forging stock, shapes	framing, masts, booms, davits, bitts, chocks, bolts, nuts, bus bars, rivets
6063	T6	tubes, shapes, rod, bar, pipe	masts, booms, low strength

Note on pipe: "Sch." in a manufacturer's inventory list refers to schedule numbers, and this replaces the old method of rating by standard (sch.40), extra strong (sch.80), double extra strong (sch.120), and triple extra strong (sch.160). Alloy 6061 pipe of sch. 40 and sch. 80, and alloy 6063 pipe of sch. 5, 10, 40, and 80 are readily available as stock items. Alloy 6061 is considerably stronger than 6063. Non-standard sch. 120 and 160 are standard in some diameters but not usually stocked by a warehouse. In the aluminum alloys a builder may have any desired shape extruded for the cost of the die, which is generally quite reasonable; to this cost he must add a minimum poundage and a setup charge. At times these charges can be offset by a labor saving.

For extensive welding of stainless steel, especially when the finished welds must have a visual neatness without grinding, the Gas Tungsten Arc method is best. Of the numerous grades available, the chromium nickel (austenitic) type 304 has low carbon content, provides good corrosion resistance after welding, and is available in sheet, plate, round bar, half ovals, bars, angles, and pipe. This type is used where subsequent heat treatment is impossible. Type 316L has better corrosion resistance than type 304 and should be used for low-magnetic purposes. The ELC (extra-low carbon) grade of type 316L offers high resistance to inner granular corrosion caused by carbide precipitation in the weld zone.

Lead is extensively used for shielding, sound barriers, battery box liners, and ballast, and must be insulated from the steel. This can be done in numerous ways, many dictated by the end use of the lead. In the case of ballast areas, the steel should be coated with a wash consisting of pure Portland cement prior to laying the bricks or ingots of lead. These should be laid in a grout of four parts clean sand to one part cement, and capped with a mixture of three parts sand to one part cement and, when cured, painted with a waterproofing paint. The alternate method is to cap the cement with a steel plate, but one should do this only when the ballast is to be absolutely permanent.

Wood bearing directly against metal should not be exposed to the weather, as it will create a never-ending poultice corrosion problem in spite of the sealants used to protect the steel and the bedding compounds used for the wood. In places aboard the vessel where wood should be pretreated, it is best to treat it with nonmetallic compounds only, to eliminate any leaching and resultant metallic corrosion. On the interior of the hull where ceilings allow adequate air circulation, cargo battens or open grates can usually be attached or otherwise fitted directly to the steel, provided it has been well painted. When a solid liner, cargo hold decking, joiner bulkheads, watertight bulkheads, and paneling are fitted, not only must the steel be well painted, but the wood/steel faying surface must also be bedded with a suitable compound such as asphalt, silicon rubber, polysulphide, or some other inert compound that will effectively reject moisture. The raw ends of the wood, especially plywood, should be painted thoroughly, and direct butting of the wood against the shell should be avoided whenever possible.

Asphalt and other bituminous compounds are very effective for protecting steel, especially in wet or damp areas, such as the bilge. They should never be used in the engine room or any other location where oil is present, since they are oil soluble. On sailing vessels the ballast may be bedded in asphalt materials, and in most vessels the cargo hold and bilges outside the engine areas are also suitable for this type of coating. Note, however, that the odor connected with asphalt and bituminous compounds may possibly taint some dry cargoes.

Whenever dissimilar metals come in contact in a marine environment, electrolysis will occur, with potentially disastrous consequences. Table 7 lists the various metals in order of their electrical (galvanic) potential. The greater the difference between values, the stronger the galvanic interaction between two metals not isolated from each other.

Even before its keel has been laid, a steel vessel may already suffer from a corrosion problem, if the materials have been improperly handled and allowed to weather badly. Whenever possible, materials should be stored under cover, dry and well aired. Steel, if stored outside, should be raised off the ground on sleepers to minimize corrosion, since wet ground accelerates rusting. The better the storage, the less work required prior to use.

All materials used in the construction of a vessel have a bearing on each other, not only in terms of direct costs, but also in terms of the additional cost of isolating them from each other. The transition labor involved in the actual attachment of the various materials varies considerably and is hard to estimate. Once the isolation is accomplished, then you can continue working the secondary material without regard to the primary material as long as the isolation is not breached. For instance, once a wooden nailer or sleeper has been bolted to a steel frame, then a wooden bulkhead, joiner bulkhead, cabin sole, ceiling, or any other wooden item can be attached directly to the nailer or sleeper without further concern about the steel.

The last word on any subject is never spoken, but on the theory that the attempt can be useful, I'll try anyway. With regard to materials, unless you as the builder have an unlimited budget and are unconcerned about the ultimate cost, it is definitely in your best interest to try to understand all of the materials entering into the

**TABLE 7. Electrical or Galvanic Potential of Metals, Assuming Vessel Speed
of 4½ to 7½ Knots**

Name	Approximate Potential (volts)	
Graphite	+0.3 to +0.2	Most noble (cathodic)
Ni-Cr-Mo	+0.08 to −0.03	
Titanium	+0.05 to −0.05	
Ni-Cr-Mo-Cu-Si	+0.05 to +0.02	
Ni-Fe-Cr	+0.04 to −0.02	
Stainless 316	0.00 to −0.10	
Stainless 304	−0.05 to −0.10	
Ni-Al-Bronze	−0.15 to −0.22	
70-30 copper nickel	−0.17 to −0.23	
Lead	−0.19 to −0.24	
80-20 copper nickel	−0.21 to −0.27	
90-10 copper nickel	−0.22 to −0.28	
Tin-bronze	−0.24 to −0.32	
Silicon-bronze	−0.26 to −0.29	
Manganese-bronze	−0.27 to −0.33	
Admiralty Metal	−0.27 to −0.35	
Copper	−0.30 to −0.37	
Tin	−0.31 to −0.34	
Brass	−0.30 to −0.40	
Al-Bronze	−0.31 to −0.42	
Low-alloy steel	−0.57 to −0.63	
Mild steel	−0.60 to −0.72	
Cadmium	−0.70 to −0.74	
Aluminum Alloys	−0.76 to −1.00	
Zinc	−0.96 to −1.30	
Magnesium	−1.60 to −1.63	Least noble (anodic)

*The difference in potential between a base metal and a nobler metal may be more, but is usually less,
than the tabular difference shown in the table, and is further affected by temperature and velocity. For
example, stainless steels will generally increase in negative (less noble) potential by about 0.30 volts
at very low velocities, bringing them closer to, say, mild steel. The speeds chosen are representative of
sailing vessels.*

construction of your vessel. In doing so, the estimating of costs and the purchasing
of materials become second nature, and you develop the ability to evaluate new
products as they come on the market. I'm not suggesting that anyone needs to start
with a backyard blast furnace; however, knowing your medium *is* fundamental.
Diligent study is always worth the effort in the long run.

3

▽

STEEL
BOATBUILDING
EQUIPMENT

Tool catalogs are every builder's "wish book." No matter how well-equipped the builder, there is always some tool that he would like to own, even if it is not on the "must have" list, let alone the "could use" list. Most of us have trouble admitting we could really do without that certain new tool—that it is more of a new toy than a necessity. Without much effort you can become "tool poor." When this happens productivity decreases rather than increases, as you spend too much time setting up and using specialty tools to do what you could have done equally well with general purpose tools in a fraction of the time. On the other hand, the opposite extreme is equally bad, for when you must convert your sparse assortment of tools every time you attempt a different job, you not only lose time, you also discover that tools are seldom good at a job for which they were not designed, even though they can be adapted to that purpose.

There is much truth in the adage that "tools do not a craftsman make." Visit any yard and you can prove it just by observing a journeyman at his trade. Note the fluid motion, the minimum effort, and the pace he maintains. In my yard, owners of a vessel under construction often wanted to "work with us and sort of pick up the trade." Usually they started with a burst of activity during the first hour, encouraging the rest of us to work a little faster with such cheerful jibes as "No wonder boats cost so much . . . I can do it faster . . . This is fun," and so on. About two hours later they were asking, "When do you guys take a break?" Two more hours—after taking a break while the rest of us kept working—and they would be asking, "When do you break for lunch?" When informed that there was still another hour to go, they usually hung around a few minutes, then discovered they had to go to town but would be back for the afternoon. The hardier ones got back by 3:00 PM and tried to do something that required neither lifting nor moving until quitting time at 5:30 PM, at which time they never failed to observe that we had worked for 10 hours at about the same pace. As efficient at quitting time as when we started in the morning, we had accomplished a great deal, and tomorrow we were probably going to do the same, while the owner would need a day of rest. In my yard we worked 10-hour days, with no breaks except one-half hour for lunch. There were no windows in the shop, no music from radios, and no other distractions; to my ears the hum of welding machines and the sounds of hammers and grinders were music. I paid well and had good men and good equipment. I am not a saint, but in the ship and boatbuilding profession there is a fine line between profit and loss that one must never lose sight of if he expects to remain in business.

I concede that some builders are amateur only in the sense that they are not professionally employed in the boat and shipbuilding trade. Plenty of people with varying degrees of skill will build or are presently building small vessels for themselves; they may have to spend more time thinking out how to adapt their knowledge to boatbuilding than will those employed full time in the industry, but in my eyes they are still "builders," not "amateurs." Some, of course, must acquire one or more completely new skills in order to start a building project. I remember teaching a young lady the fundamentals of welding in about 30 minutes, with a couple of hours spent explaining lofting, cutting, and other miscellaneous odds and ends of boatbuilding. Within three years she launched a fine 48-foot steel schooner. Thus, in my mind, the lack of boatbuilding experience does not imply an inability to acquire the skills needed to competently complete the task of building a boat.

This consideration has a direct bearing on tools. In the case of a one-time project, the vessel inherits the tools that the builder already has in his workshop plus some others purchased as needed. They may not always be the "ideal" tools for the job, but are simply tools that will suffice. In most instances they will include an assortment of hand, portable electric, and bench-mounted tools. When faced with the purchase of a new tool, you must consider its future use after the vessel is built. One of the advantages of metal boatbuilding is that, for the most part, the tools used in a home woodworking shop will also be needed for the interior as well as some of the deck structure. If you have some woodworking tools already, you may only need to add a few heavy-duty, industrial-grade tools for working the steel, and these will enhance the home workshop after the vessel is built. Fortunately for the builder of steel vessels, a basic set of heavy-duty tools will work correctly regardless of the size of vessel built and will not outlast their usefulness, unlike traditional wooden shipbuilding tools, which were proportioned to the size of the vessel being built, so that the tools needed for a larger vessel would be grossly out of place in a home workshop.

When selecting a tool, you should certainly consider whether it will be used only during construction, or whether it will be included in the inventory of the vessel. When a vessel is extensively cruised, a good selection of tools will be needed for maintenance, alterations, and repairs. The tools available in many foreign and domestic yards leave a lot to be desired, and often one remembers with a sigh a tool discarded or left behind that would now work better than the best available.

In order to carry enough tools aboard to be reasonably prepared for normal maintenance, you must decide whether to depend on shore power only or to include an independent power source as part of the vessel's equipment. If you choose independence, you will have to select tools cautiously, making sure the amperage requirements of a particular tool do not exceed the continuous rated output of the source. Smaller sailing and motor vessels most often carry electric hand tools powered by portable gasoline generators of 500 to 1500 watts. These inexpensive units are small and light enough to be dinghied ashore for use in repairing spars, sails, dinghy, or whatnot. On larger vessels that have an auxiliary diesel generator permanently installed, you may have to remain afloat if the generator is water-cooled; if it is air-cooled, you will be able to work while hauled out, but still won't be able to move the unit. The capacity of the larger generators ranges from 3 kilowatts (3000 watts) on up, 7½ kilowatts being more than enough for most welding machines and for air compressors if air-powered tools are used. Many countries use 50- rather than 60-cycle current, and some (but not all) tools will operate on either 50 or 60 cycles. In some areas, only 220-volt current is available, and this must be split to obtain 110 volts.

The prime disadvantage of working with electrical tools is the necessity of being in a dry area, as well as avoiding any other risk of grounding yourself and getting electrocuted. A ground fault device in the power line will eliminate this risk and is a must in any boatbuilding project. Other disadvantages include the cost of the tools themselves, their weight, and their maintenance. The wide variety of small, inexpensive electric tools makes them an attractive buy, but repairs often exceed the cost of a tool; this puts them in the category of expendable items. In many instances, however, the idea of a throwaway tool is in itself not only appealing but justified.

If, in the beginning, you can select the best and safest without regard for cost, then you should choose air-driven tools; however, one is seldom in this position. Despite the lower cost, light weight, and minimal maintenance costs of the air tools themselves, the initial cost of a compressor of adequate size is a major factor, especially when it exceeds the total cost of going all-electric. This is the basic reason that most small yards and shops of amateur builders are not so-equipped. But the case is not as simple as it seems. For example, a 7-inch heavy-duty air grinder demanding 11 cubic feet of air per minute (cfm), weighing 6½ pounds, and reaching 4500 rpm, lists for $190; the same quality in electric at 15 amps, 18 pounds, and 8000 rpm lists for $450. In other tools the price differential is not as great, but air tools normally run one-half to three-quarters the price of electric tools of the same quality and capacity. An air compressor with a 3-horsepower motor, delivering 22 cfm plus 13 cfm free air at 125 psi, costs $775. Thus, the difference in cost between a ¾-horsepower compressor used for paint spraying, at $450, and a 3-horsepower compressor that could power many air tools and a small sandblaster, at $775, suggests that you should seriously consider having all air-powered tools right from the beginning. The increased utility may offset the extra price, and in larger vessels a compressor can later be incorporated into the on-board equipment.

A great many small, table-type bandsaws, circular saws, jointers, routers, and other shop tools will suffice for a one-time project and still prove an asset in the home workshop after the vessel is complete; alternatively, you might sell them to someone else who is building a vessel. These tools are convenient in that they are light and easily portable; however, you should not expect production work from them, since there is no substitute for the standard, commercial machinery normally used within the industry.

The tools necessary to build a steel vessel can best be itemized by job and relative importance. This will allow you to see where a particular tool is used for more than one purpose and to decide what you absolutely must have, what would help to speed up the task at hand, and what should be considered one of those ultimate additions you *could* make. Bear in mind that quite often a home workshop will already possess some of these items, since they are useful for other purposes besides boat-building.

● **Lofting and patternmaking.** *Needed:* pencils; erasers; compass; straightedges (wood, 8 and 12 feet long); steel tape 50 to 100 feet long; steel tape (pocket) 6 to 12 feet long; 10-point hand saw; hand rip saw; block plane; smoothing plane; jointer plane; 24-inch framing square; 8-inch carpenter's square; bevel square; 3-pound machinist's hammer; claw hammer; wire-cutting nippers; small metal vise or woodworker's vise; compass saw; coping saw; chalkline; hand drill; tin snips. *Useful:* sabersaw; portable circular saw; disc sander; orbital sander; power stapler; ⅜-inch electric drill. *Ultimate:* 12-inch bandsaw; 8-inch table saw; 6-inch jointer; drill press.

● **Working steel.** *Needed:* oxygen-acetylene burning outfit with gauges; 50 feet (minimum) of dual hose; striker; goggles; welding machine with 50 feet (minimum) of cable to rod holder; welding helmet; welding gloves; chipping hammer.

●**Frame making.** *Needed:* portable grinder; small wrecking bar; Vise-Grips; anvil (3-inch thick steel plate, 12 by 24 inches, or 150-pound-minimum horn type); 8-pound sledge hammer; temporary platen (can be made by using the hull's shell plating). *Useful:* permanent steel platen for assembly; tilting-frame metal-cutting cutoff bandsaw; table-mounted drill press. *Ultimate:* bending platen with hold-down dogs, bending posts, and other accessories; needle scalers.

● **Keel assembly.** *Needed:* six 12-inch C-clamps; two pipe clamps with various lengths of pipe threaded on one end. *Useful:* quick-acting clamps rather than C-clamps.

● **Frame erection.** *Needed:* twelve 8-inch C-clamps; 24-inch level; line level; piano wire; two small turnbuckles; block and tackle (handy-billy rigged). *Useful:* quick-acting clamps rather than C-clamps.

● **Longitudinals, chines, sheer pipe.** *Needed:* two 10-inch adjustable wrenches; ⅜-inch chain in various lengths (2, 4, 6, and 8 feet, etc.) plus several shackles to fit the chain. *Useful:* two ½-ton come-alongs; a 24-inch to 36-inch pipe wrench; C-clamps as above.

● **Plating.** *Needed:* heavy-duty 7-inch portable grinder, or heavy-duty 7-inch disc grinder-sander; 2-pound ball peen hammer. *Useful:* needle scaler; Dynafile (from

Dynabrade, Inc.); 4-inch heavy-duty grinder; soft-pack slow-speed disc sander; 7-inch heavy-duty sander; tool and die grinder.

• **Machinery installation.** *Needed:* pipe threading dies at least capable of chasing damaged threads; pipe vise; small hand-held tube bender; ½-inch portable drill; die set; feeler gauges; hand pump to test tanks; air pressure gauges; socket wrenches; torque wrench; miscellaneous mechanic's hand tools. *Useful:* small air compressor. *Ultimate:* large air compressor.

• **Sandblasting.** *Needed:* compressor delivering 125 pounds of pressure at 125 cubic feet per minute. This can be rented on a per diem basis, as may a sandblasting machine (many individuals and yards own their own). You will also need a place to store the sand, which normally comes in 100-pound bags and must be kept dry. In many sections of the country, there are companies that will sandblast to white metal and prime paint for less than it costs to rent the equipment, let alone own it. In this case, it makes sense to consider owning a much smaller compressor, say a 3-horsepower, that will do spot blasting and other small blasting jobs as well as run a paint sprayer and air tools.

• **Interior and exterior joinerwork.** *Needed:* wood chisels; wooden mallet; rubber mallet; claw hammer; hand saws (8-, 10-, and 12-point); rip saw; whetstones; augers; bits; drill; squares of various sizes; screwdrivers; nail sets; awls; scribes; compass; smoothing, jointer, jack, and block planes; 2-foot cabinetmaker's rule; pencils; knife; spokeshave; drawknife; hatchet; several sizes of cold chisels; several sizes of adjustable wrenches; workbench; bench vise; dogs. *Useful:* electric drill; electric router; sabersaw; bandsaw; table saw. *Ultimate:* 6-inch jointer; molder-planer; 12-inch (minimum) thickness planer; drill press; wet and dry vacuum cleaner; 8-inch worm-drive Skilsaw; belt sander; orbital sander; hand-held planer.

• **Sparmaking.** Same as joinerwork. If homemade clamps are used for a one-time effort, you would not need to purchase more clamps; however, for a 50-foot hollow wooden spar, 100 quick-acting steel bar clamps would not be too many. For a solid spar, using only hand tools, a broadax and an adze would save time; however, a worm-drive Skilsaw plus a hand-held, motor-driven planer would accomplish the work even faster.

• **Rigging.** *Needed:* marlinspikes; fids; wire splicing vise; hammers; pliers; Vise-Grips; serving mallet; knife. *Useful:* hydraulic Nicopress crimper with the required die sizes.

• **Fittings.** Metal fittings and hardware require the same tool assortment as those used to build the vessel.

• **Painting and varnishing.** *Needed:* brushes; rollers; sponges. *Useful:* airless paint sprayer. I add this reluctantly, as much time and money can be wasted by trying to spray finish a vessel, except for the interior of the bare steel hull and the exterior priming and barrier coats. The finish color coats require masking off. While a paint sprayer is required with many of the urethane finishes that are popular these days, other paints, including high gloss alkyds, varnish, and others, can be applied with a brush by a good painter. Except for a high-grade yacht finish, a roller coat that is brushed simultaneously is excellent, and a straight roller coat is quite acceptable on commercial vessels and most distance-cruising vessels.

If you are considering building a metal boat, you should not let the seemingly endless list of required tools discourage you. If most of the work can be done with power tools, then many of the hand tools need not be purchased—for example, planes (you really would require only a block plane). The same holds true for saws. A good 12-point saw is all you need; however, I realize that some people prefer to do everything by hand that can possibly be done—hence the list.

Building Site

The selection of a building site takes priority over the purchase of any equipment. You must determine the limits of available electrical capacity; in many areas there is a limit to what power company electric lines will carry without either increasing the transformer size, running in a special line, or both, all of which is costly. Should you have access to three-phase power, this might also influence the purchase of any new equipment. If power is not available at all, you will have to generate your own.

It is always easier to build a vessel under cover, or at least partial cover, because of the unpredictability of the weather. The cover need only be temporary, and indeed, in many municipalities this is the maximum you can attempt without building permits. A building, shed, or barn is, of course, ideal. In any case, bear in mind the following safety precautions: you should never build on a wood floor; the area around the vessel should be cleaned of any debris; and any holes should be filled, loose rocks and stumps cleared away, and weeds and grass mowed down. Sparks, slag, and pieces of molten metal always present a fire hazard, and the presence of any oils an explosive hazard; wood and other absorbent combustibles thus create a serious danger underfoot. It is desirable to have a work area measuring at least 10 feet more all around than the length and breadth of the vessel, and at least 5 feet higher than the total depth from the bottom of the keel to the highest point of the cabin. Where an existing shed or building lacks only height, it is often possible to dig a trench about 6 feet wide to accommodate the keel. If the vessel must be built in the open, it helps to trench around the immediate area to assure drainage of rainwater. Overhead power lines within 30 feet in any direction of the vessel should be considered lethal unless fully isolated by a barrier from the building site. If you plan to build more than one vessel, then it would be best to bury the electric cables at least 3 feet underground. Then no one—including incoming trucks, cranes, and heavy equipment—will have to worry about electrocution.

Welding Equipment

The arc welding power source may now be selected, and this choice should be carefully thought out prior to purchase. Small shipyards use two basic methods of welding. The most popular, which is also the least expensive to purchase, is the Shielded Metal Arc method (which uses stick electrodes covered with a flux coating). Shielded Metal Arc is totally manual: the maintenance of the arc, feed of the filler metal, joint travel, and guidance of the electrode are all manually regulated, making this the most versatile of all welding methods. By contrast, the Gas Metal Arc method (also called Metal Inert Gas or MIG) is a semiautomatic process in which the machine maintains the arc and the feed of the filler metal, and the individual only provides the joint travel and the guidance. This method requires a shielding gas in order to accomplish the weld and is faster than Shielded Metal Arc as well as cleaner, since no chipping is required after the weld is completed. Because of the gas envelope around the electrode, it is difficult to use outdoors if there is a breeze blowing; temporary windbreaks are often needed, as they also are inside shops with ventilation blowers. The first cost of Gas Metal Arc welding machines runs several times that of the Shielded Metal Arc machines. For a one-time building project, Shielded Metal Arc is the best way to go. Even in small contract yards with only two or three people welding, it is difficult to justify going to Metal Inert Gas welding unless one person can work exclusively on welding production. Gilbert Klingel ran a one-man yard with minimal equipment, yet turned out vessels up to 77 feet in length using only the Shielded Metal Arc method. In my own yard, with a bit more but still very unsophisticated equipment, I was able to build as many as six vessels at one time, and I could build vessels up to 80 feet long. I always used the Shielded Metal Arc method on my steel hulls. Only when I started building in aluminum did I purchase Metal Inert Gas welding equipment, and never used it for anything but aluminum. Therefore, unless otherwise stated, wherever I talk about welding I am referring to the Shielded Metal Arc welding process because it is versatile, simple, inexpensive, and does not require ideal conditions to work.

In the United States, the purchase of a welding machine that will operate on single phase 220-volt 60-cycle current will allow you to weld anywhere electricity is available. If you buy one of the smaller units, you can plug it into any circuit able to accommodate a standard household clothes dryer. This means that the current available for welding will be limited to about 200 to 250 amps, but this is more than enough for welding steel vessels up to 100 feet. Indeed, the only limitations imposed by these smaller power sources are on the size of the welding electrode you can use and on the duty cycle of the machine. Electrodes of $\frac{5}{32}$-inch diameter will be about the maximum you can use; using this diameter, you will have a 20- to 30-percent duty cycle at the maximum output of the machine. Since duty cycle translates into the percentage of time during a 10-minute period that the machine can be used, you will be able to weld for two to three minutes out of every 10 at maximum output. At first you might think this sounds like a severe limitation, and that you should seek a 100-percent duty cycle; not so. In small steel shipbuilding, one seldom consumes half an electrode at a time without having to move a few feet before using up the remaining portion (except on very heavy shell plating). Moreover, the area just welded must be chipped clean of weld flux and the new area wire-brushed in the way of the next segment to be welded. The most diligent welder will find it difficult to maintain five minutes of welding out of every 10 for a whole working day, but even if he could, this would not justify purchasing a larger machine, since reducing to the next lower diameter of rod will normally yield a 50- to 60-percent duty cycle, and a further reduction of one diameter often results in a 100-percent duty cycle. Ship and boatbuilding demand very few heavy weldments, and these are always welded with multiple passes. Shell plating is always welded inside and out. Thus, small-diameter rods are preferred, and in fact, many yards limit the rod diameter to a maximum of one-half the thickness of the shell plating, the minimum being ³⁄₃₂-inch diameter rods, the smallest that are generally available for mild steel.

Once you have chosen a basic method, you must next decide whether to purchase a machine capable only of AC welding, or one with AC/DC capability. The former machines are the least expensive and can be used for the construction of the entire vessel. Arc blow is seldom a problem with AC equipment, although the disposition rate and penetration are not as versatile as with DC welding. Selection of the proper electrodes easily overcomes any disadvantage of AC welding in these respects, however. The dual machines capable of both AC and DC do have several advantages and are, of course, more expensive. The DC feature allows you to change the direction of current flow: straight polarity (electrode negative) is used for shallower penetration and higher disposition rates, such as on thin metal; reverse polarity (electrode positive) is used where deep penetration is required. Hard-surfacing electrodes, many of the electrodes used to weld cast iron, and those used to weld aluminum alloys all require DC voltage. If very much pipe has to be welded, then DC is a better choice than AC.

Several of the small welding machines can accommodate carbon arc equipment, which is used for welding aluminum and copper alloys, heating, bending, straightening, and soldering. Some also allow Gas Tungsten Arc welding (TIG) if they have a high frequency mode built in or can drive a separate machine having a high frequency arc starter. Fortunately, most welding supply houses are staffed with knowledgeable people rather than order-takers, who will be able to advise you on choosing equipment with these capabilities. When it is economically possible, you should choose equipment that will permit expansion or upgrading at a later date, to avoid its becoming redundant or obsolete.

Once the capacity of the power source has been determined, you may select the size of the electrode cable. Determine the length by adding together the total length of the electrode and the work (ground) cable. Rather than having two cables to trip over, builders customarily install a permanent ground cable that can be buried, or use an insulated ground bar connected to the welding machine by a short length of cable. In this case, a 50-foot length of welding cable would be cut into a 48-foot length for the electrode and a 2-foot length to the ground bar, and if the ground bar were 10 feet long, we would then calculate the size of wire for a 60-foot length. If the maximum current were 150 amps, size No. 2 would be correct, as it would be up to a total cable length of 150 feet. A machine capable of 250 amps could use size No. 2 but would be limited to a total run of 100 feet, and if 150 feet were required, then 1/0 wire would have to be used. After studying your building site, the approximate position of the vessel, and the size of the vessel itself, you can make a final determination of cable size and length. As a rule of thumb, the length of the vessel plus 40 feet gives the cable length to order for the electrode holder. On larger vessels you can reduce the cable length somewhat by siting the welding machine near the center of the vessel. The difference in effort of dragging No. 2 versus 1/0 cable each day will be enough to make you cautious about the setup.

The welding machine, and indeed, all machinery, must be protected from the elements when you are building out in the open. You should plan on a small shed for this purpose, or wheels will have to be used on all heavy equipment to permit easy moving after each day's use.

Metal cutting in small steel boat and shipbuilding is generally done by oxygen-acetylene torch, since the equipment is fairly inexpensive. If money were of no concern you might consider adding plasma arc cutting capability, since it would allow you to cut all the metals used in the construction of the vessel with the least distortion. Oxygen and acetylene bottles are supplied by local plants that specialize in this service. In some localities you can own the bottles, but in other places ownership is prohibited by law, and you must rent the bottles from the company, usually with so many days allowed for consumption before a daily demurrage commences. Paying demurrage can become expensive over the construction time of the vessel, so you will do well to shop around even to a more distant city to obtain the most favorable rental. In general, two large bottles of oxygen are consumed per large bottle of acetylene. Some builders prefer using short hoses (50 feet) and thus must have a cart to move the bottles to the position nearest where they are to be used. I prefer not to move the bottles, keeping them lashed to a building or a post away from the vessel and using longer runs of hose. Never lay the full bottles on their sides, as this can damage the regulators. I stress again that the area in which the bottles are used and stored must be kept clean, well aired, and *free of any oil*, as oxygen under pressure coming in contact with oil will cause a fire and quite probably an explosion if it feeds back to the bottle. Always replace the caps on empty bottles, and never accept a bottle from a supplier unless it has a cap. You can purchase the regulators, hose, torch, tips, and striker from the local gas supplier or from a welding supply house.

Welding rods are supplied in water-resistant cardboard boxes and, in some instances, watertight tins. Once you open a box or tin, it is imperative to keep the rods dry and as moisture-free as possible. Most welders just stick a handful of rods in their back pockets or carry them in a small leather bag fastened around the waist; usually an hour's worth is about the maximum that need be exposed at any given time. Low-hydrogen rods must be kept and used in a heated condition. For common rods, you can convert a small refrigerator to an oven by installing a 100- to 150-watt light bulb and cutting a small vent hole to eliminate the moisture. Some people use ovens fitted with light bulbs or else small heating elements. Several manufacturers produce ovens specially designed for heating rods. The smaller, portable sizes will hold 50 to 70 pounds of rod and have the advantage that you can site them close to where you are working, thus not having to overload your hip pocket.

When more than one vessel is under construction at the same time, it is often possible to automate some of the work, especially in making long cuts, cutting holes, and doing much of the welding. The rule of thumb (it sometimes seems that all boat and shipbuilding is thumbs) is that, counting setup time, if the job can be done faster and better automatically than a skilled man could do it, then automate. In my yard, employing fewer than 12 people, limited automation increased production enough to avoid hiring four extra workers. Quite obviously, in a one-man shop there will be a limit to any automation. The Weld Tooling Corporation manufactures the BUG-0 systems used in many yards for specialized automation.

Brushes are used by the dozen, especially wire brushes. For years, I have purchased these items from two companies, Torrington Brush Works and Advance Brushes, Inc.

Items for general shop outfitting and material handling are usually purchased locally; much can be found in surplus stores and junk yards. These items include bins, lockers, and sinks; unloading equipment such as skids, ramps, and rollers; ladders; plate lifting clamps; chain hoists; and hand winches. If your time is important, you can get all of these things from a supply house such as SHD in Boston that specializes in this equipment. SHD also carries in stock the V-groove drop-forged casters with a capacity of 6,000 to 8,350 pounds per wheel in 6-, 8-, and 10-inch diameters. These wheels are excellent for moving and launching cradles. The groove fits inverted angle iron, laid down free or on ties as a rail. On concrete, the flat portion of the wheel may be used without the angle. The casters are also available with swivel bases should you need to move cradles in any direction other than ahead or astern. Some of the companies that manufacture these wheels are listed below.

Individual builders, as well as small shipyards, normally deal exclusively with local welding supply houses rather than directly with the factory. By purchasing name brand equipment, you will insure that the warranties are valid and any application problems can be referred back to experts. Thus, I would strongly advise against buying off-brands, house brands, and bargain-basement brands. Another factor you should keep in mind is the repair of tools. Eventually, every tool needs repair or service, and it is much better when this can be done locally.

The list that follows indicates firms that I have done business with in the past, or whose equipment I have used to my complete satisfaction. It is not all-inclusive; however, should you see these names in your welding supply company, you can rest assured they stand for good and reputable companies.

Arc welding power sources:

Airco Welding Products, 575 Mountain Ave., Murray Hill, NJ 07947
ESAB Welding Products Division, P.O. Box 7949, The Woodlands, TX 77380
Hobart Brothers Company, P.O. Box EW-452, Troy, OH 45373
Lincoln Electric Company, 22801 St. Clair Ave., Cleveland, OH 44117-1199
Miller Electric Mfg. Co., 718 South Bounds St., Appleton, WI 54911
Union Carbide Corporation, Linde Division, P.O. Box F-600, Florence, SC 29501

Cutting equipment:

Airco Welding Products, 575 Mountain Ave., Murray Hill, NJ 07947
Arcair Company, Rt. 33 N, Box 406, Lancaster, OH 43130
ESAB Welding Products Division, P.O. Box 7949, The Woodlands, TX 77380
Smith Equipment Div., Tescom Corporation, 2600 Niagara Lane North, Minneapolis, MN 55441
Union Carbide Corporation, Linde Division, P.O. Box F-600, Florence, SC 29501
Uniweld Products, Inc., 2850 Ravenswood Rd., Fort Lauderdale, FL 33312

Electrode holders, clamps, lugs, connectors:

Airco Welding Products, 575 Mountain Ave., Murray Hill, NJ 07947
Bernard Division, Box 667, Beecher, IL 60401
Jackson Products, 5801 Safety Dr. N.E., Belmont, MI 49306
Tweco Products, Inc., P.O. Box 12250, Wichita, KS 67277

Ovens:

Henkel, Inc., P.O. Box 1322, Hammond, LA 70401
Phoenix Products Company, Inc., 4715 N. 27th St., Milwaukee, WI 53209

Brushes:

Torrington Brush Works, Inc., Torrington, CT 06790
Advance Brushes, Inc., 12501 Elmwood Ave., Cleveland, OH 44111

Safety and health equipment, welding helmets, gloves, protective clothing:

Elliott Glove Co., P.O. Box 5525, Compton, CA 90224
Jackson Products, 5801 Safety Dr. N.E., Belmont, MI 49306
Lincoln Electric Company, 22801 St. Clair Ave., Cleveland, OH 44117-1199
Morse Safety Products Company, 18103 Roseland Ave., Cleveland, OH 44112
Wolverine Glove Co., P.O. Box 8735, Grand Rapids, MI 49508

Portable electric tools:

AEG Power Tool Co., 1 Winnenden Rd., Norwich, CT 06360
Black and Decker, U.S., Inc., 626 Hanover Pike, Hampstead, MD 21047
Robert Bosch Power Tool Corp., 3701 Neuse Blvd., New Bern, NC 28560
Dayton Electric Mfg. Co., 5959 W. Howard St., Chicago, IL 60648
W.W. Grainger, Inc., 5959 W. Howard St., Chicago, IL 60648
Hitachi Power Tools USA, Ltd., 4487-F Park Drive, Norcross, GA 30093
Makita USA, Inc., 12950 E. Alondra Blvd., Cerritos, CA 90701
Milwaukee Tool Corp., 13135 W. Lisbon Rd., Brookfield, WI 53005

Rockwell International Corp., Power Tool Div., 401 N. Lexington Ave., Pittsburgh, PA 15208
Skil Corporation, 4801 W. Peterson Ave., Chicago, IL 60646

Portable air-powered tools:

ARO Corporation, The One Aro Center, Bryan, OH 43506
Ajax Tool Works, Inc., 10801 Franklin Ave., Franklin Park, IL 60131
Black and Decker, U.S., Inc., 626 Hanover Pike, Hampstead, MD 21047
Chicago Pneumatic Tool Div., 2200 Bleecker St., Utica, NY 13501
Cob Industries, Inc., P.O. Box 870, Larchmont, NY 10538
Dotco, Inc., Rte. 18 East, Hicksville, OH 43526
Dynabrade, Inc., 72 E. Niagara St., Tonawanda, NY 14150
Florida Pneumatic Mfg. Corp., 2900 High Ridge Rd., Boynton Beach, FL 33435
Ingersoll-Rand Power Tool Div., 28 Kennedy Blvd., East Brunswick, NJ 08816
National-Detroit, Inc., 1590 Northrock Court, Rockford, IL 61131
Rockwell International Corporation, Power Tool Div., 401 N. Lexington Ave., Pittsburgh, PA 15208
Thor Power Tool Co., Stewart-Warner Corp., Rte. 9, Roweland Dr., Johnson City, TN 37601
Universal Mfg. Co., Inc., 1168T Grove St., Irvington, NJ 07111
U.S. Industrial Tool and Supply Co., 13545 Auburn, Detroit, MI 48223

Air compressors:

Curtis-Toledo, Inc., 1905 Kienlen Ave., St. Louis, MO 63133
Dayton Electric Mfg. Co., 5959 W. Howard St., Chicago, IL 60648
Emglo Products Corp., Johnstown Industrial Park, Johnstown, PA 15904
Gardner-Denver Compressors, 1800 Gardner Expy., Quincy, IL 62301
Ingersoll-Rand Power Tool Division, 28 Kennedy Blvd., East Brunswick, NJ 08816
Kellogg-American, Inc., Box 159, Rte. 125, N. Kingston, NH 03848
LeRoi Division, Dresser Industries, Inc., P.O. Box 90, Sidney, OH 45365
Worthington Div. Compressors, McGraw-Edison Co., 270 Sheffield St., Mountainside, NJ 07092

Heavy ironworking equipment:

E.G. Heller's Son, Inc., Box 416, Tarzana, CA 91356
Hill Acme Co., 1201 W. 65th St., Cleveland, OH 44102
Metal Muncher, Div. of Center Engineering Co., Inc., P.O. Box 192, Rte. 3, Clay Center, KS 67432

Building platens:

The Acorn Iron & Supply Co., Delaware Ave. & Poplar St., Philadelphia, PA 19123
Weldsale Company, 2151 Dreer St., Philadelphia, PA 19125

Clamps:

Adjustable Clamp Co., 414 N. Ashland Ave., Chicago, IL 60622
James Morton, P.O. Box 3991, Batavia, NY 14020
Wetzler Clamp Co., Inc., 11th St. & 43rd Ave., Long Island City, NY 11101

Miscellaneous—Wheels:

Albion Industries, 800 Clark Rd., Albion, MI 49224
Bishop-Wisecarver Corp., 2104 Martin Way, Pittsburg, CA 94565
Casters & Wheels for Industry, Inc., 1339-T Sun Ave., Elmont, NY 11003
Hamilton Caster & Mfg. Co., 1637-97 Dixie Hwy., Hamilton, OH 45011
Ohio Brass Co., 380 N. Main St., Mansfield, OH 44902
Wellington Machine Co., 133 Dewolfe St., Wellington, OH 44090
Xtec, Inc., TSP Wheels, 211T Township Ave., Cincinnati, OH 45216

Automated Systems:

The Weld Tooling Corporation, 3001 W. Carson St., Pittsburgh, PA 15204

General Outfitting:

SHD, P.O. Box 13T, Sycamore Ave., Medford, MA 02155

4

$\triangledown$

BASIC
SCANTLINGS

The theme song of a construction plan is the *scantling plan*, often referred to as the *midship scantling section*. This plan is the designer's way of saying to the builder, "This is the way this vessel will be constructed; these are the sizes of materials that will be used; and when there are exceptions to this plan, they will be shown on the construction plan and construction sections plan, or in special details." When constructing a steel vessel, the builder should strive to maintain a standard that will not only produce a strong, fair, and economical hull, but will utilize the material to its fullest potential without excess weight.

DETERMINING SCANTLINGS

Scantlings generally derive from the standards devised by regulatory bodies or else from the designer's own rules, evolved from successful vessels of a particular type. Some designers use length as the sole criterion for developing scantling sections; others consider length, depth, and breadth, but treat the hull as if it were a simple box. Both of these methods disregard displacement and can result in structures that are either too heavy (overbuilt) or too light (underbuilt). I prefer to analyze the hull shape, the intended speed (if designing a power vessel, especially one with a planing hull), the waters in which the vessel will operate, and the displacement; from these I arrive at a basic scantling scheme that accentuates the virtues of steel. For me, displacement and length are the primary considerations, while depth and beam are secondary.

Distortion will result when the scantlings are ill-conceived. For example, light plating over heavy framing results in a starved-horse appearance, while the use of light framing in conjunction with heavy plating will cause the hull to shrink on its frame and buckle it. In the best construction, the framing and plating have the same thickness, so that the throats of the fillet welds connecting the frame to the plate can form true 45-degree angles. Except in vessels of more than 30,000 pounds displacement, however, this is seldom possible, since the framing would be so thin that it would buckle under its own weight while being set up, and little or no margin would exist for long-term corrosion. When absolutely necessary, framing up to two times the shell thickness can be used. Any more than this will produce "quench effect" problems in making fillet welds and any continuous welds, such as those in way of the fuel and water tanks. Exceptions to this rule would be the bearding welds along box keels, bar keels, the stem, the horn frame, and to heavy-walled pipe.

As for the shell plating itself, with the exception of box sections and barges, the upper limit for cold-forming plating is ⅜ inch (15.3 pounds per square foot), but since such plates are seldom used on vessels under 100 feet of deck length, this imposes no practical limit on the small-scale builder.

SOME REPRESENTATIVE SCANTLING SECTIONS

The best and really the only way to learn good construction practice outside a working yard that builds a variety of craft is to study as many plans as possible. To this end, I have organized this chapter around a series of representative illustrations, and much of what follows will simply comment on the scantling sections themselves. By spending some time studying these sections, both the seasoned and first-time builder may, I hope, learn something about the relationship between hull form and scantlings. Special attention should be paid to distinctive construction details of different sizes and types of hulls (flat-bottom, V-bottom, multi-chine, and round-bottom), alternative ways of constructing sound sections for each type, and the various relationships between plate thickness and framing on different hulls.

Flat-bottom hulls are seen in the sharpie, garvey, dory, and scow hull forms in the United States, and in other generic types, such as the Dutch grundels and botters, the Thames sailing barges, and many of the Chinese junks.

Figure 7 shows a 36-foot ketch-rigged sharpie yacht, framed both transversely and longitudinally. Her centerboard is, almost by necessity, sited well off the centerline in order to achieve reasonable accommodations.

Figure 8 shows the section of a 78-foot three-masted sharpie cargo schooner, one of the largest of her type ever built. Because of her extreme length-depth ratio, she has been strengthened by a longitudinal bulkhead that divides the cargo hold 5 inches off the centerline. This bulkhead also forms one side of the centerboard trunk. The trunk protrudes above the main deck in order to hold a centerboard large enough to assure proper sailing ability, and to reduce the scantlings of the deck beams as well as the thickness of the deck plating. The centerboard trunk is located off-center to lessen the distance that the mainmast must be offset on the opposite side, and also to allow for a smaller width of keel. This vessel has no engine; for long-term maintenance reasons, none of her water tanks are integral with the hull.

Figure 9 shows a 33-foot 6-inch motor dory of the St. Pierre type well detailed and

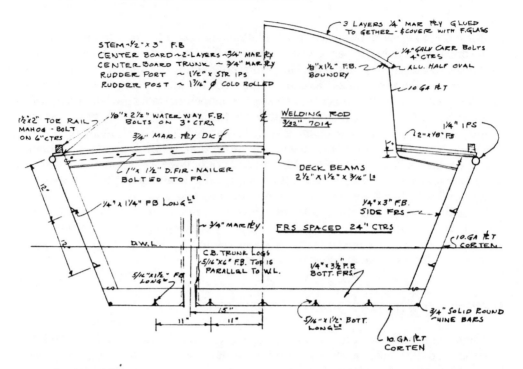

Figure 7. *Scantling section of a 36-foot ketch-rigged sharpie yacht.*

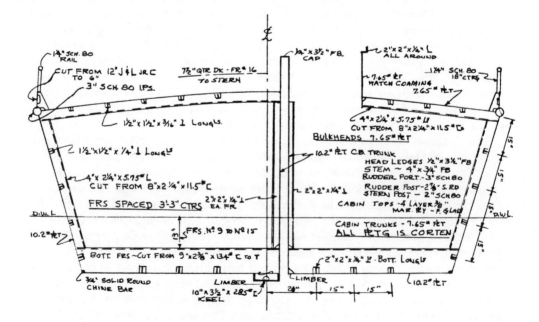

Figure 8. *Scantling section of a 78-foot three-masted sharpie cargo schooner.*

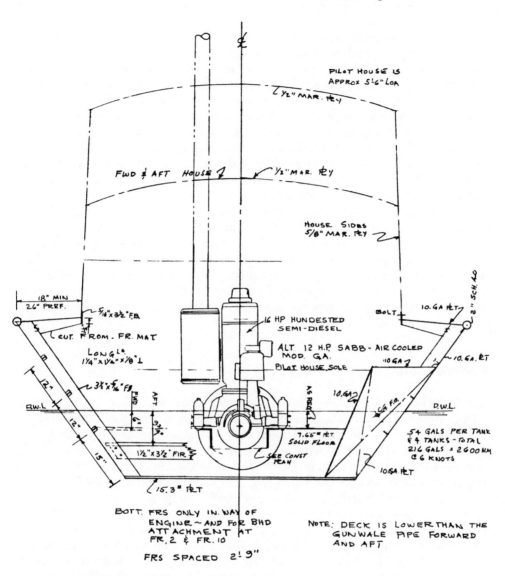

Figure 9. *Section of a 33-foot 6-inch St. Pierre–type motor dory.*

described by John Gardner in *National Fisherman* magazine and in his *Dory Book* (International Marine Publishing Company, 1978). This particular example is designed for Caribbean cruising with a range of 1,000 nautical miles, eliminating the need to refuel in many of the islands where fuel costs twice what it does in the U.S. It represents one of those rare instances where extra-thick bottom plating is more an asset than a detriment. Here, thicker bottom plating is used to offset the weight of superstructure and to lower the vertical center of gravity. Such a vessel will accommodate two persons in reasonable comfort and, with very low horsepower, achieve a cruising speed of 6.0 knots and a maximum speed of 7.0 knots.

There has been a growing tendency for owner-builders and some designers to use extra-heavy bottom plating in an attempt to reduce the amount of ballast needed to bring a vessel down to her lines. Some also do so for the added strength this is supposed to give; however, most do it solely for economic reasons. On a few double-ended hull forms and dories, thicker plating will not cause harm in the static condition, but in almost all counter or transom hull forms it will cause the longitudinal center of gravity to move aft. Typically, the girth at a point 10 percent aft of the forward end of the waterline (from bearding line to deck) about equals the girth at 10 percent forward of the after end of the waterline, but in many hull forms the girth of the extreme forward bottom section is less than half that of the after bottom section. This means that a change in plate thickness will affect the ends unequally. Such a change in weight distribution will always affect the dynamic responses of a vessel, and she will be slow to rise in a head or following sea. Such vessels are known as plungers, divers, or submarines. The opposite is equally as bad: with weights concentrated amidships, any vessel (other than many of the canoe-bodied IOR boats) will hobbyhorse and will not drive in a seaway, spending its time pitching and looking at the moon.

V-Bottom Hulls

V-bottom construction (often referred to as single-chine, which is incorrect because a flat-bottom boat also has but one chine per side) is used throughout the world, not only in metal but also in wood and fiberglass construction. It has the advantage, for the most part, of using straight sections in the framing, and has enjoyed the reputation of simplicity both in design and construction. This reputation is not entirely deserved, because the actual simplicity of any given design always depends on too many "ifs." If straight sections are used throughout, the forward bottom sections will have a fore-and-aft twist, necessitating the use of narrow plates for the forward 10 to 15 percent of the bottom length. If the frames are curved to conform to a cylindrical or conical section (developable surface), then the labor is increased in framing, although in some hull forms, such as planing power vessels, the use of developable forebodies can increase the strength of the plating, allow lighter plating, and confer other benefits. For slamming into a sea, such vessels need a chine forward, designed to function as a spray rail. A developable forebody with convex sections is seldom dry, and is normally avoided in sailing vessels for this reason. I have always found it better to design the best forebody for seakeeping ability regardless of some increase in labor cost.

In spite of the popular notion that designing V-bottom and flat-bottom hulls is simple, they are just as difficult to design as any round-bottom hull, because so few controlling lines generate the design that an error in judgment means a poor design with no way to prove out the errors. In my opinion, this explains why people heaped scorn on these vessels in the past. In fact, there were some sterling examples, in many instances superior to their round-bottom counterparts. In metal construction one seldom encounters the horrendous problems forming a V-bottom hull that were so common in the past with some of the V-bottom wooden hulls. My own experience has been that in wood a round hull is always the easiest to construct, while in metal a round hull is the most difficult.

Figure 10 shows a 42-foot schooner; over 300 vessels have been built to this design, and it exemplifies the light construction possible in a steel ocean-cruising yacht.

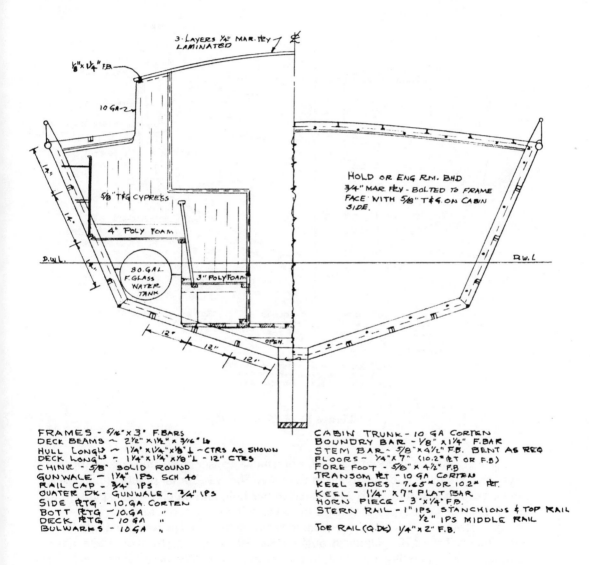

FRAMES - 5/16" x 3" F.BARS
DECK BEAMS ~ 2½" x 1½" x 3/16" L
HULL LONG'S ~ 1¼" x 1¼" x 1/8" L - CTRS AS SHOWN
DECK LONG'S ~ 1¼" x 1¼" x 1/8" L - 12" CTRS
CHINE - 5/8" SOLID ROUND
GUNWALE - 1¼" IPS. SCH 40
RAIL CAP - ¾" IPS
QUATER DK - GUNWALE - ¾" IPS
SIDE RTG - 10. GA CORTEN
BOTT RTG ~ 10.GA "
DECK RTG ~ 10 GA "
BULWARKS - 10 GA "

CABIN TRUNK - 10 GA CORTEN
BOUNDRY BAR - 1/8" x 1¼" F.BAR
STEM BAR - 5/8" x 4½" F.B. BENT AS REQ
FLOORS - ¼" x 7" (10.2" RT OR F.B)
FORE FOOT - 5/8" x 4½" F.B
TRANSOM RT - 10 GA CORTEN
KEEL SIDES - 7.65" OR 10.2" RT.
KEEL - 1¼" x 7" PLAT BAR
HORN PIECE - 3" x ¼" F.B.
STERN RAIL - 1" IPS STANCHIONS & TOP RAIL
                ½" IPS MIDDLE RAIL
TOE RAIL (Q.DK) ¼" x 2" F.B.

Figure 10. *A 42-foot schooner yacht.*

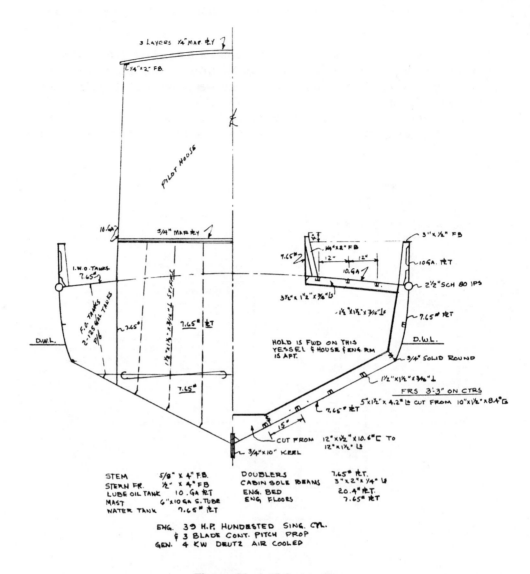

Figure 11. *A 45-foot troller.*

Figure 11 shows a 45-foot troller. This one had a cruiser stern, and curved topside sections were used in order to fair in the ends. She was, for all practical purposes, round-bottom in the forward 25 percent of her hull, and much more expensive to build than the later types that used the wide seine or square stern.

Figure 12 shows a 66-foot three-masted fishing schooner. She was fitted with long-range fuel tanks of 3,700 gallons throughout the fish hold, in the form of saddle tanks, with an additional 500-gallon tank in the engine room. The hold tanks are never empty, because salt water replaces the fuel oil drawn off to replenish the main working tanks, so the vessel retains the same stability and trim regardless of the amount of fuel consumed. Auxiliary fishing vessels use machinery to maintain hold

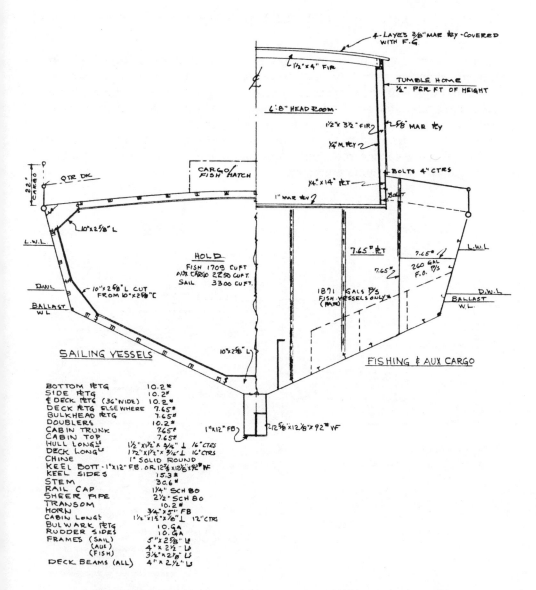

Figure 12. *A 66-foot three-masted auxiliary fishing and cargo schooner.*

temperatures, so they require a large fuel capacity to get their cargoes to port in prime condition. This same vessel, built as an auxiliary cargo carrier, had a total fuel capacity of just 500 gallons. Note that the lower portion of the keel is an I-beam that also meets the cooling requirements for the engine by functioning as a heat exchanger.

Multi-Chine Hulls

Multiple chines are used most often when a vessel's displacement becomes so great in proportion to its length, beam, and depth that a V bottom would become boxy. This refinement applies more to sailing vessels than to power vessels, as an increase in beam of the latter is often beneficial for both powering and stability, whereas in sail an increase in beam often adversely affects sailing ability and ease of handling and could also require a larger sail plan, and thus a larger crew.

Figure 13 shows the section for a 38-foot schooner-rigged cargo yacht of the coaster model. A fine carrier, she is often built for commercial purposes without an engine, to gain the maximum cargo space.

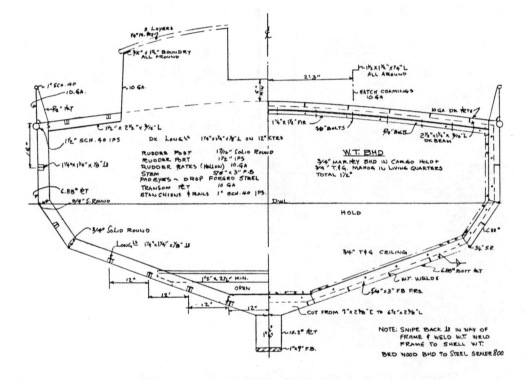

Figure 13. *A 38-foot schooner-rigged cargo yacht.*

Figure 14 shows the section for a 54-foot three-masted pinky fishing and cargo schooner of the clipper type. Two of these vessels are presently employed in the Pacific fisheries, and have auxiliary engines. As cargo vessels, some are fitted with an auxiliary; however, most remain pure sailers.

Figure 15 represents two auxiliary brigs designed for the cargo and passenger trade. An extra chine was necessary in this case to lower the engines and obtain the proper shaft angle without having to increase the depth of hull.

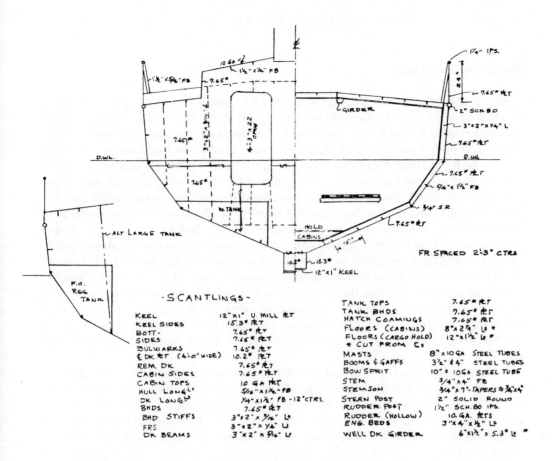

Above: Figure 14. *A 54-foot three-masted pinky fishing and cargo schooner.* **Below: Figure 15.** *An auxiliary brig for the cargo and passenger trade.*

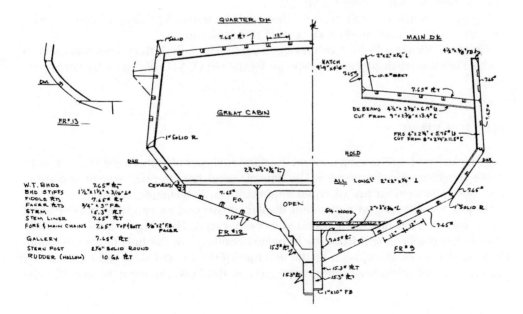

Round-Bottom Hulls

Round-bottom hull forms are the most difficult to build because they have virtually no straight sections. All frames must be bent, and all the plating is curved in at least two directions. A builder contemplating this form of construction needs more equipment than is necessary for other hull forms. Most of the framing can be worked cold if you have a building platen with the appropriate fixtures. By proper spacing of the bending post and dogs, the frame material can be worked around with a tool called a "squeezer." When angle frames are used, the post will need resetting for the port and starboard halves, but if flat bar frames are used, one setting is sufficient. Some yards have furnaces to heat the material white hot for bending (or to any lesser color). This is much faster than cold bending. Another alternative method involves building a hydraulic bending machine, which again allows the builder to work the metal cold. However, this method is slower than cold working on a bending platen, as you must arrive at the correct amount of bend by hit and miss—at least on the ones I have used. There is still another alternative: using a power hammer (preferably) or hand hammer to elongate one edge of the material, thus causing a curve. Three- to four-inch wide material can be done in this manner if your arms hold out.

A plating model is a must for round-bottom construction; attempting hit-and-miss layup of plating is just asking for a lumpy hull. Due to the numerous extra welds required, it is desirable to work with at least 7.65-pound plate ($\frac{3}{16}$-inch) to lessen the distortion, using longitudinals rather closely spaced and transverse framing spaced at two to three times the distance that would be used with transverse framing alone.

Figure 16 shows a 79-foot round-bottom fishing and cargo schooner of a burdensome model, which proved to have too large a capacity for fishing and not enough for carrying cargo. Heavily canvased, she required a large crew. In her later life she became a full-powered vessel.

Figure 17 shows a 53-foot trawler. Her displacement of 51 tons (114,240 pounds) requires a substantial amount of steel in her structure.

Figure 18 shows a 45-foot ketch-rigged yacht. Her 3-inch thick keel was used to reduce her ballast-displacement ratio under the old CCA (Cruising Club of America) rules.

SHELL PLATING

The thickness of shell plating used on the different types of hulls varies so much as to make generalizations impossible. The type of vessel, her intended area of operation, and her displacement are of equal importance in determining the thickness. For example, a yacht sails at a constant displacement, and so can use lighter plating than, say, a similar hull form intended to carry cargo. The cargo vessel may easily double her displacement from the in-ballast condition to the fully laden condition. Vessels that work in ice, such as the fish tugs of the Great Lakes and many ocean trawlers, require heavier plating, especially in the bow. Suffice it to say that the

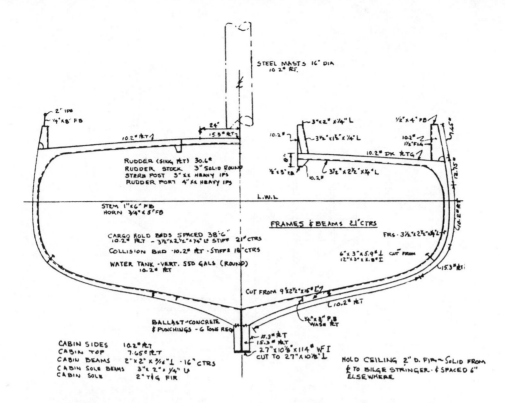

Above: Figure 16. *A 79-foot round-bottom fishing and cargo schooner.* **Below: Figure 17.** *A 53-foot trawler.*

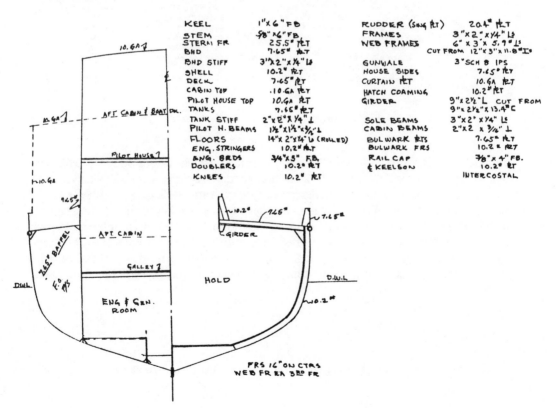

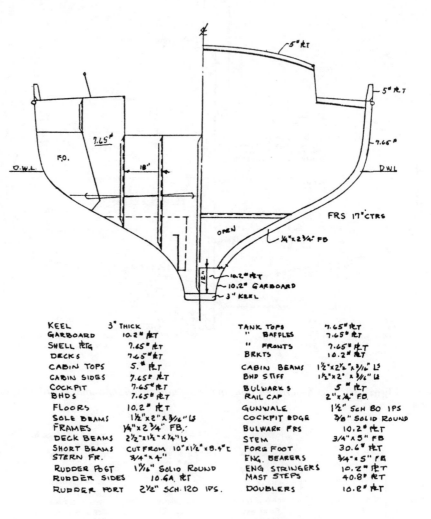

Figure 18. *A 45-foot ketch-rigged yacht.*

KEEL	3" THICK		TANK TOPS	7.65# flT
GARBOARD	10.2# flT		" BAFFLES	7.65# flT
SHELL PTG	7.65# flT		" FRONTS	7.65# flT
DECKS	7.65# flT		BRKTS	10.2# flT
CABIN TOPS	5.# flT		CABIN BEAMS	1½"x2½"x3/16" LS
CABIN SIDES	7.65# flT		BHD STIFF	1½"x2" x3/16" LS
COCKPIT	7.65# flT		BULWARKS	5" flT
BHDS	7.65# flT		RAIL CAP	2"x¼" FB.
FLOORS	10.2# flT		GUNWALE	1½" SCH 80 IPS
SOLE BEAMS	1½"x2"x3/16" LS		COCKPIT EDGE	3/8" SOLID ROUND
FRAMES	¼"x2¼" FB.		BULWARK FRS	10.2# flT
DECK BEAMS	2½"x1¼"x¼" LS		STEM	¾"x5" FB
SHORT BEAMS	CUT FROM 10"x1½"x8.4# L		FORE FOOT	30.6# flT
STERN FR.	¾"x4"		ENG. BEARERS	¾"x5" FB
RUDDER POST	1 7/16" SOLID ROUND		ENG STRINGERS	10.2# flT
RUDDER SIDES	10.6A flT		MAST STEPS	40.8# flT
RUDDER PORT	2½" SCH. 120 IPS.		DOUBLERS	10.2# flT

minimum plating you can use is ⅛-inch for small vessels (about 30 feet), while the heaviest plates would not exceed 5/16-inch at 79 feet. The displacement of a vessel is judged by the nondimensional displacement-length ratio, defined as displacement in tons divided by $(.01 \times DWL)^3$. The smaller this number, the lighter the plating can be, within reason. If plating weight is reduced too much, however, so much framing will have to be added to recover transverse and longitudinal strength that the advantage will be lost. Thus, a 79-foot vessel with a displacement-length ratio of 200 should be able to use light plating, but 3/16-inch may be *too* light, requiring too much additional framing.

CHINES

Chines take a wide variety of forms, and the choice of the best one for a vessel

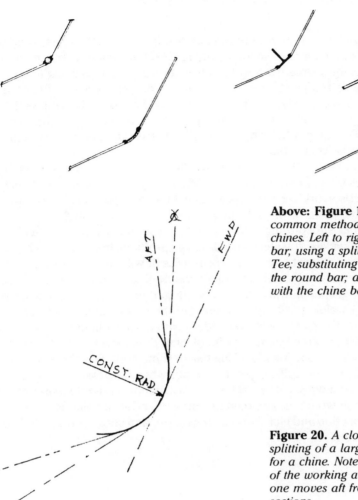

Above: Figure 19. *The most common methods of building chines. Left to right: with a round bar; using a split pipe; using a Tee; substituting a flat bar for the round bar; and dispensing with the chine bar altogether.*

Figure 20. *A closer look at the splitting of a large-diameter pipe for a chine. Note that the chord of the working arc increases as one moves aft from the forward sections.*

depends on the hull shape. Figure 19 shows the most common methods of building chines. The most universal is the round bar type, which bends readily and is normal to all planes. Sometimes builders will use small diameter pipe in lieu of solid rounds; however, the probability of internal corrosion makes pipe chines a poor choice. Probably the worst feature of the rounds is that the minimum feasible size is ⅝-inch diameter, and most builders prefer ¾-inch diameter unless the frames are closely spaced. These dimensions present a problem on the internal welds, for unless the plating is quite thick, a trough is formed between the plating and the round. Moreover, good weld penetration requires greater heat (amperage) than would otherwise be needed. This means you must be very careful after welding to fill any remaining space between the round and the plating with cement or some other compound to assure drainage. The welding must be done in very short increments, with long skips between increments, or the chine will probably deform.

To overcome the appearance of a sharp corner at the chine, some builders will split a large pipe into lengthwise segments, using a constant radius to bridge the included angle. In the forward sections, where the chine angle is obtuse, this means that the chord of the segment is only ½ inch, whereas amidships it might have to be 4 inches or more to bridge the more acute chine angle. Radiusing the chines will reduce the displacement a bit compared to leaving them hard, but unless the radius is large, the difference will be small. This type of chine is better than the round bar if the vessel will be hauled with lifting straps, and it also eliminates the weld problems associated with the round bar.

The T-bar chine is another style used to alleviate the ills of round bars. In some hulls it enhances the appearance, while in others it gives the illusion of poorly fitted plates that have been bridged with a piece of flat bar. It is much easier to use than the split pipe, and the stem of the Tee always bisects the chine angle.

On certain hulls, substituting a flat bar for the round bar makes for a clean weld inside and out; however, you still face a drainage problem. In each frame bay you will have to drill or cut at least one limber; otherwise, it will mean resorting to cement, which in this instance will be more objectionable than in the case of round bar.

Some builders dispense with chine bars altogether when using heavier plating, which is best for welding, without a doubt. On the other hand, great care must be taken when fitting the plates, lest you end up with a wavy chine line. I think that, in spite of its virtues from the builder's point of view, doing away with chine bars is not structurally as sound as using a backing bar of some sort. The chines are the most vulnerable portion of the hull, subject to damage when the vessel is grounded out or bumps submerged ledges, rocks, and other obstructions. I don't mean to say that a round-bottom hull would escape damage altogether, but a chine is at the extreme fiber of the hull section and lacks an easy transition, so it should enjoy a little extra in the way of strength.

DECK EDGES

The deck edge, gunwale, or sheer (whichever the designer wishes to call it) is normally the widest portion of the frame, amidship at least, and forms the junction of the side and deck plating. I have shown a number of ways of treating this detail in Figure 21. When the pipe is 3 inches or less, it is customary to include the whole pipe in the structure even if it is Schedule 80 (heavy wall thickness). There are two ways of using it: welding the deck plating flush with the top of the pipe, or raising the pipe so that the deck plates, if extended, would intersect its center. Most fishermen prefer the former construction, which makes decks easy to clean and allows them to drain completely. It has the same advantages on commercial vessels that carry animals and autos on deck. However, the inside weld is poor at best and requires extra care while welding, lest you miss some slag and have some inclusions and voids in the welds. Builders prefer the intersecting method because it makes for easier welding; the time saved in welding more than offsets the extra labor in notching out for the bulwark stanchions. With this type of deck detail, the builder must insert one or more pipes at the low point of the deck to drain off those couple of gallons that will not drain over the sheer pipe. These drain pipes angle outboard and should be of

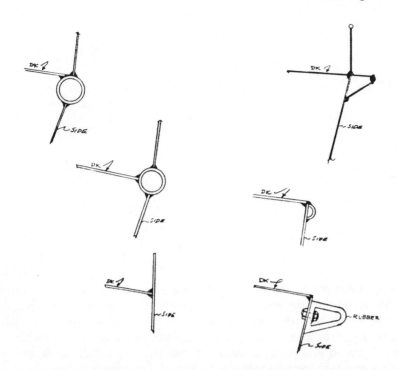

Figure 21. *Several ways of treating the junction of side and deck plating. On the left, top to bottom: incorporating a whole pipe, the deck plating being flush with the top of the pipe; deck plating (if extended) intersecting the center of the pipe; deck butting to side plating, with sides continuing upward to form bulwarks. On the right: deck plating continuing outward past the sides to meet a round bar and closer plate; a split-pipe gunwale; a heavy rubber gunwale.*

stainless steel, and the outside lip should protrude about ⅛ inch or so to prevent streaks on the topsides. In tugs and many other types of working craft that must lay alongside larger vessels, wharves, drill rigs, and other structures, very heavy sheer pipes are required, normally split in half and welded to the shell of the vessel. Because of the diameter and wall thickness, they must, for the most part, be worked in place by heating.

Heavy rubber gunwales provide the best cushion and eliminate carrying tires over the side as fenders. No one has ever devised anything so nice for slamming up against pilings all night. Not that the rubber is all that absorbent, mind you, but at least in the morning you don't feel as if you spent the night in a cement mixer. To mount a rubber gunwale, bolts should be welded to the hull at the intervals required by the manufacturer. On some hulls with strongly flaring topsides it is desirable to knuckle the plate in way of the fender. Another gunwale-fender arrangement sometimes used calls for letting the deck plating continue out over the side plating. Brackets are then welded at each frame to both the side and deck, with a round bar of 1 inch or so fitted to the end of the bracket. The deck is then welded to the top and a closer plate is welded to the bottom of the round bar and to the shell. This type of fender takes a good deal of extra welding and fitting, and any pinholes in the weld will

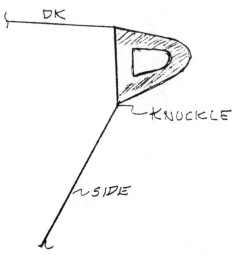

Figure 22. *A knuckle in the side plate in way of a rubber gunwale.*

lead to a corrosion problem difficult to cure. Banging into pilings can dent this steel fender and can also rupture the welds, causing leaks. Finally, if the vessel is slab-sided or has tumblehome, then the shell and deck may join without a protective pipe or fender, or, if there are bulwarks, the side plating may continue up, in which case the deck merely butts to this plate. In larger vessels this is a critical area, and no plate, opening, or anything, should terminate without a generous radius.

CENTERBOARD TRUNKS

In all vessels that need them, centerboard trunks are a structural asset when properly built, but potentially a structural weakness when poorly built. Figure 23 indicates the most common methods of incorporating them. The usual method is through the keel itself, with the centerline of the slot and that of the vessel coinciding. In this instance enough room must exist along the outboard side of the trunk and the side of the keel to assure a proper weld, not only for the trunk itself but for the bottom and sides of the keel joint. In shoal-draft shallow hulls, this can be done by forming the keel from a channel having sufficient flange depth to form the bearding line joint also. The gross width of the trunk plus 8 inches is about the minimum keel breadth for this construction, as Figure 23 indicates in the case of a 58-foot schooner hull. The keel itself is beveled on the outside of the slot to give the required joint design, and the whole then has 100-percent joint efficiency.

Sometimes you may find it easier to offset the trunk by the half-width of the keel, with the centerline of the mast offset a half-width of the keel to the opposite side—perhaps to avoid having the mast straddle a trunk, which of course would be possible, but expensive. The diameter of the mast dictates the minimum width of the keel in this instance, and thus determines the scantlings. If the width of the keel is less than the mast diameter, there will be insufficient room for the mast step and the collar (ring) in which to step the heel of the mast. Customarily, the trunk side in such cases serves as a leg of the step reinforcing, with the centerline bracket directly over

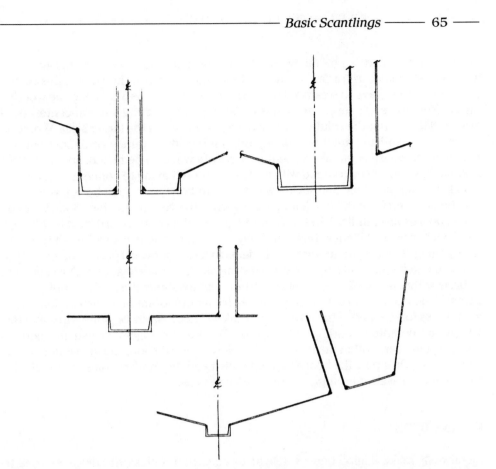

Figure 23. *Common methods of incorporating a centerboard trunk. Clockwise from top left: through the keel (in this case, on a 58-foot shoal-draft schooner hull); beside the keel; as a bilge board normal to the shell plating; and well offset from the centerline in a flat-bottom vessel.*

(and often incorporated as an extension of) the keel sides, and the outboard leg of the step welded to the shell plating.

Some vessels use bilge boards, which are customarily set normal to the shell—that is, at right angles—even though this may occur at the turn of the bilge. As mentioned in regard to flat-bottom sharpies, it may prove necessary to move a trunk several feet off the centerline to permit some sort of an accommodation plan. I have not done this with anything other than sharpies, but to allay any fears that this harms the sailing qualities, let me say that it seems to make little difference just as long as the slot remains parallel to the fore-and-aft centerline of the vessel.

The head ledges of all centerboard trunks need to be at least double the thickness of the trunk sides, since for the most part they can only be partially welded on their insides, and it seems rather pointless to weld continuously on one of the inside edges and omit the other.

A word here about centerboards might be helpful. They like being made of wood, and a steel trunk likes for them to be made of wood. In a shoal-draft vessel having a centerboard that is long relative to the length of the hull, the board in the down position, if it is made of metal, will certainly lower the hull's center of gravity and increase stability. In order to have sufficient strength, however, this metal centerboard will have to weigh at least four times as much as a comparable wooden board. Now the engineering problems of raising and lowering a metal centerboard are not difficult, but the solution is expensive, especially in the larger sizes. Worse, in a seaway, when lying ahull or running off, the board is entirely or almost entirely raised. If the board is metal, the center of gravity will also be raised, and a prudent seaman has enough to contend with in a gale without having to concern himself with stability. A simple block and tackle will suffice to hoist a wooden board, which can also be dropped from the trunk for painting while the vessel remains afloat. Wooden centerboards are not light. In the 78-foot sharpie, the centerboard is 23 feet long, 6 feet 9 inches wide, 3 inches thick, and weighs one ton. The trunk width is 3 ½ inches net opening. In some yachts with insufficient draft for windward performance but too much to qualify them as true shoal-draft designs, the centerboard trunk will be built entirely within the keel, or else will protrude slightly above the keel but not into the cabins. The centerboard in such yachts is frequently of metal construction and is sometimes foil-shaped. If the latter, the trunk will necessarily be quite wide, and this will permit complete welding of the inside. Such an arrangement usually requires vertical guide bars within the trunk itself, however, and the long-term maintenance is a nightmare. Dropping the board to paint both it and the trunk requires a Travelift for the smaller vessels, and a pit for the larger vessels.

ENGINE BEDS

Metal hulls make engine beds a delight to construct, unless the designer tries to squeeze them into the minimum space. The frame spacing is normally halved in the way of the engine, or extra-deep floors are added. The stringers (engine bed) should run either from bulkhead to bulkhead or to extra-deep floors. The intermediate frames and floors should be deepened and their tops leveled off fore and aft to provide walking room. The top flange of the bed can consist of a heavy flat bar, but the webs need not have great thickness; if they do, the welding to the shell plating will crack sooner or later, and possibly split the plating due to the normal vibrations of the engine and the torque it imparts. Whenever possible, lightening holes should be provided in the webs, not only to reduce vibration but also to assist access to the bilges and engine for cleaning.

In vessels with box keels, the area directly below the engine can often serve as the working fuel tank, kept full by gravity feed from one of the main tanks. Due to free surface effects, no more than one tank should ever be used at the same time. Figure 24 shows some of the details of an engine bed and the keel tank. Fuel fills should go to within 2 inches of the bottom of the tank, as this eliminates froth when filling the tank. The return fuel lines should also go to the bottom of the tank in order to reduce the chances of trapping air in the fuel system. If any tank is to be sounded manually, a striker plate should be welded to the shell in way of the sounding tube. Vents to all tanks must open well above the fill pipe. If fitted with whistles, they will warn you when the tank is about to overflow.

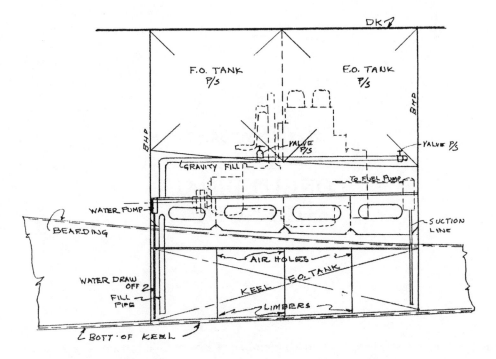

Figure 24. *Some details of an engine bed and keel fuel tank.*

One rarely finds detailed drawings of the complete engine room because it is a complex arrangement to draw, but designers usually indicate on the scantling section any auxiliary generators, compressor foundations, and other machinery fixtures. Thus you may begin to form an idea of how best to run the piping and wiring; however, a final determination cannot be made until you can physically get into the space.

It is, of course, incumbent on the builder to follow the scantling and construction plan furnished by the designer. Although the availability or scarcity of certain stock steel sections may occasionally dictate scantling modifications, unless the builder has enough experience in the construction of a particular type of vessel, he must more or less accept the drawings as prepared. Never try to outguess the designer.

5

▽

TRANSVERSE AND LONGITUDINAL STRENGTH

Shell plating is the principal strength member of a steel hull. Indeed, in very small vessels, transverse and longitudinal framing may be dispensed with altogether, since the shell has rigidity by itself. Using a continuous stem, keel, and stern bar as a means of attaching the two sides provides an additional margin of strength and will prevent the vessel from buckling if suspended from the ends only. The addition of gunwale bars in the form, say, of an angle, will prevent the hull from collapsing if pressure should be applied athwartships or if the vessel should be heavily laden. Many vessels, such as lifeboats, have been built in just this manner. Larger vessels, too, could be built in similar fashion, but the structure would of necessity become inordinately heavy, until ultimately, a vessel of normal hull form would weigh so much that it would sink immediately when launched.

There are basically two categories of forces to contend with, those affecting the longitudinal and the transverse strength of the hull, although in certain types of shallow hulls and in large, open vessels, one must also take account of a third factor, the torsional (or twisting) force. Designers and builders use certain terms to describe the way a vessel distorts in response to various stresses. If the vessel were suspended from her ends and the center of her hull deflected downward, the resultant change in shape would be called "sagging"; if she were supported only in the middle, and the ends then drooped, this would be called "hogging." If she were not rigidly supported athwartships, her sides would flex, a process known as "panting." When a vessel's bow is, say, forced to starboard while at the same instant her stern is forced to port, she is subject to "racking" (at sea) or "twisting" (ashore). These conditions have manifold causes: overloading, rough seas, pitching, rolling, stranding, and inadequate or weak structures, among others. It is, of course, imperative that a vessel's hull not only be watertight and that all exposed enclosures

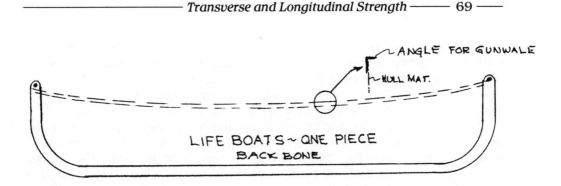

Figure 25. *Lifeboat construction, showing the one-piece stem, keel, and stern bar, with further stiffening provided by gunwale bars.*

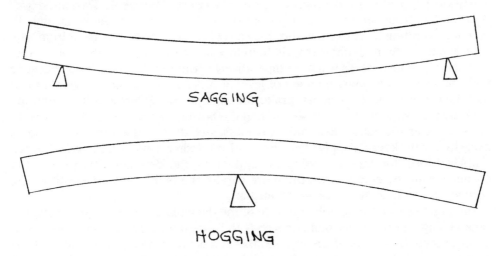

Figure 26. *Sagging versus hogging.*

be weathertight, but that she not change shape under normally imposed stresses. Rigidity is best accomplished by the use of internal framing, both transverse and longitudinal, to support the plating, and by deck beams to keep the sides separated at a fixed distance.

For boatbuilding purposes, two common words have special meanings. To *strain* means to cause a change of form or size by the application of an external force or forces. Strain differs from *stress*, which describes, in alternate contexts, either a force acting upon and tending to deform a body, or a body's internal resistance to deformation. The intensity of the applied or resisting force is expressed in pounds per square inch. Equating a vessel's hull to a box beam or girder is a simple way for a designer to conceive and calculate what is in fact a rather complex problem. For his part, the builder, owner, or master should be aware of how stress and strain affect a vessel during launching, after taking on cargo, in a seaway, and under other circumstances.

The designer will do everything necessary to assure structural integrity, but it is in the builder's hands to prevent faulty workmanship that would cause the vessel to break up under normal use, and to see that none of her structure fails. The general notion that material contributes most to the quality of a vessel is not quite true— workmanship also has a great influence on the quality of hull produced.

It is always a mistake, for example, to underestimate the need for strong welds and ample stiffening members in a vessel's deck. To visualize why this is so, imagine a horizontal, thwartships line drawn through a vessel's midsection so as to pass through the vertical center of gravity, which lies on the vessel's centerline. The intersection of this line with the centerline (seen as a vertical line in the sectional view) is called the *neutral axis*. If the vessel is a barge with its deck and bottom of like construction and weight, the neutral axis will lie exactly at the mid-depth of the hull, and the forces of stress and strain acting on the vessel will be evenly distributed over deck and bottom. In most craft, however, decks are not continuous, due to hatchways and cabin trunks, and they may be of lighter plating than the bottom. The neutral axis of the material mass will therefore lie closer to the bottom of the hull than the top, and stresses will be comparatively greater in the deck region because they are acting on a longer moment or lever arm. A structural analysis would show that the upper edge of the sheer strake, for example, being farther offset from the neutral axis, experiences more stress than the bottom of the keel. If the keel were three feet from the neutral axis and the deck six feet, the stress at the deck would be twice that of the keel. By applying such casual approximations, you can visualize in a simplified form the strength calculations done by the designer. The greater the distance from the neutral axis, the more careful the builder must be with welds, notches in the structure, and workmanship.

The practice of welding only one side of the deck plating and the joint between deck plating and the sheer plate or pipe is to be deplored. The resulting weld can never exceed 85-percent efficiency, and this at a point of maximum stress! Cuts or openings located at the extreme fiber of the hull, such as scuppers and boarding doors, can also detract from strength in this critical area. Their corners should be rounded and their cuts ground smooth. Joints of plating should never be lined up with hatches and trunks, and seams of plating should be kept clear of all longitudinal and transverse framing. Failure in sharp corners, or "notch effect," occurs when the stress becomes so great in a concentrated area that the involved plate or member tears. I have seen cracks in 1-inch plate run across a deck from a hatch corner to the riveted waterway plate. All corners must be rounded.

Flat-bottom vessels over 50 feet with little depth of hull are subject to numerous stresses normally associated only with large shipbuilding, as are some riverboats, scows, and barges. Designers of such vessels are always aware of these stresses. Sailing vessels are always subject to racking strains, especially in a seaway; thus, they require doublers, thicker plates, or both in their deck structure in way of the masts. Since many of the smaller ones lack bulkheads, the beams should be well-kneed to the frames, and sometimes web frames may be incorporated. In lengths below 80 feet on deck, sailing vessels with full keels have few worries longitudinally. A vessel with an extreme cutaway forefoot and a long counter stern can be strengthened enough along the centerline to eliminate the need for excessive shoring when

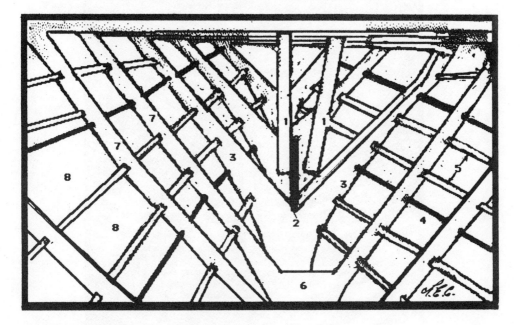

Figure 27. *Sketch of a bow framing configuration. Numbered parts are as follows: (1) spurling pipes; (2) centerline chain locker bulkhead; (3) web frames; (4) chines; (5) longitudinals; (6) deep floors; (7) regular frames; (8) shell plating.*

drydocked. Unlike their wooden counterparts, steel boats of this type display little tendency for their ends to droop and cause hogging. One need not worry much about strength in sailing yachts, as their shape assures adequate depth of hull; their keel structure, being rather massive in proportion to the remainder of the structure, can be considered ballast. These yachts, of course, do not have to support any heavy loads other than their own structural weight.

Trawlers, trollers, shrimpers, and other fishing vessels of similar hull form are akin to full-keel sailing vessels, and have few longitudinal or transverse strength problems. When breaking ice, the Great Lakes fish tugs often have almost 50 percent of their length out of the water as they ride up on the ice to crush it. These vessels do need their whole forebody bottom reinforced longitudinally, and must have deep floors. The fishing vessels that can run into problems are the ones with exposed struts supporting the propeller, free-hung rudders, and the ability to plane.

Motor yachts achieve most of their depth of hull with freeboard. Structural weights above the waterline must therefore be controlled carefully, lest the vertical center of gravity rise so far that it impairs the stability of the vessel. In the United States, at least, motor yachts are more often than not overpowered and overequipped. This, with the normal load of fuel necessary to get them from one marina to another, plus their tremendous water capacity for their size, poses some problems in regard to longitudinal strength. These problems can usually be solved by incorporating several full or partial metal transverse bulkheads, plus longitudinal connecting bulkheads for the fuel and water tanks. The engine beds, when run

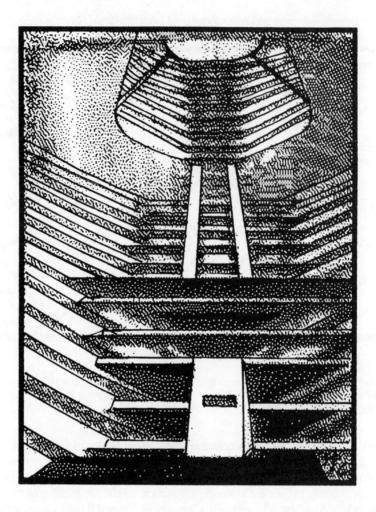

Figure 28. *Sketch of a round-bottom fishing schooner that was built using only transverse framing. The floors are wood, which simplifies the installation of the hold ceiling, and her rock ballast can be well-stanchioned down.*

between and connected to transverse bulkheads, form excellent fore-and-aft girders. One should not use wood decks and deckhouses to give strength, but rather, should depend on the steel structure entirely.

Table 8 gives a partial list of weldments used in construction. It can serve as a guide. I have generally based these weldments on the American Bureau of Shipping rules. Sizes are correct for the thinner member being welded. The spacings in some instances deviate from ABS standards; they derive from the standard construction of vessels built by The Colvin Manufacturing Corporation and the Colvin Shipbuilding Company.

Table 9 is a partial list of weldments developed in my yard for use when the basic design of the vessel incorporated transverse web frames and closely spaced longitudinals. Experience showed that the amount of welding required by Table 8 would cause a great deal of needless distortion on certain hull forms, so in this method of construction the amount of unsupported plate determines the spacing of longitudinals. The calculation for unsupported area is based on T-bar longitudinals, assuming a stem of at least the same thickness as the shell plating. Therefore, with ⅛-inch plating and 3-foot 3-inch frame spacing, the maximum longitudinal spacing could be 19 inches on the bottom and deck, whereas the topsides could have 21-inch spacing if the longitudinals were parallel to the sheer, but only 17-inch spacing if parallel to the waterline. Using the maximum spacings results in a hull structure suitable for light-displacement sailing vessels. In normal construction, the transverse frames could be uniformly spaced 38 or 39 inches and taken as a modular reference length for working out accommodations: one frame space for a water closet, two frame spaces for a berth, and so forth. Half-frames are introduced in the way of the engine rooms, forward of the collision bulkhead, and aft in the way of the rudderpost and stern tube. Longitudinals are then spaced as follows:

⅛" (5.0 lb.) plate	12" centers
³⁄₁₆" (7.65 lb.) plate	15" centers
¼" (10.2 lb.) plate	18" centers
⁵⁄₁₆" (12.75 lb.) plate	21" centers
⅜" (15.3 lb.) plate	24" centers

In my yard we made frequent exceptions to the rule, depending on the hull shape. Too much welding adds nothing to strength and, in fact, weakens the structure.

Table 10 indicates the welding rods most commonly used in steel boatbuilding, along with the minimum and maximum amperages that would be required. Other rods are used occasionally, but the ones listed are the most general. Electrodes of smaller and larger diameters are available, but ³⁄₃₂ inch, ⅛ inch, ⁵⁄₃₂ inch, and ³⁄₁₆ inch are the most common sizes, and all a builder needs.

Sharp corners and edges must be avoided at all times. You must always grind them to a radius—the size matters little in most instances. Sharp corners will not hold paint, are apt to chafe lines if on deck, and above all, can cut or injure the crew. Torches leave a ragged cut, which, if in a stress location, will be apt to tear. Grind them. "Beautifying" your work takes just a few minutes and will pay for itself by easing maintenance.

The builder can and usually does make many of the items used in rigging a vessel. Little can be done about their location, but by eliminating unnecessary reinforcements, one *can* do a lot to prevent them from fouling or from causing stress.

Using ASTM A-242 plating (sold under the trade name Corten) will increase the longitudinal strength of the vessel, provided the thickness of the plating has not been reduced to save weight. Reducing weights to the extreme minimum used to be quite a fad, but increased labor costs and the small margin left for corrosion and strength negate the assumed benefits of weight reduction after a point. It is always desirable to reduce structural weight, of course, especially if in doing so one also increases structural strength and cuts down on labor.

TABLE 8. Partial List of Weldments for Vessels of 80 Feet or Less

Item	Connections	Not Over 3/16"	PLATE THICKNESS Above 3/16" to 1/4" inclusive	Above 1/4" to 5/16" inclusive	Above 5/16" to 7/16" inclusive	Above 7/16" to 33/64" inclusive
Single-bottom floors	Center keelson	1/8" double continuous	3/16" double continuous	1/4" double continuous	1/4" double continuous	1/4" double continuous
	To shell frame spaced 30" or less	1/8"-1½-12-S	3/16"-2½-12-S	1/4"-3-12-S	1/4"-3-9	1/4"-3-8
Floors, nontight, double bottom	Solid floors to center vertical keel	1/8"-1½-10-S	3/16"-2½-10-S	1/4"-3-10	1/4"-3-8	1/4"-3-6
	To inner bottom	1/8"-1½-12-S	3/16"-2½-12-S	1/4"-3-12-S	1/4"-3-9	1/4"-3-8
	Solid floor stiffeners	—	3/16"-2½-10-S	1/4"-3-10	1/4"-3-8	1/4"-3-7
Watertight and oiltight	Peripheries of floors in double bottom	—	3/16" double continuous	3/16" double continuous	1/4" double continuous	1/4" double continuous
Girders, webs, and intercostals	Center girder, rider plate, and shell to bar keel	1/8" double continuous	3/16" double continuous	3/16" double continuous	1/4" double continuous	1/4" double continuous
	Longitudinals (continuous and intercostal) in way of engine	—	3/16"-2½-6	1/4"-3-6	5/16"-3-6	5/16"-3-5
	To bulkheads or decks	—	3/16"-2½-12-S	1/4"-3-10	1/4"-3-8	1/4"-3-6
Frames, nontight	To shell (spaced 30" or less)	1/8"-1½-12-S	3/16"-2½-12-S	1/4"-2-12-S	1/4"-3-9	1/4"-3-8
	To tank top and margins	1/8" double continuous	3/16" double continuous	1/4" double continuous	5/16" double continuous	3/8" double continuous

Frame brackets	To frames, longitudinals, and deck	⅛" double continuous	³⁄₁₆" double continuous	³⁄₁₆" double continuous	¼" double continuous	¼" double continuous
Bulkheads	Stiffeners to nontight structural bulkheads and stiffeners on deckhouse sides and aft ends	⅛"-1½-12-S*	³⁄₁₆"-2½-14-S*	³⁄₁₆"-3-12-S*	¼"-3-12-S*	¼"-3-9*
	Stiffeners to watertight bulkheads	—	³⁄₁₆"-2½-12-S	¼"-3-12-S	¼"-3-9	¼"-3-8
Bulkhead stiffener brackets;	To stiffeners and to decks	⅛" double continuous	³⁄₁₆" double continuous	³⁄₁₆" double continuous	¼" double continuous	¼" double continuous
watertight and oiltight		—	³⁄₁₆" double continuous	³⁄₁₆" double continuous	¼" double continuous	¼" double continuous
Foundations	Main and auxiliary engine	⅛" double continuous	³⁄₁₆" double continuous	¼" double continuous	¼" double continuous	⁵⁄₁₆" double continuous
Decks	Beams, transverses, or longitudinals to deck	⅛"-1½-12-S	³⁄₁₆"-2½-12-S	¼"-3-12-S	¼"-3-9	¼"-3-8
	Beam knees to beams and frames	⅛" double continuous	³⁄₁₆" double continuous	³⁄₁₆" double continuous	¼" double continuous	¼" double continuous

* To have pair of matched intermittent welds at ends same length and size as increments.

Note: S=staggered. All thicknesses and other dimensions are in inches. Where more than one number is given (e.g., ⅛"-1½-12-S), the first number refers to fillet width, the second to length of weld increment, and the third to spacing between weld centers. "Staggered" means spacings are given between welds occurring on opposite sides of a joint; where staggering is not indicated, spacings are for a chain-welded joint. Dimensions given for double continuous welds refer to fillet width.

TABLE 9. Partial List of Weldments for Vessels That Are Longitudinally Framed in Conjunction with Transverse Web Frames

Connections	Plate Thickness		
	⅛"	3/16"	¼"
Floors to flat keel	⅛" double continuous	3/16" double continuous	¼" double continuous
Floors to shell	⅛"-¾-12-S	⅛"-1½-12-S	¼"-2-12-S
Floors to center vertical keel	⅛" double continuous	3/16" double continuous	¼" double continuous
Floors to stiffeners	⅛"-¾-12-S	3/16"-1½-10-S	¼"-2-10-S
Peripheries of watertight and oiltight floors	⅛" double continuous	3/16" double continuous	3/16" double continuous
Center girder–rider plate and shell to bar keel	⅛" double continuous	3/16" double continuous	3/16" double continuous
Longitudinals (continuous and intercostal) in way of engine	⅛"-1-6	3/16"-1½-6-S	¼"-2-6
Bulkheads and decks	⅛"-¾-6	3/16"-1½-12-S	¼"-2-10
Frames to shell	⅛"-¾-12-S	3/16"-1½-12-S	¼"-2-10
Frames to tank tops	⅛" double continuous	3/16" double continuous	3/16" double continuous
Frame brackets to frames, longitudinals, and deck	⅛" double continuous	3/16" double continuous	3/16" double continuous
Bulkhead stiffeners to nontight structural bulkheads and stiffeners on deckhouse sides and aft ends	⅛"-1-12-S	3/16"-1½-14-S	3/16"-2-12-S
Bulkhead stiffeners to watertight bulkheads	⅛"-1-12-S	3/16"-1½-12-S	¼"-2-12-S
Bulkhead stiffener brackets to stiffeners and decks	⅛" double continuous	3/16" double continuous	3/16" double continuous
Bulkheads, watertight and oiltight	⅛" double continuous	3/16" double continuous	3/16" double continuous
Foundations, main and auxiliary engines	⅛" double continuous	3/16" double continuous	¼" double continuous
Decks—beams, or transverses, or longitudinals to deck	⅛"-1-12-S	3/16"-1½-12-S	¼"-2-12-S
Beam knees to beams and frames	⅛" double continuous	3/16" double continuous	3/16" double continuous

Note 1: S=staggered. Unless otherwise noted, welds are chain welds.

Note 2: It is assumed that the maximum unsupported panel area will be: ⅛" plate—4 sq. ft. or less; 3/16" plate—6 sq. ft. or less; ¼" plate—8 sq. ft. or less. Where this condition is not met, welds in Table 8 should be used.

TABLE 10

AWS E-6010: a DCEP (direct current, electrode positive) rod. Can be used in any position and for all welding of mild steel. Has a sodium-cellulose base coating. Resultant weld has deep penetration. Available in four sizes. The 3/32-inch rod requires from 40 to 80 amps; the 3/16-inch requires from 140 to 250 amps. A 'dirty' rod that produces a lot of weld splatter. Of limited use in light plating, where there is no need for penetration since both sides are welded. A good choice for heavier framing. The grandfather rod of shipbuilding.

AWS E-6010 IP: Also available from some companies. Iron powder additive gives a smoother arc and less splatter than the sodium-cellulose coated rods, yet retains all other characteristics of the E-6010. Available in three sizes. The 1/8-inch requires 70 to 130 amps; 3/16-inch requires 140 to 225 amps.

AWS E-6011: An AC all-position rod with cellulose base. All the features of the E-6010, including deep penetration, with little splatter. Available in four sizes. The 3/32-inch requires 50 to 70 amps; the 3/16-inch requires 160 to 190 amps.

AWS E-6012: A DCEN (DC, electrode negative) or AC all-position rod with moderate penetration. Available in four sizes. The 3/32-inch requires 35 to 85 amps; the 3/16-inch requires 140 to 240 amps. Used in small-craft construction, but should be avoided in plating over 3/16 inch. Really limited to single-pass fillet applications.

AWS E-6013: An AC/DC (either polarity) all-position rod with mild penetration. Available in four sizes. The 3/32-inch requires 45 to 90 amps; the 3/16-inch requires 150 to 230 amps.

AWS E-7014: An AC/DCEN all-position rod with iron powder coating and mild penetration. Four sizes available. The 3/32-inch requires 80 to 125 amps; the 3/16-inch requires 200 to 275 amps. Because its chemical composition closely matches that of Corten steel, it was used in my yard for welding mild steel to Corten or for Corten seams, with the understanding that a single pass would be used on all seams, and that prior to any external welds, seams would be ground back to sound metal. Use of this rod is limited to 3/16-inch plating or less. In high-stress areas, E-7018 is used.

AWS E-7016: An AC/DCEN rod. Not generally used on vertical down welds. Four sizes available. The 3/32-inch requires 65 to 110 amps; the 3/16-inch requires 180 to 255 amps. A low-hydrogen rod; must be kept heated prior to use.

AWS E-7018: An AC/DCEP all-position rod. Four sizes available. The 3/32-inch requires 65 to 110 amps; the 3/16-inch requires 180 to 255 amps. Also a low-hydrogen rod; must be kept heated prior to use.

Where it is appropriate to save weight, the designer will call for lightening holes in a vessel's reinforcing members. The centers of such holes must be no farther from the supported plating than a distance equal to one-third the depth of the beam; the total cross-sectional area of the holes as viewed end-on in a cross-section of the member must not exceed 15 percent of the cross-sectional area of the member itself (including the flange, if there is one); and the depth of the holes may not exceed 40 percent of the depth of the member. If you follow these rules, the structure will be lighter but no weaker. Larger holes can be made but require reinforcement, which is expensive and adds weight. *Never* use holes to lighten the flanges. Web frames, deep floors, and longitudinal stringers are the normal areas in which holes are cut. A design asking the builder to drill out all floors, frames, and longitudinals is likely a poor design, an exception being when holes are necessary to reduce the registered tonnage of a vessel otherwise too great to enter a given trade.

All holes made for lightening purposes must be freed of any roughness or sharp edges by careful grinding or filing. When drilling holes for galvanized bolts, allow $\frac{1}{64}$ inch more than the bolt diameter for up to $\frac{3}{4}$-inch diameter bolts, and $\frac{1}{32}$ inch more for bolts over $\frac{3}{4}$-inch diameter. Where piping runs through a deck or bulkhead and must be welded, it is necessary to have a clearance of 4 inches on pipes 3 inches or less in diameter, and up to 6 inches on 8-inch pipe, in order to assure sufficient space for the welder to work.

When curtain plates are attached to the deck edge as a continuation of the side plating, or if they are attached to the railcap of the bulwarks, the joints must be given a generous transition radius. Figure 29 shows a typical curtain plate. Such large holes require reinforcement.

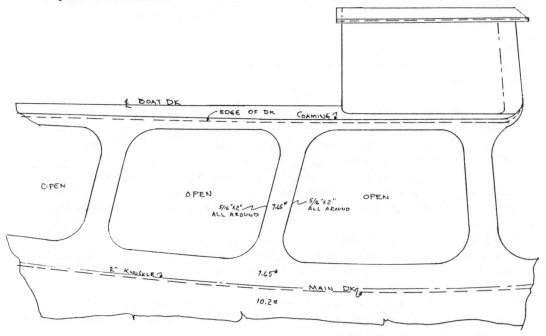

Figure 29. *A curtain plate on a 58-foot trawler.*

In wooden vessels, the stresses imposed during launching, drydocking, land storage, stranding, overloading, and sailing in heavy weather were often severe enough to cause permanent deformation, as structures slipped from their original locations. It always made me sad to see some of the larger wooden sailing vessels that had lost their sheer after a few years of service. Hogging and racking led to the need for increased rigging tension, which in turn exerted even more pressure on the already strained hull, making it slightly deeper as the mast bore down on the keel. In a seaway these boats began to spew their caulking, causing them to leak even more than usual, which was certainly wearisome for their crews as they pumped to keep afloat and to reduce cargo damage. A good friend often told me that he went to sleep each night with a prayer that he would never again have to sail in a wooden vessel. Metal vessels can, of course, suffer all the ills common to wooden vessels; however, vessels less than 100 feet in length and of normal scantlings are usually so strong that this is a rare occurrence. If the designer has done his job, and the builder his, the owner or operator will never have to lose sleep worrying about an unsound vessel.

6

▽

ESTIMATING
COSTS

To estimate the approximate cost of a sailing vessel, you need only the sail and spar plan, provided the plan also contains the sparmaker's notes, sailmaker's notes, equipment notes, and rigger's notes. For a power vessel you need only the outboard profile with specifications for engine, fuel capacity, auxiliary engines, and equipment notes. With the addition of the interior arrangement plan and one frame section, plus the scantlings of the vessel, which may be on a typewritten sheet, you should be able to come close to figuring the actual cost with just a few hours' work. If you are a professional builder, you may then quote an initial estimate to a prospective client; if you are an amateur builder, this exercise will give you an idea of the magnitude of the project ahead.

If you should be awarded the contract or decide to build the vessel for your own account, the final estimate will be subject to receipt of the complete plans and specifications (if any). Unless the designer or owner makes substantial changes to the initial sail and spar (outboard profile) and interior arrangement plans, your first estimate will in all probability come within a percent or two of your actual costs, and your profit margin should be sufficient to absorb any slight difference without forcing a change in bid. Occasionally, builders bid high initially and, upon reviewing the plans, find they can lower the cost, but this happens rarely. On the other hand, a builder who comes in way over his estimate when he finalizes a bid may find some doubt cast on his ability. Labor and time prohibit a minutely detailed cost analysis, which is certainly not normally justified until after the vessel's completion, when it may be used for future reference. Therefore, accurate estimation is as necessary a building skill as accurate lofting or fitting.

The builder must use a quick but reasonably accurate method for estimating the weight of steel the vessel will need, and the amount to be ordered. The one I have used for many years is to multiply the length on deck times the molded beam, times three, times a factor that ranges from 0.65 to 0.85, depending on the fullness of the vessel's ends. The product is the shell area in square feet. Knowing the plating weight per square foot, I multiply the weight by the area by 1.6 to 1.7 to obtain the hull weight. Hull weight multiplied by 0.60 gives shell weight, and multiplied by 0.40 gives structural weight of frames, longitudinals, keel, floors, and other members. Steel bulkheads I treat as rectangles, multiplying the beam on deck times the depth of hull (deck edge to bearding) times the plate weight, with no allowance for shape, and figuring the drops (waste pieces) as being equal to the weight of the stiffeners. This approach to estimating weight of bulkheads is faulty for a barge-like hull form but quite reasonable for many other forms. The cabin trunks I ignore if the cabintops are of wood, on the assumption that the weight of the displaced deck and its framing equals or exceeds the weight of the trunk sides and ends; that is, I calculate the weight of the deck plating as if it were uninterrupted by cabin trunks. If the cabintops are of steel, I again treat the deck area as an uninterrupted surface, but in this instance I add the total area of cabintops to the uninterrupted deck area for weight calculations, in effect counting the plan area of the cabin structures twice. This is for sailing vessels. For motor vessels the deckhouses, being large, are estimated as separate units and added to the hull weight. I never make any deductions when using this formula.

If the scantlings are available, a more accurate method is to calculate the weight of a one-foot-wide section that girths the vessel amidships, divide that weight by the girth of the midship section to get the vessel's average weight per square foot, and then multiply that figure by the approximate square footage of hull and deck surfaces. Table 11 gives the numbers to employ with this method for the 42-foot 7-inch pinky schooner that illustrates this book. The total girth weight of 335.5 pounds is divided by 36, which is the girth in feet calculated from the 12-foot breadth of deck, 20.7 feet of shell girth, 1.64 feet of keel sides, one foot of keel girth, the diameter of the sheer pipe, and the width of the railcap. The result is 9.32 pounds per square foot. Multiplying the breadth of the deck amidships by 3 would give the same result in this instance, and for most vessels this rough-and-ready method gives a good approximation. Now, 42.7 feet (the length on deck) times 12.0 feet (the molded beam) times 3 times 0.75 gives 1,152.9 (or 1,153 square feet) for the shell area, and 1,153 multiplied by 9.32 gives 10,746 pounds of steel by the long method. The short method yields 1,153 times 1.65 times 5.65, or 10,479 pounds of steel, so the agreement is good. The bulkheads 3, 5, 8, and 12, according to calculations, need an additional 1,195 pounds of steel. Thus we may summarize:

Shell plating $=$ 10,479 $\times$ .60 $=$ 6,287 @ \$.38 $=$ 2,389.12
Bulkhead plating $=$ 1,195 @ \$.38 $=$ 454.10
Structure $=$ 10,479 $\times$ .40 $=$ 4,192 @ \$.20 $=$ 838.40
TOTAL \$3,681.62

TABLE 11

Item	Area or length in midship section (feet or square feet)	Unit weight (pounds per foot or per square foot)	Frame spacing (feet)	Total weight (pounds)
Shell plating	20.70	5.65		117
Frame	19.20	3.72	3.25	22*
Deck beam	12.00	3.07	3.25	11.3
Floor		9.75	3.25	3
Deep floor	1.00	6.80	3.25	2.1
Keel sides	1.64	7.65		12.5
Hull longitudinals	12.00**	1.80		21.6
Keel	1.00	33.10		33.1
Chines	4.00	1.91		7.6
Sheer pipe	2.00	5.02		10.0
Railcap	2.00	3.83		7.7
Deck longitudinals	11.00	1.80		19.8
Deck plating	12.00	5.65		67.8
Total				335.5

*This number is arrived at by multiplying the length of the frame in the midship section by the unit weight of the stock, and dividing by the frame spacing.
**There are 12 longitudinals, each having a 1-foot length through the representative section.

If mild steel is used in lieu of Corten, then the plating cost comes to $1,346.76 less than the above figure in prices quoted as of late 1983. The actual cost of steel varies according to tonnage purchased. Companies usually quote prices based on 10 short tons of ordered steel, and the price per pound increases progressively for every 100 pounds below this base in the amount ordered. At times you will do better to overorder, to gain the lower price per pound. Quantity extras can double or triple the per-pound cost when underordering, especially if the company adds a delivery charge; therefore, overordering makes much more sense.

In the above example the actual shell area by direct calculations was 1,143 square feet, meaning that the estimate was close. From other data in the table and the scantlings section, you could also calculate the weight of the deck and bulwarks; for this design it would come to 3,880 pounds, or 33 percent of the total weight. I mention this because some owners and builders try to outguess a designer and add more freeboard to a design. This always results in a disaster, and the same holds true for an increase in plate thickness. In this example, an increase to, say, 7.65-pound plate would entail a 35-percent increase in shell weight, or 2,643 pounds.

For some unfathomable reason, certain people set great store by a bill of materials. By and large it can tell you only what at *one time* was available to *a particular builder*, and it does not follow that the same sizes will now be available. It is always best to work from the stock list of *your* supplier's warehouse. A case in point: at one time I had a good buy on my supplier's remaining stock of 1-inch by 7-inch flat bars, enough for about 20 vessels, and so my then-new designs utilized this size whenever possible. Many other builders have since built from these same designs, several of which provide a bill of materials. The letters come in: "I can't get 7-inch bars; is it okay to use 8-inch?" or "Those Tees are not available; what about angles instead?" I had the same experience when building in wood. When my yard had its own saw and planing mill, our standard planking length was 40 feet, with widths in odd numbers and thicknesses in the rough that would dress to even quarters (¾, ⁵⁄₄, ⁶⁄₄, etc.), none of which is standard today. You just can't expect stock designs drawn five to 30 or more years ago to reflect industry's latest attempts to eliminate the once-standard sections (now known as "specialty items") in favor of the present stock sizes—really poor substitutes for what was once common. If requested to, the designer will usually supply with the study plans an alternate and up-to-date modification of the scantlings, based on what he knows to be available. Just the same, material "take off" requires but a few hours of "by guess and by golly" estimating, during which time the builder becomes familiar with the design, the structure, and the designer's method of depicting the vessel. This familiarity will pay off handsomely during the course of construction.

Displacement generally offers a poor method of costing a vessel, since it reflects ballast, fuel, engine, joinerwork, and outfitting weights, all of which vary considerably from vessel to vessel or design to design. Similarly, gross tonnage (a measurement ton of volume) can be manipulated depending on the owner's requirements. You can measure a vessel one way to yield 100 gross tons, then turn around and structurally redesign the same vessel to yield only 10 gross tons. Any rule of thumb based on volume or weight alone has the same inherent limitations. Even the weight of raw steel going into the vessel can mislead you, because a given mass of steel can be assembled in numerous ways. The scantlings and the shape of the hull determine the hull cost of the vessel, and all other items must be figured separately as independent entities.

Knowing the quantity of material in a vessel, you must still reckon with welding and fitting costs to arrive at an accurate cost estimate. Using the Pinky as an example, there are 20 full-length, double-fillet welds per side: railcap (2), bulwark to deck (2), deck to gunwale pipe (2), side to gunwale pipe (2), upper chine (4), lower chine (4), bearding (2), and keel side to bottom (2). Using a 50-foot average for each, that gives 1000 feet of welding per side. If ⅛-inch electrodes and 7 feet of finished weld per hour are assumed, then it follows that 143 hours will be required to weld up each side and, with perfect fitting up, you will consume about 300 pounds of welding rod. Next, let's imagine a design with only a single chine and the same plate weight. This will eliminate 200 feet of welding, 29 hours of labor, and 60 pounds of welding rod per side. Also, it will lead to savings in plate fitting, framing of the plate, and cutting between the two chines. Finally, let's say we are building a sharpie, which is a flat-bottom vessel: we can drop the keel and bearding welds, saving another 100 feet of welding, 14 hours of labor, and 30 pounds of rod per side, without counting the savings of not having to fit a plate to the bearding, keel sides, and keel.

Possibly, though not probably, each of these vessels could have the same displacement and thus about the same amount of hull material. Now the weight of hull material remains fairly constant for any given displacement, although length, breadth, and depth may vary, with a corresponding effect on gross tonnage (in vessels of the same general structure). The displacement-length ratio, which can be written as $D/(L/100)^3$, changes with length when displacement remains constant. Thus, one vessel may be 20 percent longer than another for the same displacement, and have a displacement-length ratio of 225, compared to the shorter vessel's 425. In practical terms, this means the longer vessel will be lighter (for its length) than the shorter, but it will cost more to build. The cost of the steel laid down in the yard, then, has little value as an index of total cost; however, what is done with that steel has a great deal to do with cost. In the above examples, using the sharpie as a basis for comparison, the single-chine V-bottom hull will require 14 percent more hours and welding rod per side, while the multi-chine hull will require 43 percent more labor and welding rod per side. If the vessel were round-bottom, this would add still more to welding and fitting costs. Yet all three boats have the same displacement!

Perhaps the best way to determine the cost of a vessel is to make rough estimates for each particular segment. For the Pinky, costs would break down about as follows:

lofting and templates	100 hours
10 frames @ 5 hours each	50 "
keel and deadwood	60 "
longitudinals	30 "
layout of plates	100 "
billet, trailboards	20 "
bitts, chocks, etc.	30 "
grinding external welds	50 "
stern overhang	6 "
welding	536 "
4 bulkheads @ 10 hours each	40 "
setup	15 "
plating	100 "
trunks	30 "
rudder	10 "
tanks	10 "
sole beams	10 "
grates	4 "
added margin of 10 percent	120 "
TOTAL	1,321 hours

Totaling, we arrive at 1,321 hours construction time, to the cost of which we must add: 1,000 pounds' welding rod, one bottle (large) acetylene, two bottles (large) oxygen, six grinding wheels, 20 grinding disks, two chipping hammers, four wire brushes, three cup brushes for power, and wood building blocks and shoring. (I have based these estimates on a similar vessel I built several years ago.) The professional builder multiplies the labor by the rate of pay, and adds this to the cost of the steel and other materials, neglecting overhead and burden; that, roughly, will equal the cost to construct the hull. The cost of electricity and taxes applies to all builders. The professional will also have billing, accounting, secretarial, and other miscellaneous costs to defray. All of these expenses should be worked out in relation to a month of 160 hours. Theoretically, the Pinky's hull would take 8.25 months for one man working full-time to complete, and 1.65 months in a five-man shop. The cost of doing business for this period is the burden, and is added separately to derive the total cost of construction.

One of the backyard builder's most common errors is to underestimate not only the cost of construction and material, but the time involved to construct the hull and finish the vessel. A project often becomes a matter of years—not months—and when this happens it may suffer the ill effects of inflation, health, flagging desire, and the distinct possibility that the vessel's intended use will change before it gets launched. If anything, people tend to choose designs either too large, too complex, or both to be feasible; they rarely choose too small a vessel.

The rest of this chapter, while pertaining primarily to the contract builder, applies equally to the home builder. Fineness of finish, installation of electronics, refrigeration, and so forth, are common concerns. A word of philosophy for the home builder: few people look back without saying, "I probably could have bought a boat for the same price or less and had the use of it for all those years I have spent building this one"; then they add, "but it is better than I could have bought, I know what's in it, and I did it all myself."

A one-man shop or backyard builder will require about 40 percent more time to build a vessel than a two-man team, due to lost motion in such things as fitting plates, heavy lifting, and the necessity of resorting to building jigs and fixtures to do what two people could do in minutes without jigs. A man and wife team, if they allocate the work correctly, can accomplish as much as two men. A professional one-man shop has the advantage of lower overhead, since there is no helper to pay and no fringe benefits or insurance to cover. If there is an ideal number to operate a yard, it has never come to my attention. Assuming the workers are all skilled, five seems to be about the maximum for most yards, and then units after that in pairs. In a nonunion or co-op yard, it is possible to employ workers skilled in several areas. Thus, a welder may also be a machinist and do machinery installation; another welder may be a woodworker and painter; the template maker may double as the burner who cuts out the plates, besides being the head joiner man. The more diversified the gang, the higher the production. With a less skilled work force, partial and sometimes almost total supervision is required; in this case, eight to a gang is about the most one person can handle. A supervisor produces very little, directly; however, if he can prevent costly mistakes, then he has earned his salary.

Many steel builders prefer to do only the metalwork, sandblasting, priming, and maybe engine installation before delivering the vessel to another yard or the owner for completion. This reduces the size of the work force and the amount of equipment necessary for finishing out. Moreover, the risk is much smaller and the headaches fewer.

If, however, you contract to deliver a finished boat, you will have to estimate the cost of the interior, the rigging, and the outfitting. From the sail plan you can obtain the number of blocks, feet of standing and running rigging, turnbuckles or deadeyes, number of splices needed, size and length of anchors, anchor chains, anchor rodes, mooring lines, size and lengths of all spars, and the number and area of all sails. Assorted pieces of gear such as dinghy, bilge pumps, and life jackets will also be listed. All of these items are easily priced. For a motor vessel, the pertinent information, similar to that shown on the sail plan for a sailing vessel, often appears on the outboard profile or on a separate sheet listing all the major equipment, including the size of all engines, generators, thrusters, winches, boats, and davits.

The interior arrangement plan(s) give the rest of the information necessary to work up the bid or estimate. Again, you need to make a rough material list and figure the labor for each item. A simple breakdown would include lumber, trim, and small hardware such as hinges, hasps, doorknobs, latches, and lift rings, followed by major hardware such as toilets, sinks, portlights, hatches, skylights, and prisms. Also included would be all the berths, mattresses, settees, cushions, table, galley stove, heaters and their fuel systems, and then the engine along with its controls, battery (or batteries), exhaust system, anchor winch, deck winches, and other mechanical devices. Motor vessels usually have dual controls, while auxiliary sailing vessels have only a single control. Finally, an estimate would be made for the piping and electrical systems. You won't go far wrong in your estimate if you forget the discount price of each hardware item and figure that the labor for installation approximately equals the discount. This will also cover miscellaneous nuts, bolts, and screws. It takes just as long to hang a door and fit the hardware as it does to make it, unless it is a very complicated door with raised panels and inlays.

Weather—temperature and humidity, to be specific—makes it difficult to estimate the time needed to sandblast the exterior of the hull and obtain the desired finish. The complexity of the structure, the paint system used, and the method of application also affect this variable. The interior of the hull in smaller vessels is usually not sandblasted, but wire-brushed, thoroughly cleaned and degreased, primed, and painted with anywhere from three to five coats, including the primer. Larger vessels are usually sandblasted inside. The interior will normally be insulated, ceiled, or both, and, while the steel surface does not require the high degree of finish that the exterior requires, it must receive excellent coverage and be well done in all other respects, since it is seldom seen again. Again, when estimating you should use the retail price, not the discount price, and let that cover the cost of cleanup, sandpaper, and paint buckets.

You will have an even more difficult time estimating the cost of the interior cabin finish, since only one small area at a time can be done. You would probably do best to triple the man-hours that the same surface area of exterior deck work would take, including trim.

A knowledgeable builder realizes the limitations of his yard and knows that, while he as an individual may be capable of superb craftsmanship, it does not follow that all his employees have the same skill. He will be content knowing that the vessels he builds are constructed to the best of the yard's ability. He will also understand that there is a certain fineness of finish he can achieve economically, and that trying to exceed that degree leads surely to bankruptcy; therefore, he will shy away from a design that requires more than his customary quality of work. Yards that specialize in high-quality "yacht" work cannot afford to lower their standards either, so there is room for all. Similarly, vessels being constructed by home builders may become mired in an eternal state of incompletion if the builder is unable to make realistic choices for joinery and other finish work.

When the architect or owner furnishes much of the basic materials, hardware, engine, rigging, sails, and other equipment, the builder must depend on specifications from the various vendors, such as those furnished by the engine manufacturer, so that the foundations can be built to fit. The building contract should include a clause that exempts the builder from the contract price should a vendor modify either the shape or design of a component after the order for it has been signed. This happened to me once, when an engine did not match the manufacturer's specifications for length, height, depth, width, and location of hold-down bolts; I had to remove the engine beds, relocate a bulkhead, and raise part of a deck to accommodate the changes. In another instance, face locks (to be screwed to the outside of doors and panels) were specified from a catalog furnished by the owner. The manufacturer discontinued the item, and mortise locks were substituted; however, it took 18 months to receive them. Needless to say, there was also a significant increase in labor cost, since these had to be mortised into the woodwork. The difference in installation time was 1½ hours apiece, and there were 200 of them!

The builder should also add another clause for his own protection when other parties than himself purchase and furnish materials and equipment. The clause should specify that delivery of these items to his yard must occur on or before a specified date, with stiff penalties for non-delivery, as he must either work around the missing parts or, in extreme cases, even stop all work and wait. Either way, this creates an added expense.

The majority of sailing and many motor vessels require permanent ballast. In the former, lead is the best material. If it is sited in a box keel, there are numerous advantages to using lead bricks instead of casting the ballast in place; bricks may be insulated from the steel and will have a stowage factor within a few percent of cast ballast. Where plenty of room exists, ingots may suffice; however, the bulk of ingots sacrifices space and overall density, which results in a higher center of gravity. Concrete, boiler punchings, miscellaneous scrap steel, and railroad irons have the least density of all ballast materials, and when installed properly also prove labor-intensive. If steel ballast is used, it should be in flat plates, carefully cut, cleaned, and fitted to the keel cavity, then capped over with a welded steel plate. Experience indicates that lead is by far the least expensive ballast to install in spite of its higher first cost. In any case, if practicable, only enough ballast for stability in launching should be built in, and the remainder added after launching and fitting out. This permits reasonable alterations in equipment, interior arrangement, and fuel and water capacity without extensive calculations by the designer or builder.

Either the builder or vendor may supply or install electronics for communication, navigation, and other purposes. The cost for this equipment and installation should not figure in the hull contract unless it is *always* part of the vessels normally constructed in the builder's yard. There are so many unforeseeable and laborious fitting details associated with this equipment that a separate contract should be made for the electronics.

The builder is not in an enviable position, for he has the largest investment in—and the most to lose on—any one of the hundreds of items he must build or install in the completed vessel. He not only has to contend with the architect and the owner, but with everything else that creeps, crawls, or flies, all apparently trying to prevent his completing the vessel. Indeed, has there ever been a builder who, after years of frustration, has not viewed his yard and said to himself, "Even at 5 percent interest on my investment, I would make more than I do now and have fewer headaches!" only to find himself, five minutes later, thinking about another vessel he wishes to build?

7

▽

LOFTING
AND
TEMPLATE MAKING

The purpose of the Lines Plan and Offsets (see Figure 30) is to define the shape of the vessel in such a manner that a builder may transform this small-scale drawing into a full-size vessel. To do this, he must redraw the plan full size and, in the process, fair out any humps and hollows in the individual lines, simultaneously making sure that they agree with other faired lines. This process is known as lofting. Most first-time builders dread lofting because they see no progress toward a completed vessel and fear having to do so much complex drawing when they are unsure of what they are doing. If you look at lofting step by step rather than as a whole, however, you can see an orderly progression from the very simple grid to the completed lines laid down. As with everything else in the building of a vessel, you must think only of the immediate problem and not worry about those that may show up later because, in reality, if you are accurate and thoroughly check the work you have already done, problems usually resolve themselves or present easy solutions.

Some professionals fall into rather slipshod lofting practices under the assumption that they will save money by just skimming through, fixing what has to be fixed later, if ever. Careful or not, all loftsmen dislike having to loft a poorly drawn vessel with bad offsets, and they judge a designer by the accuracy of his lines and offsets. A good loftsman can take a poor set of offsets and lay down a fair hull, but in reality he, rather than the chap who sold the set of plans, is designing the hull.

In traditional wooden vessels, many builders lofted in profile only the stem and forefoot and the sternpost to the transom. Then they lofted the molds, and that was it. On the shipway, the molds were erected and ribbands sprung around them, after which the molds were padded or shaved to suit the eye of the builder, in order that templates could be lifted for all intermediate frames. Even today, some builders use only one or two molds and the transom as the basis for constructing their vessels.

From long experience, they do produce fair hulls, some of them fine sailers; however, they can never exactly duplicate their work.

In steel construction, building by "rack of eye" is out of place and economically foolish. A few builders do it anyway, but to perpetuate such imprecise practices in a time when tool and equipment manufacturers are providing the builder with the means of ever-greater precision seems self-defeating.

Lofting is known in the trade as "laying down" the lines, and the making of templates from the mold loft floor is known as "taking off." The necessity of lofting is invariably questioned by amateurs and some builders with very limited facilities. For some reason the notion exists that, if the vessel has been built previously, the offsets are true and therefore only the sections need be lofted. Time will be saved, it is reasoned, and time is money. In the end, however, this is false economy. Regardless of the number of times a vessel has been lofted, and even if the offsets are offered as "returned" and "corrected," a competent builder will still lay down the lines full size. Why? It is the duty of the builder to reproduce with reasonable accuracy the vessel as designed, and not just an approximation. By relofting, he assures himself that the offsets are indeed true, that there are no errors in the figures, and that he himself has not made an error.

Returned offsets are corrected to the nearest ⅛ inch and sometimes to the nearest $+\frac{1}{16}$ inch, in which case, for example, an offset might appear as 10–8–6+ and be read by the loftsman as 10 feet 8¾ inches $+\frac{1}{16}$ inch; this is as close as his rule or tape reads. Only inexperienced draftsmen or designers would give an offset in sixteenths, or worse yet, in thirty-seconds or sixty-fourths of an inch, yet in fairing the lines the true dimensions lifted from the loft floor will have this much accuracy.

Unlike the builder in wood, who could pad or shave the molds to produce a fair hull, the steel builder has no option other than to be correct from the beginning. An error of $+\frac{1}{8}$ inch in one frame and $-\frac{1}{8}$ inch in the next creates a ¼-inch gap. While this might seem insignificant in, say, a 70-foot vessel with a beam of 20 feet, this error might well equal or exceed the plate thickness. Accuracy on the mold loft floor will not only improve the potential for a fair hull, but will save many hours of labor during erection. It should eliminate the misfortune of having to remove an offending frame, cut it apart to salvage as much as possible, remake it, and finally reinsert it, plumb it, and square it to the other frames. Proper lofting can also save many hours of labor in the later stages of construction. Indeed, in many yards the work done on the mold loft floor includes making the patterns for cabin trunks, hatches, mast steps, and many other items that can be constructed as subassemblies for later, sequential installation. In a properly lofted vessel, one may even go on to joiner bulkheads, shelving, cabinets, and other pieces that must conform to the vessel's hull.

TOOLS FOR LOFTING

The tools required for lofting are quite simple. You need only several wooden battens of different dimensions, a straightedge, several marking sticks, chalkline, pencils, nails, hammer, framing square, small square, bevel square, and a template of the deck camber. The battens are used for laying down long curved lines, and you will need several sizes to suit the various curves to be drawn. The deck edge of the

42' PINKY SCHOONER · TABLE OF OFFSETS ~:· · N° 169

STATION	FP	1	2	3	4	5	6	7	8	9	10	11	12	13	14	AP	T	S
HEIGHTS ABV + BEL DWL.																		
SHEER-UNDER RAIL CAP	6-2-4	5-7-7	5-4-3	4-10-2	4-4-7	4-0-4	3-5-0	3-7-0	3-5-7	3-5-6	3-6-7	3-9-0	3-10-6	4-0-5	4-3-2	5-1-2	5-9-3	5-7-6*
MAIN DK EDGE	4-3-5*	3-10-1	3-7-4	3-2-6	2-10-1	2-6-3	2-3-2	2-1-3	2-0-2	2-0-1	2-1-2	2-3-4	2-4-6	2-8-0	3-0-1	3-2-5	—	—	—
UPPER CHINE	3-2-7*	2-2-6	1-9-2	1-0-1	0-5-6	0-1-5	0-0-4	0-1-2	0-0-2	0-2-2	0-5-7	0-11-1	1-2-3	1-6-0	1-10-0	2-8-0*	—	—	—
LOWER CHINE	2-10-7*	1-6-3	0-10-6	0-1-7	0-11-0	1-4-5	1-7-5	1-8-3	1-7-2	1-3-7	0-10-6	0-3-0	0-1-7	0-7-4	1-1-7	2-5-7*	—	—	—
BEARDING LINE	SEE	SEE	1-5-2	2-9-0	3-1-5	3-4-3	3-6-0	3-7-4	3-8-4	3-7-2	3-3-0	2-4-3	1-7-5	0-8-7	0-4-1	—	—	—	—
GHOST ₵			1-7-4	3-0-0	3-4-3	3-6-4	3-8-0	3-10-0	3-9-1	3-5-4	2-7-3	1-10-4	0-11-1	0-2-2	—	—	—	—	—
BOTTOM OF KEEL	LINES	1-9-0	3-10-4	← STRAIGHT LINE ←							5-9-0 →	← SEE LINES →		3-0-1 →		—	—	—	—
HALF BREADTHS																		
SHEER-UNDER RAIL CAP	1-0-0-3	2-6-7	3-4-0	4-6-2	5-4-0	5-9-7	6-0-7	6-1-6	6-0-7	5-9-6	5-4-2	4-6-4	4-0-4	3-5-7	2-11-1	1-9-3	1-3-6	0-10-0*
MAIN DK EDGE	SEE	1-9-3	2-7-4	4-0-2	4-11-7	5-7-3	5-11-0	6-0-0	5-10-6	5-7-0	5-0-4	4-1-2	3-6-0	2-9-4	2-0-0	0-1-2	—	SEE	—
UPPER CHINE	1-0-5	1-11-3	3-5-0	4-6-4	5-3-4	5-8-2	5-9-5	5-3-3	4-7-6	3-8-0	3-0-5	2-4-5	1-7-2	—	—	—	—	—	—
LOWER CHINE	0-7-7	1-5-0	2-8-0	3-6-7	4-2-0	4-5-5	4-6-4	4-5-0	4-1-3	3-7-0	2-6-7	2-3-7	1-9-0	1-1-1	—	—	—	—	—
BEARDING LINE	LINES	0-0-2	0-0-6	0-3-3	0-4-0	← STRAIGHT LINE →			0-4-0	0-1-4	0-3-6	0-1-2	0-3-2	0-2-4	0-2-4	0-1-2	—	LINES	—
												0-1-2	0-1-4	0-3-0	0-1-5	2-3-0	0-11-5	0-5-0	

LOWER EDGE OF BULWARK 3-6-0 · 2-10-5 · 2-3-0 · 0-11-5 · 0-5-0

NOTES: 1. OFFSETS GIVEN IN FEET, INCHES, & EIGHTHS OF AN INCH TO THE INSIDE OF SHELL PLTG, UNDERSIDE OF DECK & BOTT OF KEEL

2. DECK EDGE OFFSETS ARE TO A FAIR EXTENSION OF SIDE SHELL TO DECK & SHEER-DECK EDGE PIPE OR FENDER NOT INCLUDED-SETS ON #169-3

3. GHOST ₵ IS FOR FAIRING PURPOSES & SHOULD BE USED-BEARDING LINE IS THEN AUTOMATICALLY FAIRS FROM HALF BREADTHS

4. DECKS CAMBER 1" PER FOOT OF HALF BEAM

5. THE * IS THAT LINE EXTENDED TO A PERPENDICULAR FOR FAIRING PURPOSES ONLY ₵ THE TRUE HEIGHT IS OBTAINED WHERE IT INTERSECTS THE HULL

6. CABIN TRUNK SIDES TUMBLE HOME ½" PER FOOT OF HEIGHT-ENDS ARE VERTICAL

7. WHEN 2 OFFSETS ARE IN SAME BOX THE UPPER IS THE BEARDING ₵ THE LOWER IS THE KEEL WIDTH

Figure 30. *Reproduced on this and the following two pages is the Lines Plan and Offsets of the Pinky, Colvin Design No. 169, the building of which is described in this text. Length over the rails, 50 feet 8½ inches; length between perpendiculars, 42 feet 8 inches; length on designed waterline, 36 feet 1 inch; molded beam, 12 feet; draft on designed waterline, 5 feet 9¾ inches; displacement on designed waterline, 38,000 pounds. The Lines Plan was drawn to a scale of ¾ inch equals 1 foot.*

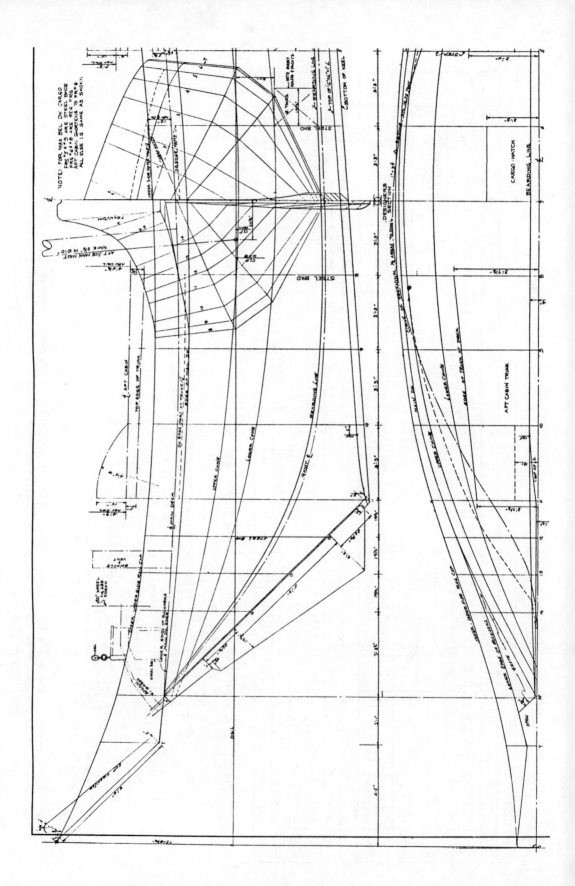

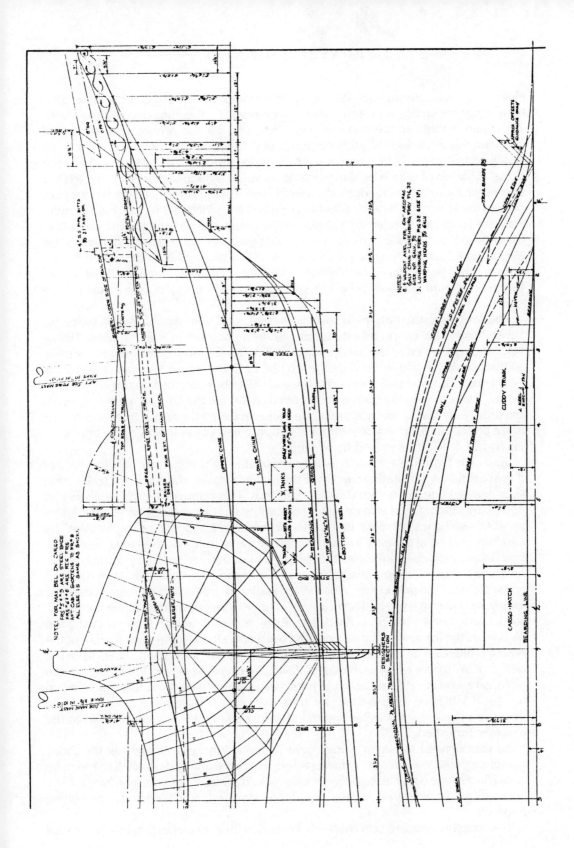

Pinky illustrated throughout this book, for example, would require a wide, stiff batten, say 1½ inches wide and about ½ inch thick. Its bearding line and the ghost centerline would require two different sizes, one for the pronounced curvature between frame 10 and the after perpendicular (AP) and between frame 4 and the designed waterline (DWL), and one for the more gently curved segments between these. A batten of ½ inch by ¾ inch would be about right in the former case, while a batten similar to the deck-edge batten would serve in the latter. To lay down the plan view of the Pinky, you would probably use a batten ½ inch by 1 inch. A builder must exercise judgment in selecting the size of the battens to be used for any given line. There is no ironclad rule that could or should be followed other than this: *always use the stiffest batten that can be readily bent to a fair curve.* Should the batten be too limber, it will lie happily at each offset to be faired but will not actually fair the line; however, should the batten be too stiff, the line will develop flats or even false curves.

The length of the battens is also important, and you should ideally splice up several pieces to obtain a batten that will do a complete line all at once. This is seldom done on a one-time basis, so several battens are often "leap-frogged," that is, shifted along the line in overlapping lengths until the whole line has been faired. When doing this, you must not scribe the end still to be continued, as this end will not be fair. Rather, when you move the batten to continue the line, permit it to overlap the previously faired line by at least one frame space on the easy curves and two or more on the hard curves. In general, a batten one-half the length of the line to be faired will need to be moved three times.

To lay the batten, place a nail, usually a twopenny or threepenny, on either side of it near each frame or station line. Once the batten is down, check the line by bending over and sighting the batten through your legs. This removes the visual distortion caused by sighting right side up. Any irregularities will be readily apparent. If you see none, this still does not mean that the line is perfectly fair, so it must be "proven" by carefully removing the nails at each station or frame that was used to lay down the line. If the batten does not move, the nails at one station are reset and the nails at the next one removed. Should the batten move in or out to become fair, then the nails are set to hold the new curve. When every station or frame in the design is used for lofting, it is customary to pull several nails at once to test the batten. When the batten moves and a new position is fixed, you absolutely must recheck by removing the nails from the frames or stations next forward and aft, to assure that the lay of the batten is indeed true. This explains why the loftsman requires good offsets from the designer. With poor offsets, where few, if any, are correct as given, lofting becomes a nightmare, and in extreme cases the loftsman is forced to do the actual designing on the mold loft floor. In this case, he tries to maintain the profile as close to the designer's drawing as possible and then fair in a hull that looks similar to what the designer furnished.

An experienced loftsman would have a multi-chine vessel such as the Pinky completely laid down, ready to make patterns, in two working days. With a helper, he could do it in one day. The first-time builder would probably require five days, mostly because he is not used to the squatting, stooping, and bending that lofting requires.

The straightedges are best made of plywood, with a minimum length equal to the maximum half-beam of the vessel if you are only making one. To make only one straightedge is poor economy, however. Several sizes are handy—for example, 8 feet, 10 feet, and 12 feet—and you will use them constantly throughout the construction of the vessel. The width must be at least 1 inch per foot of length, and I have found a ⅜-inch thickness handy.

Marking sticks are also best made out of plywood, and they, too, should be straight. Two or three are sufficient, with their lengths similar to the straightedges, but they need not be more than 2 inches in width. To avoid confusion, some loftsmen use one edge for, say, the deck edge half-breadths, and another edge for the rail half-breadths. Turning the stick over, they then mark the half-breadths on one edge for the upper chine and on the other for the lower chine. When they have no further use for those marks, they erase them or sand them off, then reuse the stick for the next set of marks that need to be transferred. The marking sticks are used to pick up the faired dimensions exactly, since to use a tape or rule at this moment would yield inaccurate measurements.

The chalkline used to strike long lines, or any line for that matter, should be as thin as possible. Most builders will usually substitute a smaller diameter line for the one furnished with the case when purchased. A 30-pound fish line (stranded type) lays down a very fine line when snapped. The common type used in house construction lays down a coarse line of ⅛ inch or more, which in boat and shipbuilding is considered not much better than one put down with a mop.

Pencils are used for marking the lines. Some prefer the carpenter's type, which has a flat, rectangular lead. I prefer the common office type with about number 2 lead, sharpened with a standard office pencil sharpener. You should scribe the finest line you can see. Several pencils are needed to scribe, say, a 50-foot line. Dull pencils, dull soapstones, and dull tools have no place in a shipyard.

THE MOLD LOFT

A mold loft in its finest sense is a separate building, a loft over one of the shops, or a gallery permanently set aside just for lofting and patternmaking. Such lofts have their own power tools—bandsaws, table saws, planers, and jointers—in addition to the usual workbenches and hand tools. Extensive facilities usually imply a large work force, and generally, the larger this is, the more extensive are the lofts.

In many small yards a temporary loft is set up, and dismantled after the lines have been laid down and faired. The templating is limited to that required for the stem, keel, deadwood, horn, and transom. If the hull is round-bottom the individual frames will also be taken off, but in single- and multi-chine construction, as long as the frame sections are described by straight lines, frame templates are not usually made. Rather, the dimensions of each frame are transferred directly to the framing platen with a marking stick and laid down as full frames. Once the frames have been made and checked, the loft can be taken up, but a wise professional builder will utilize the loft for much more than the minimum. He will store the lofting work, especially if it is on plywood, until it is either needed again or is, finally, of no further use to him.

Although they lure with the prospect of compactness and convenience, paper lofting and paper patterns are really worthless because they are subject to too many distortions. Increasingly, loftsmen do draw on dimensionally stable Mylar, often with the aid of a computer. Mylar is used in computer lofting of body plans, and sometimes for complete lofting of small craft. For large vessels, however, the Mylar must be secured to a floor and the final patterns lifted just as if the loftsman had laid them down directly on the wood. Then, too, even well-made wooden templates need careful handling, but you must handle Mylar with even greater care.

The primary advantage of computer lofting is that it produces a correct and faired body plan, thus guaranteeing the fairness of any longitudinal section; this does away with lofting waterlines, diagonals, and buttocks unless the need arises for a particular line. However, if you use a computer, the stem, stern, keel, and deadwood should still be laid down manually, full size, so you can easily lift and check the templates. Computer lofting is especially useful for round-bottom designs, but take warning: at least some methods of computer fairing generate lines that may differ slightly from those indicated by the designer, and a vessel laid down by the conventional method could come much closer to the actual design.

In my yard, due to space limitations, we used temporary lofting areas such as the sail loft or spar shop. If these were in use, then the area set aside for the actual construction of the vessel was used. We always made the loft floor of the best marine-grade plywood available, painted flat white, and of the same thickness as berth bottoms, shelving, and laminates used in cabintops. That way, each vessel eventually consumed her loft floor and saved me the taxes on a permanent loft and materials. The owner benefited from my lower overhead and the labor saving of using the coat of flat paint as a primer.

You can determine from the lines plan of the Pinky (Figure 30) that an area of 13 feet 6 inches by 54 feet 7½ inches is the minimum required to lay down the lines full size, providing the necessary depth and length. Using standard sheets of plywood, the economical dimensions become 16 feet by 56 feet, or 28 sheets. The plywood must be laid down on a flat surface, fastened to the adjoining sheets at each corner with a sheet-metal tab, and the whole given a coat of sealer followed by two coats of flat white, well thinned. There is always a temptation to use a roller to speed up the application of the sealers and paint, but the resulting surface is *not* smooth and will make the lines a bit jiggly. Also, it will wear down pencils faster than a smooth surface. A small, airless sprayer works fast and with excellent results. While slower, a paint brush will yield the best surface of all. If a perfectly flat surface is not available, then it will be necessary to construct a subframe that will give the desired level plane on which to lay the plywood. This must, of course, be strong enough to support the loftsman while he is working, without deforming.

LOFTING FULL-SIZE

There are several methods of lofting, each of which has advantages as well as disadvantages. I will illustrate the three most popular methods, using for my example the pinky hull form because it has all the features to be met with in most designs, and also some rarer features such as a floating fo'c's'le deck, overhanging false stern, and billet (a carry-over from wooden vessels, where it was a functional structure). As a multi-chine design, it is a bit more complex than the single-chine, flat, and V-bottom hull forms, although it is not as complex as a round-bottom hull.

The easiest method of lofting to describe and grasp is done full-size on a grid at least as long and deep as the vessel itself. When space considerations make this impossible, the lines may be laid down in fore-and-aft halves superimposed, or else on a scale foreshortened for length. The latter two methods become quite straightforward with practice, but for the moment, let's concentrate on lofting full-size, assuming that enough space exists to make it feasible.

The Grid

First you will need to establish a working grid on the loft floor, proportioned to the lines of the vessel. Start with the *baseline*, a lengthwise line running from end to end of the floor, or at least a couple of feet beyond the ends of the hull. Depending on the designer's scheme for referencing heights on the hull profile, this line may correspond to the DWL or some other line parallel to it (perhaps a line touching the deepest point of the keel, so that all heights can be expressed as a plus measurement above the baseline). In any case, you must locate it on the floor, leaving enough room above to draw that portion of the profile situated above the designer's baseline, plus a bit more for projecting the expanded transom and any elevated structures, such as cabin trunks, that will be lofted for the purpose of making templates.

Next, you will need to establish a centerline for the half-breadths (or plan view), parallel to the baseline and offset from it far enough to allow lofting the half-breadths without interfering too much with the lower portion of the profile.

Finally, you must erect perpendiculars to the baseline and centerline, these perpendiculars to represent frame stations. These will extend the full width of the floor, since, when lofting begins in earnest, the same lines must represent the same frame stations on both the profile and half-breadths.

A chalkline may be used to snap the base and center lines, provided it is quite fine and the end points of the second line to be drawn have been offset from the ends of the first accurately enough to ensure true parallels. When they have been laid down to your satisfaction, scribe them in with a sharp pencil.

Figure 31 shows the loft floor with the grid marked and identified. After establishing this grid, you are ready to start laying down the lines. The plans for the Pinky indicate offsets for heights + (above) and − (below) the DWL, following my standard practice. The DWL, then, becomes the baseline for the profile. Under no circumstance should a joint formed by several sheets of plywood be used for any line in lieu of a struck line that is straight and true. The centerline of the plan view is not given as a dimensioned line on the plans, and thus may be located to suit the loftsman. For the sake of clarity, it is desirable to site this line so that the half-breadths do not cross the DWL when the latter is also used as the profile base. Some loftsmen do prefer to use the DWL as the baseline for the half-breadths, but this leads to numerous lines crossing areas where several templates will or may be

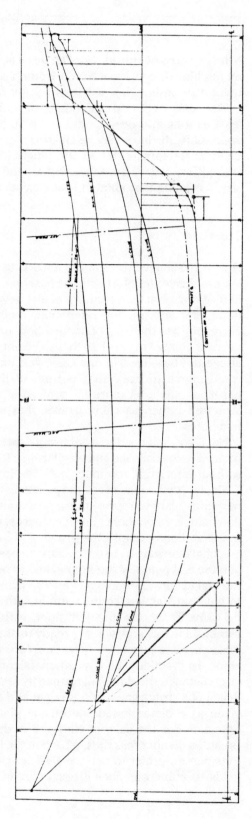

Above: Figure 31. *The mold loft floor with the grid marked and identified.* **Below: Figure 32.** *The maximum extent to which the Pinky's profile may be laid down prior to laying down the half-breadths.*

lifted—for example, the keel and the cabin trunks. In Figure 33 the centerline has been sited below the profile and at a distance below the DWL that prevents the half-breadths from crossing the DWL. The vertical lines in the drawing are the frame lines, spaced according to the Lines Plan. All lines are labeled at each end, or at top and bottom. During lofting, you will find on numerous occasions that adding further identification avoids confusion.

Laying Down the Profile

Figure 32 shows the profile of the vessel as laid down, and represents the most that may be laid down at this time from the offsets given plus other dimensions indicated. Further development of the profile must wait until the half-breadths have been laid down. The small circles superimposed on some lines indicate the use of extended lines and additional dimensions not given in the table of offsets but shown on the Lines Plan. What this drawing shows applies only to flat-bottom, single-chine, and multi-chine vessels. In round-bottom hull forms, the upper and lower chines do not exist and will not appear. The ghost centerline, sometimes also called the fairbody line, should always be drawn in for all hull forms; however, if it is not shown by the designer, then to obtain this line you must wait until the frame or mold sections are drawn before you can find it. This line, if viewed from above, is a straight line; viewed in profile on the loft floor (or the designer's profile drawing), it describes a curve connecting the points where frames, if extended to the centerline, would intersect. Nonexistent in the finished hull (and hence a "ghost"), this line nevertheless has an important use in lofting, namely to ensure that the frame ends lie fair at the centerline, without any humps and hollows when viewed in profile. If the ghost centerline produces an unfair curve when the batten is sprung around the points that define it, then it should be faired and the frames altered to suit, except in the case of certain unusual hull forms having a designed-in knuckle.

Laying Down the Half-Breadths and Sections

Figure 33 shows the half-breadths laid down from offsets given. The half-breadth of the bearding line is laid down last for reasons given later. Verticals will have to be extended downward to intersect the centerline to produce the end points for the sheer, main deck, upper chine, lower chine, and the bearding line where it intersects the stem. In round-bottom hulls, only the half-breadth of the keel bottom and the main deck line could be drawn at this time.

Next, depending on the design (that, is whether it is drawn to the actual frames or to design or mold stations), the half-sections should be drawn as shown in Figure 34. If numerous transverse frames are used, one need not use all of them at this time, since their final shape will depend on the fairing of the chines in flat, Vee, and multi-chine hulls; waterlines and buttocks are needed and faired only when concave or convex sections are used in the ends of such vessels. In round-bottom hulls, there being no chines, the fairing must depend entirely on waterlines, diagonals, and buttocks to prove the lofted shape. When mold stations are used, one normally lofts all of them. Designers who are or have been builders will normally design steel

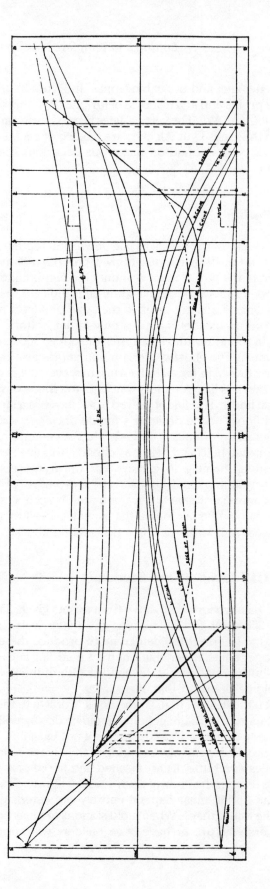

Figure 33. *The maximum extent to which half-breadths may be laid down from the offsets given*

vessels on the actual frame stations required in the finished vessel, for this saves time on the mold loft floor as well as in the preparation of other plans. When designs are prepared around design or mold stations, these must be faired before the actual frames may be lifted from the loft and faired as a separate body plan.

Fairing the Lines

The remainder of the lofting may commence only after the profile of the hull, the half-breadths for the keel, and the half-breadths for the deck are proven fair. Once these lines have been proven for fairness, they must not for any reason or whim be altered in order to fair in any of the other lines, or you will be inviting chaos. In round-bottom hulls, the procedure is to next fair in the mold stations or selected transverse frames directly from the offsets to form the body plan. Then, picking up the faired section (body plan) offsets for half-breadths, these measurements are transferred to the plan view of the hull and faired longitudinally. Buttocks are transferred from the body plan as heights on the profile and faired longitudinally. Diagonals are laid down in a separate area for clarity, as previously mentioned, and faired longitudinally. Numerous errors may be discovered, since the body plan was faired from offsets given. Then, by the longitudinal layout of these offsets, you must go back to the body plan and mark in the offsets that were corrected longitudinally, fairing as you go. You may discover that the longitudinal offsets cannot produce a fair body plan. Where discrepancies occur, you will note them and transfer them back to where they originated and again refair this line longitudinally until all lines are in agreement. In doing this, the buttock lines are parallel to the centerline in plan view, and a buttock line will cross a waterline (curved in plan view) at a precise distance forward or aft of a frame. This point of intersection must be identical in profile, where the waterlines are projected as straight lines and the buttocks are curved. The diagonals are not lofted in the profile portion of the hull nor on the plan view of the hull as each diagonal is assumed to be normal to its own plane.

In flat, Vee, and multi-chine hulls, the actual frames or molds (that is, the body plan) are not drawn until after the longitudinal fairing of the lines has been done, since the individual segments of the frames in the body plan are straight between points. The Pinky's lines do not have buttocks, diagonals, or waterlines to be faired, since the chines, when faired in profile and plan view, are all that are needed to fill in the actual shape of any section between the faired-in half-breadth of the deck and the ghost centerline. The principle for lofting the chines is similar to that of the waterlines and buttocks. Fairing the half-breadths, body plan, and profile is a progressive job, and you will shuttle back and forth some between the three sets of lines before they all agree, but they *will* agree sooner or later. If in doubt as to the fairness of waterlines or chines, you can always lay down more sections in the doubtful area to gain more data points.

In round-bottom vessels the number of frame fairing stations needed to lay down faired half-breadths, heights, and diagonals will vary according to the shape of the vessel. To use every frame for fairing purposes when lofting a round-bottom hull would result in too much drawing and redrawing of unproven lines. Generally, a slender hull with fine ends needs the least number of frame stations for fairing, and

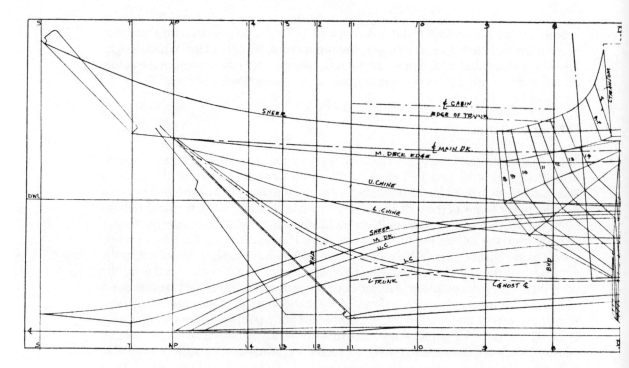

frames may be chosen to yield a spacing of one-fifth to one-eighth the length of the hull on deck. On the other hand, a full-bowed vessel may need all frame stations for fairing in the first quarter of her length and then a wider spacing, perhaps every third or fourth frame, thereafter. Canoe sterns and some of the character types with tucks and galleries will need to use all the frame stations in the stern. Of course, all frames will be lofted eventually, after the fairing has been done. If, in fairing, the loftsman finds his batten slack or a line doubtful, he will add an intermediate frame station to prove the line before scribing it in. Generally, the designer will delineate the difficult areas of the hull with more frames or stations, and the loftsman will instinctively recognize these as areas that might pose some problems in fairing. If cant frames are shown (additional frames, not square to the centerline, used in very full-ended vessels), all of these must be lofted with the primary frame stations.

Deck and Other Lines

Once the half-breadths have been laid down and faired, you may add the centerline of the deck to the profile drawing, since it may now be determined from the faired lines. It is curved in profile, since it follows the sheer, but its height above the sheer diminishes toward the ends of the vessel, as the half-breadth of the sheerline diminishes. The Lines Plan notes the camber of the deck as 1 inch per foot of half-

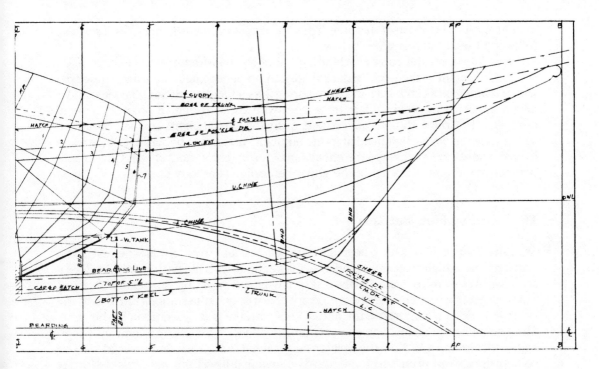

Figure 34. *The completed lofting.*

beam. Some loftsmen find it easier to use a full-size pattern of the deck camber to determine the height at each frame or mold station; others do it mathematically. They measure out from the centerline to determine the half-breadth of each frame, and then, knowing that the rise of the deck is one inch per foot of half-beam, they calculate the rise to the centerline. Thus, 3 feet 9 inches of half-beam will mean 3¾ inches of rise. If a pattern of a deck beam is constructed, measurements can be found from it directly.

In the Pinky design the fo'c's'le deck at frame 5 is 6½ inches above the main deck and intersects the forward perpendicular (FP) where the stem crosses. The location of the fo'c's'le deck edge is not yet known, but the centerline is a straight line, so this may be scribed in. Once the frame sections have been laid down, the edge of the fo'c's'le deck is determined by measuring outward from the centerline. (This cannot be done until the frame sections are laid down, since all frames in this area flare, and the deck intersects somewhere between the "main deck extended and the sheer.")

Note also that since the lines are faired to the centerline, and the sternpost has a siding given, it is now possible to scribe in the bearding line. Measure outward from the centerline in plan view one-half the siding of the sternpost, and scribe a parallel line. Since the plating will be flush with the forward edge of the stem bar, which has a half-side of ¼ inch, the bearding line practically coincides with the stem face from just forward of station 2. The cabin trunks, cargo hatch, and the foredeck hatch should also be scribed in at this time. Then the transom can be finalized and scribed, following the directions given below.

Figure 34 shows the completed lofting. All of the half-frame sections have been scribed in, and now the fo'c's'le deck edge can be determined, after finding by trial where it lands on each frame and then fairing it as a half-breadth in plan view and a height in profile to assure a fair agreement with the determined points. The final outlines of the frame stations are scribed, using the faired heights and half-breadths. At this time the partial bulkhead at frame number 5½ can also be scribed, since a line from the faired lower chine to the ghost line determines its exact shape. Once again, you can see the importance of the ghost centerline (fairbody line).

The Bearding Line and Keel

After the frame sections have been faired in, it is prudent to determine the rest of the bearding line, which is the intersection of the keel side with the bottom frames. There are several reasons to make this the last step whenever possible. To begin with, it will now represent a true and fair line with respect not only to the stations but also to the ghost line. Equally important, the actual keel material is decided upon at this time. The Lines Plan indicates, and the scantlings call for, a 6-inch by 6-inch by 1-inch angle oriented as a V. Now the builder may have this in stock, but it could also be back-ordered and promised for yesterday, meaning it will not be available for six months, if ever. Maybe the nearest distributor has the section, but charges $400 for delivery. So it goes. The owner wants less draft, changes the ballast from lead to iron, adds tankage in the keel sections, *ad infinitum*. On the economic side of it all, a 9-inch by 1-inch universal mill plate (flat bar, FB) is available for one-tenth the cost of the angle and can be delivered *now*. I don't mean to suggest that this always happens or that the builder is incompetent if he didn't have the keel on hand long before signing the contract or beginning the lofting. We all live or should live in a practical world, and these days, stockpiling for years in the future is not practical. Builders must depend on their suppliers, and they in turn on theirs, so minor changes must be contemplated at times in order to progress with the work. Of course, it would be intolerable for a builder to change all the scantlings to suit his whim or his suppliers *if* the materials called for were standard for the industry.

The keel *is* the most frequently changed portion of the hull structure below the main deck; however, once finalized, it must always remain unchanged or none of the floors will fit. The width of the keel should be the same as a standard mill plate (FB) or shape if it is parallel-sided for at least 50 percent of its length; otherwise, the edges of the keel will have to be flame cut and ground after cutting to finish them. Moreover, deep floors on parallel-sided keels can also be cut from standard FB if the keel conforms to a standard width. Being rectangular in section, they need only be cut for length, and this saves labor in scribing, cutting, and grinding the long sides, which would be necessary if they were a nonstandard width.

If a change in keel width has been made, it is only necessary to change the half-breadth to find the new points of intersection for the bearding line on the body plan. This, of course, should follow relofting the bearding line in the half-breadth plan, using offsets that reflect the actual dimensions of the keel stock used. An increase or decrease will change the parallel portion of the keel bottom and some of the other floor widths before and after the parallel section. The bearding must eventually diminish with a fair line to the original endings determined by the stem and sternpost.

Let us assume, however, that no change in keel width, and hence in half-breadth, will be made on the Pinky. We find that the floors, frame 4 to frame 10 inclusive, are parallel-sided and will have a molded half-breadth of 4 inches. For each half of the body plan (forward and after sections), we scribe a parallel line four inches off the centerline; its intersection with frames 4 through 10 defines the bearding line for that segment of the keel. Offsets for the remaining frame stations are transferred from the half-breadths up to the frames to determine where they intersect. Once these points are established, the heights will be transferred to the frame station lines, and the profile of the bearding line can be faired and scribed. We have now all but finished lofting the Pinky.

OTHER LOFTING METHODS

Before proceeding, I should emphasize that the lofting method already shown yields the most usable information without additional relofting to obtain templates, and is superior to other methods for clarity. Two others are quite common, however, and used by experienced loftsmen.

Lofting by Halves

Figure 35 shows a method used when a larger vessel than the yard normally constructs is to be lofted, especially when building on such a scale will not be repeated. In this method, the vessel is lofted full size and true length, but in two halves. The fairing of the forward half is stopped a bit more than one frame aft of amidships, that is, just aft of frame 8 in the Pinky example. Using a common frame, in this case frame 2, and marking this also as No. 7, the loftsman now strikes in all frames aft of No. 7 to the stern and labels them with new numbers. Thus, frames 7 and 8 will appear twice in both profile and plan, once in the forebody and again in the afterbody. Taking his offsets for frames 7 and 8 from the lofted forebody (not the table of offsets), he then lofts the afterbody of the hull, starting at No. 7; this results in an afterbody profile and plan superimposed on the forebody. The loftsman assumes that No. 7 was fair when he lofted the forebody, because he faired through No. 8; however, to be sure, he will refair both halves without making any changes to No. 7. After fairing the afterbody, he checks to see if No. 8 is also fair at all points previously found in laying down the forebody. If it is not, he must find the error and fair again, this time assuming that frames 5, 6, 9, and 10 are established and fair in the correct line for Nos. 7 and 8. Sooner or later, both halves will agree in all overlapping stations.

Aside from the confused web of intersecting lines it creates, and the need to reloft

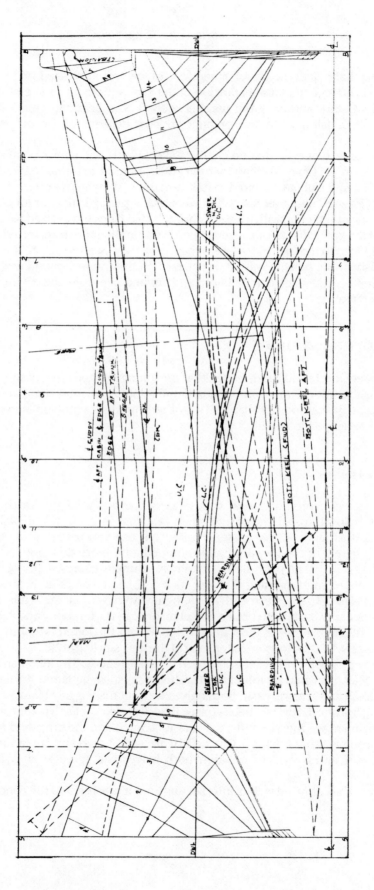

Above: Figure 35. *Lofting of the Pinky full size, but with overlapping forward and after halves.* **Below: Figure 36.** *A method of lofting in which heights and half-breadths are full size, but the hull length is foreshortened, in this case to one-half its true dimension.*

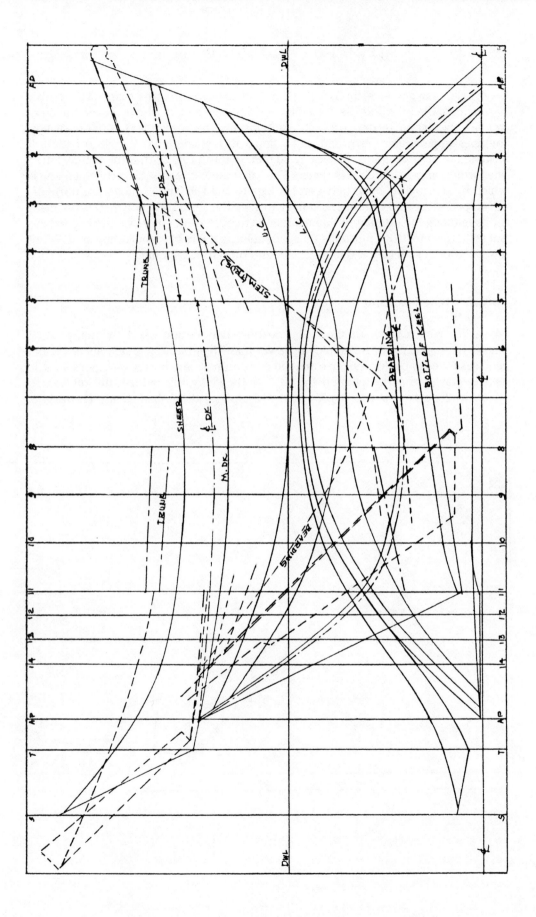

the overlapping portions, this is a good method and gives the true shape of the ends. I have shown the afterbody as dotted lines for the sake of clarity; however, in actual practice they would be drawn as solid lines, just like the forebody. On small drawings, the lines appear quite crowded, but when you consider that the size of the loft assumed in my example is 16 feet by 40 feet, you will realize that the actual, lofted lines would appear much less dense. The loftsman can easily discern which line is which by putting his head between his legs to sight it. The sections are normally developed at the end stations, as shown, to keep the central section of the floor clear for developing the templates. Some loftsmen use different colors for the two halves, but I find this more of a nuisance than a benefit, as the light in the lofting areas is not always good, especially if one must depend on natural lighting.

Foreshortened Lofting

Figure 36 illustrates a method of foreshortened lofting used by many small shipyards, especially those employing fewer than 10 persons. It is very accurate and requires little space, for the lines are laid out one-half, and in rare instances as little as one-quarter, the true length of the hull. For the Pinky, this reduces the loft floor to 16 feet by 28 feet (14 sheets of plywood) when lofting at one-half length. The heights

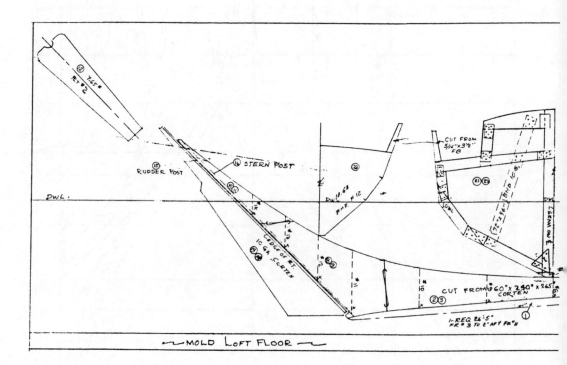

and half-breadths are true, full-size measurements. The ends become very distorted; however, all measurements will remain correct and fair and will produce a fair line again when the length is corrected. The body plan is drawn about the midship section, as in ordinary full-scale lofting, but is not shown here for the sake of clarity. After fairing by the foreshortened method, at least the bow and stern must be relofted to their true size. With straight keels, especially those with parallel sides, the rest of the backbone may be ignored; however, if the keel has pronounced curvature or other irregularities, the whole profile including the keel should be lofted.

TEMPLATE MAKING

The moldloftsman has now done the bulk of his work and can commence making templates, made of sheet metal, masonite, plywood, or normal plank wood. In my own yard, we always used ¼-inch marine plywood in preference to other materials, since it was stable, light, and easily cut with a sabersaw or bandsaw. The sheets were precut into 5-inch strips; the remaining thin strip was used as a marking stick. By using marine plywood instead of a cheaper grade, we never had to worry about any material in the yard being unsuitable for inclusion in the finished vessel, should the

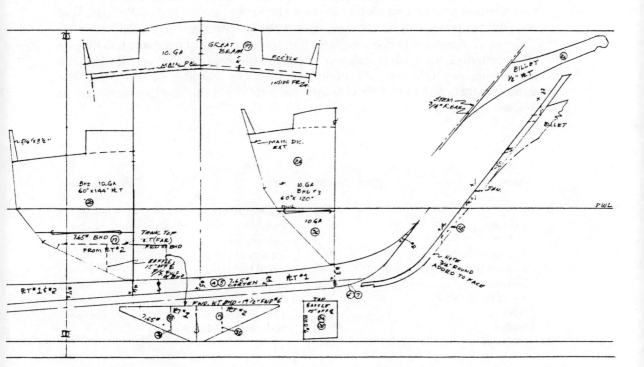

Figure 37. *Several of the templates for the Pinky (including the backbone template) that can be lifted from the mold loft floor.*

occasion arise. This also applied to staging, scaffolding, and the like: if it was there, it was usable.

In making the templates, either twopenny galvanized common nails, with the protruding end nipped off, or air-driven staples can be used. The latter have the advantage that each staple equals two nails, is much faster to drive, and does not require the nipping of its ends. The pieces of the template should be cut for exact fit, and not used as spiling planks, as would be normal in wooden shipbuilding. Exactness in metal construction cannot be overly stressed. In my yard, once the templates had been used, they would be pulled apart and reused until there was no wood left. In a 50-foot hull, four to five sheets of plywood were sufficient for all the templating necessary to construct the vessel.

The first templates made will be those for the stem and forefoot. The billet shown on the Pinky drawings would probably not be used on a commercial vessel because of the cost, but usually would be included on a vessel finished as a yacht. In any case, the template for it is made separately and fitted to the stem. The forefoot template must be notched to fit the keel.

Next the loftsman will make the template for the keel sides (deadwood), and in doing so will take account of the keel material actually available, since the template joints must agree with joints practical to make in the steel stock used. In the forward and after ends (forward of frame 4 and aft of frame 10) the keel tapers toward the centerline, and true girth lengths will be needed to assure the correct plate width where this keel side plate lands on the frames. More vessels are fudged in these areas than are done properly, so it is best to have a butt joint near the ends of the keel. That way, the templates can be checked against the hull proper.

Figure 37 shows backbone templates and several others of the many that may be lifted from the floor. Each is assigned a number, and, if more than one piece is to be made from any template, the additional numbers will also be indicated. The templates that can be lifted directly from the loft floor in the example shown are as follows:

Name	Piece Number	Name	Piece Number
keel	1	deadwood	2–5, 8–11
forefoot	6–7	transom	12
rudder	13–14	rudderpost	15
sternpost	16	bottom of bulkhead 6	17
forward watertight bulkhead	18–19	top of bulkhead 6	20
bulkhead 8	21–22	bulkhead 12	23
top of bulkhead 3	24	stem	25
billet	26	deep floors	27–33
baffles	34–35	bottom of bulkhead 3	36
great beam	37		

Not shown or numbered but also picked up and templated will be:

floors 2, 3, 11-14	6 pieces	bulwark frames 3, 6, 8, 12, great beam	12 pieces
forward trunk sides	2 pcs.	aft trunk sides	2 pcs.
aft trunk end	1 pc.	cargo trunk sides	2 pcs.
cargo trunk end	1 pc.	fender frames	28 pcs.
companion sides	4 pcs.	forward hatch	4 pcs.
companion tops	2 pcs.	trailboards	2 pcs.
mainmast step	1 pc.	watertank bottom plate	1 pc.
watertank top	1 pc.	watertank end pieces	2 pcs.
centerline bulkhead, rope locker	1 pc.	centerline bulkhead, chain locker	1 pc.
battery foundation	7 pcs.	binnacle coaming	4 pcs.
bitt bracket	1 pc.	after perpendicular and transom stanchions	4 pcs.

This makes a total of 124 pieces, and if you consider that each piece made directly from the framing platen without templates can be checked on the mold loft, then the total is 215 pieces directly verifiable. If the Pinky had auxiliary power, additional templates might include fuel tanks (sides, ends, and tops), engine beds, stern tube, and boss framing—about 12 to 16 more templates.

In larger vessels the list of templates would expand to include each piece of framing and, of course, more frames and probably several longitudinal bulkheads. In a typical 80-foot three-masted schooner, for instance, the total number of templates lifted from the mold loft floor would come to 600—more if she had auxiliary power.

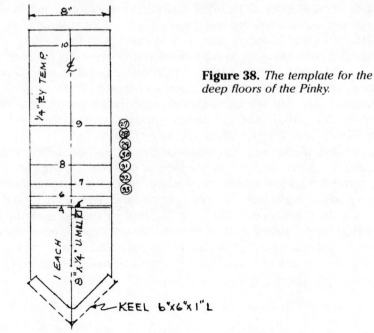

Figure 38. *The template for the deep floors of the Pinky.*

The deep floors (frames 4 through 10) have a common width and bottom and differ only in length; thus, a common template for all need only be a bit longer than the deepest floor, with the others marked for proper length (Figure 38). Templates for all other floors are made as individual pieces.

Although this step comes a bit later than templating, I should point out that when the keel angle is ready to be scribed for cutting and grinding, all the frame stations will be center punched, scribed, and numbered on it. *In metal vessels the frame is always set on the side of the scribe mark toward the midship frame.* This is the opposite of wooden construction, where the frames are *away from* the midship frame. Wood frames are beveled (dubbed) fair, whereas metal frames are not. The frame line on any loft floor is good for only *one edge* of the frame.

SCRIBING PLATES FOR CUTTING OUT

I cannot stress the importance of the mold loft enough. You might ask: "What about the one-man shop; what about the two- or three-man shop; is such extensive template making really desirable for a small operation?" The answer is always an unqualified *yes*. The difference between profit and loss is slender in all small shipyards, but the few hours needed to properly loft and make templates will be more than compensated when you cut the material. Figure 39 indicates how this is done, assuming that you have two 60-inch by 240-inch, 7.65-pound plates. Each will weigh 765 pounds and cost about $300 (in 1984)—enough to make you think twice about wasting any steel if you can help it. The various templates that require this plate weight are juggled around the plates to minimize the waste. The whole process takes one person about 30 minutes, and once you are satisfied, each template is clamped or otherwise secured and the plate scribed for cutting. After removing the template, you should identify the marked piece with the same markings as the template. The remaining unused portions of the plate will be used for doublers, brackets, and keel supports during construction. Utilizing, say, 95 percent of the plate area means that you will have 38 pounds of scrap left over, or $15 loss per plate, plus one-half hour of layout time and eight hours for making the necessary templates. I doubt that this many pieces could be cut from the same two plates by trial and error in 40 hours, with the same or less scrap.

The competent loftsman will make sketches of his templates against the plates and material that are available in the yard or on order for the construction of the vessel, referencing these sketches to a plate number. It is not uncommon in a well-run yard using this system to find a plate or two and some shapes left over, with little scrap from the original order, which is better than wasting material and having a large scrap pile. Regardless of the size of the vessel, a goodly amount of "paper doll" sketching takes place throughout the course of construction, since a few minutes' sketching often saves not only hours of time and material but costly mistakes.

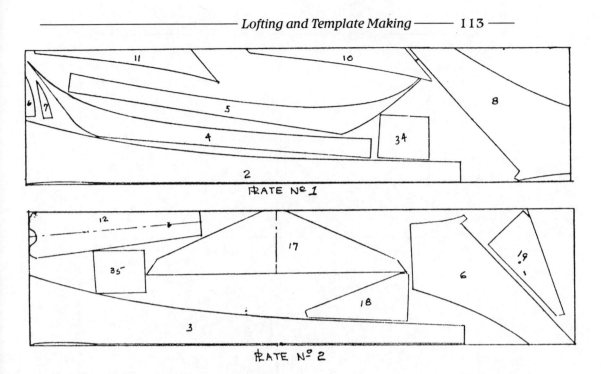

Figure 39. *The method of arranging templates for parts of the Pinky requiring 7.65-pound plate, minimizing the scrap from two 60-inch by 240-inch plates.*

WORKING ON THE FRAMING PLATEN

Figure 40 shows a temporary framing platen made from three sheets of 60-inch by 192-inch, 10-gauge material. These sheets will later be used in the plating of the hull (two on the bottom in the midship portion and one on the deck). At this time, however, they will be laid out and tack welded together to form a platform 16 feet by 15 feet. The spacing of the tacks will depend in part on the floor or frame upon which the plates are laid to form the temporary platen (this floor must be flat in all directions and if it is not, it will have to be leveled, as in the case of the loft floor). A centerline is struck that will represent the centerline of the hull, and the DWL is next struck at right angles to the centerline. Note that neither of these lines will utilize a natural seam in the sheets. Note, too, that when the temporary platen is lifted and the sheets or plates are ready to use in the construction of the vessel, the side used for working the frames must *always* face the *inside* of the vessel.

Yards with more than one vessel under construction at the same time find a permanent platen the best solution for laying down frames. If elevated to a comfortable working height above the floor or ground, it also becomes a useful working area for subassemblies. In this case, the platen usually has one or more vises, anvils, and fixtures near one edge for bending deck beams, collars, and other curved parts. The minimum plate thickness for such a platen is ⅜ inch (15.3 pounds); however, the heavier the plate used, the less the distortion caused when working hot pieces. Yards that habitually build round-bottom hulls work on very thick bending

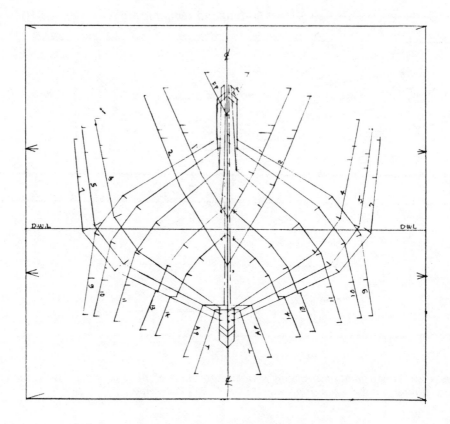

Figure 40. *A temporary framing platen.*

slabs or platens containing a series of square holes into which various tools can be fitted.

Since frames 3, 6, 8, and 12 are steel bulkheads, they need not be laid down on the platen, but instead can be laid down directly on the material from which they will be cut. All other frames, however, are laid down on the platen with a marking stick, using the offset dimensions obtained from the mold loft. All points needed to lay these frames down are centerpunched into the platen and connected by lines drawn with a sharp soapstone. Should a tack weld lie in the way of any frame, it will be ground flush at this time. A short tick mark is added in soapstone as each frame is drawn, to call attention to the reference points that need to be marked and to indicate where the various pieces will join: fo'c's'le deck edge and main deck extended, on frames 1, 2, and 4; and on all frames, the sheer, the main deck edge, the upper chine, the lower chine, and the bearding line intersections. The best practice when no templates are made is to lay out both sides of the frame, making this an extra check for accuracy before you finally commit yourself. Even though, in practice, the frame pieces will be cut in pairs—the first piece cut being used as a pattern for the second piece—errors can always creep in.

In smaller vessels you should always check the pieces cut against the corresponding sections as laid down on the loft, to satisfy yourself with the

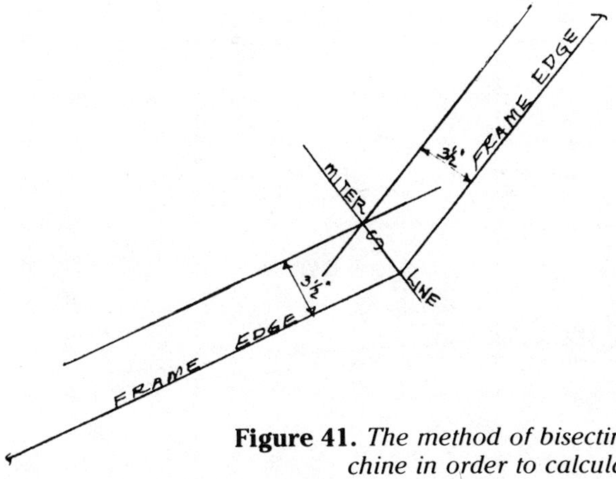

Figure 41. *The method of bisecting the angle of a chine in order to calculate the miters for the frame pieces.*

correctness of the platen layout. Some loftsmen prefer to go directly to the framing platen rather than scribe the frames on the wood floor, but in doing so lose a valuable check in case they should err on the platen layout. Always maintaining a degree of redundancy adds a safety factor that can save much time in the construction of the frames and bulkheads. In small vessels the individual framing pieces are light and small enough to allow checking each against the lofted frame stations prior to assembly. In larger vessels it is always best to make a template for each piece of the framing.

On round-bottom hulls and large single- and multi-chine hulls that have a template of each frame lifted from the mold loft, it will suffice to make duplicate halves of the frame, mark the DWL, and lay the frames down, checking the sheer of the undrawn halves for height and half-breadth.

When laying out both sides of the frames as shown, the usual practice is to lay out the forebody looking up and the afterbody looking down, with the centerline and DWL common to both; this reduces the possibility of picking up the wrong frame. The layout man would never see the complete platen as shown, unless he stood about 80 feet above it, so actually these lines are not confusing.

Before they can be assembled and welded on the platen, the frame pieces are cut to a miter at the chines. The platen provides an accurate place to lay out the miters as well as the frames themselves. To figure the miter for each piece in a joint, you simply bisect the angle of the joint. Figure 41 shows the method of bisecting any angle, in this case the chine. Working on the platen, it is best to use material the same width as the frame material, also making the bisecting line longer than actually needed to connect points, so that it can be easily picked up.

Figure 42 shows frame 5 laid out on the platen. The ⁵⁄₁₆-inch by 3½-inch flat bar (FB) used for the framing has been mitered at the chines; piece number 37 will have been cut from a template made on the mold loft floor, and serves as the great beam (GB) on this vessel. The scantling section (Figure 76) indicates a 1½-inch by 10-inch by 8.4-pound channel cut to 9 inches, the ends of which have been trimmed normal to the frame; this piece and others like it span the bottom of frames 4, 5, 7, 9, 10, and 11 (this was done to reduce the gross tonnage of the vessel). The 1½-inch by 2½-

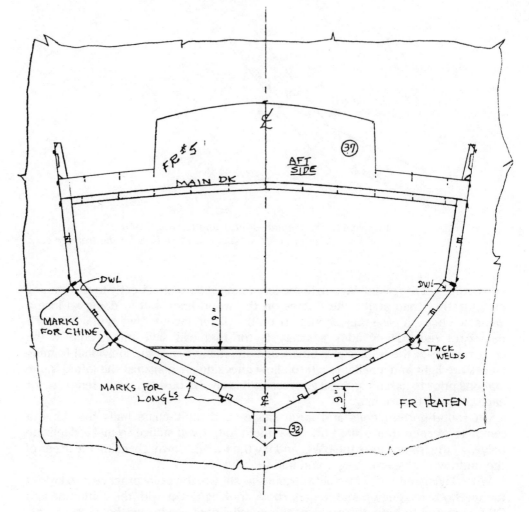

Figure 42. *Frame 5 of the Pinky laid out on the platen.*

inch sole beam is located 19 inches below the DWL, as per the Construction and Scantling plans (Figures 67 and 76). The bulwark stanchion templates are taken from the mold loft, as is the deep floor, piece number 32. Having been cut, each piece is now sited where it belongs and checked for proper fit. Where joints occur, the pieces are lifted and beveled for welding, then relaid and tacked in position on the platen. (After cutting and grinding, the bulkheads, too, are laid—not tacked—on the platen to have their stiffeners added, as it is imperative that flatness of the surface be retained.) When all are in place, the frame will once again be checked to make sure that no "walking" of the pieces occurred as they were tacked down. Once checked, all pieces will be welded together, forming a one-piece frame. As noted above, the frame lies on the aft side of the station mark; thus, the differences in material thickness of the several pieces will not affect the proper fit of the frame inside the hull, since the down side or station side of the frame is a continuous plane without any joggles, and the greater hull girth aft of the station line in the forebody or forward of the station line in the afterbody will allow clearance for thicker pieces. Finally, the welds in way of the chines must be ground smooth, so that they may be scribed for the chine bar cutout.

The frame may now be scribed, with the centerline also punched in enough places so that, should the scribe line later be obliterated, you can reestablish it; likewise, the DWL is centerpunched across the frame bars. In this instance there is a deck-joining piece, No. 37, the great beam, and on this the main deck line is also punched and scribed. Before removing the frame, mark all cuts for longitudinals, and make a punch mark where they will butt a frame without continuing (main and fo'c's'le decks). Also scribe the chines for cutting. Once again, you would be wise to check that all marks are in the frame, and the frame itself numbered and identified as to which way it should face, after which the tacks can be broken loose with a cold chisel.

At this time the frame will be weak, having been welded on one side only, so you must turn it over very carefully, elevating it on short blocks where necessary to allow for the flange on the floor plate, which now faces downward. With the frame once again on a flat plane, joints to be welded are back-chipped and otherwise prepared. Once this side of the frame is welded, the centerline should be transferred from the opposite side and scribed; however, the DWL need not be transferred. Welds on this side of the frame are not ground. The frame may now be moved elsewhere. The residual tits from the tack welds are ground flush, and the frame turned over again for the cutting of the longitudinals and the chines. Because of a tendency for warping and buckling during welding, the companionway opening will not be cut until the decks and trunk sides are in place.

VESSELS WITH CENTERBOARDS

If you are building a centerboard vessel, the centerboard trunk sides and head ledges should be lofted in their proper places on the loft floor. In most instances the centerboard is sited on the centerline of the vessel, and thus will pierce the keel. The designer will usually give the net half-breadth of the slot. The loftsman will then have to make allowance for the thickness of the trunk sides, and when marking the template for the keel will show the gross opening. Many of the larger sailing vessels have the centerboard offset to one side of the keel proper so that it passes wholly or partially through the garboard plate.

Except in certain yachts, centerboards are normally made of wood, usually in planks that are drift- and through-bolted together after shaping. It is customary to fit a galvanized half-oval along the full length of the bottom edge of the centerboard and carry it up both ends for a foot or two to prevent its being ripped off in the event of grounding. Boards so constructed have a slight tendency to sink; should they not, a portion is cut out near the after, lower corner, and lead is cast in. Sometimes a centerboard is made from three or more sheets of marine plywood, laminated together with resorcinol or epoxy glue and covered with one or more layers of fiberglass cloth using epoxy resins. Boards of this construction must have lead cast in the lower forward portion as well as the lower after portion, to give negative buoyancy. This is in addition to the half-oval grounding shoe, which should be installed outside all glass covering.

In the larger vessels, the usual practice is to ship centerboards after launching the vessel. With the vessel in deep water, the board is lowered into the water and guided into the trunk using lanyards rove prior to launching. The board is then hoisted by its own pendant aft and a temporary tackle hitched to the forward end, until it is in position for the pivot pin cap to be removed and the pin pushed home and recapped before the vessel floods.

It is a good practice to make a template of the centerboard and lay it on the mold loft floor, checking that the pin lines up properly and that the board will pivot without fouling the lofted lines of the trunk and slot. There is nothing more vexing than to find out too late that the board either does not fit or will not pivot.

LOFTING THE STERN

A canoe stern needs the same type of template as the stem. In addition, the loftsman must make due allowance for the rudderport, and also provide sufficient marks both for leveling the stern as a unit and for referencing to other level lines. Failure to do this invites the possibility of the canoe stern's being incorrectly sited on the rudderport. Worse, even though the vertical end offset might be correct (the tip of the stern set at the right height), the remainder of the plane could be off, causing a sag or hog in the sheer that would completely spoil the lines. When you have to work with a complex design, measure, mark, compare, then do it again!

Cant Frames

Cant frames—frames not square to the centerline of the vessel—are used in vessels with very full or rounded ends, and are sited to lie as close to normal with the shell plating as possible. This permits the true shape of the vessel to be maintained while at the same time giving the greatest support to the shell. It also eases the job of welding or otherwise fastening the shell to the frames, a job that would be difficult or in places even impossible if the frames were set square to the centerline and were thus forced to meet the plating at acute angles.

Figure 43 shows two types of vessels that commonly use cant frames in the stern—a three-masted schooner and a tug. Such sterns, commonly called fantail sterns, are designed for specific utilitarian purposes, by the way, rather than to suit some momentary style or fad. In the schooner, such a stern would reduce the helm when the vessel was loaded and heeled, easing the quarters without sacrificing deck space or cargo capacity. In the tug it would prevent or at least reduce the possibility of the towline fouling and capsizing the vessel.

Figure 44 shows one method of lofting a round stern and locating the cants, as well as the expansion and cutting layout of the stern plate for a 68-foot schooner. The stern is lofted in plan and profile, as with any other type of stern. The extent of offsets

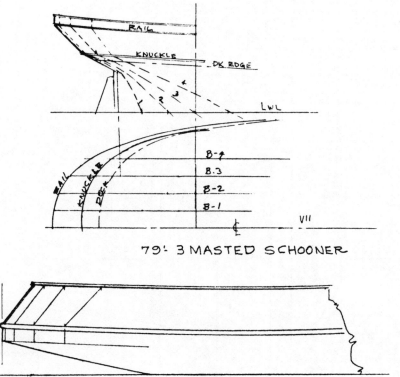

RAIL
KNUCKLE
DK EDGE
LWL
B-4
B.3
B-2
B-1
VII
RAIL
KNUCKLE
DECK

79'· 3 MASTED SCHOONER

65'· TUG

Figure 43. *Two vessels having cant frames in their sterns.*

given will vary from one design office to another; some will furnish only offsets for heights and half-breadths, while others will also furnish dimensions along each buttock to define the plan view of the chine and main deck extended. Seldom will the cants themselves be shown or the offsets given for them, the hope being that the loftsman will do a good job of locating the cants and properly lofting the whole stern as the designer imagined it.

Were cants not used in this vessel, frame 18 would be a half-moon shape, with its deepest point at the centerline. Internal welding of the chine would be impossible for about 20 inches off centerline on either side, and would offer no support for the chine and almost none for the deck edge. If frame 18 were eliminated and buttocks (longitudinal frames) used in lieu of cant frames, selecting for example the intersection of cants B and D at frame 17 as the site of buttocks, there would be fair support for the chine but almost none for the deck. If a stiffener were inserted where frame 17 joins the chine, it would land at such an acute angle that welding, aside from going against good building practice, would cause distortion in the stern plate. Using the cant frames A, B, C, and D solves these problems by subdividing the entire stern into reasonable segments, providing the maximum support with the minimum

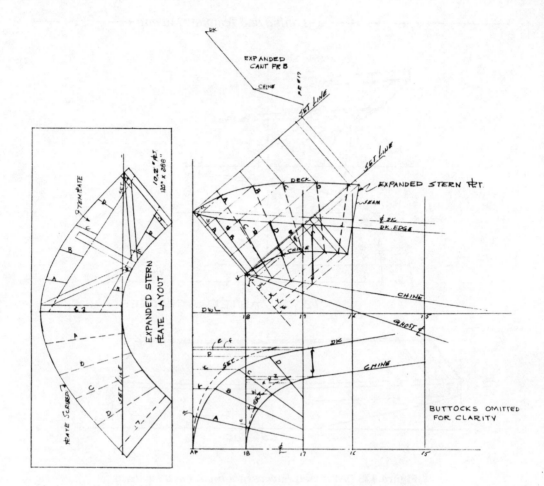

Figure 44. *A method of lofting a round stern and locating the cants, and the expansion and cutting layout of the stern plate for a 68-foot schooner.*

framing and weight. A loftsman might find it expedient to lay down one or two extra waterlines intersecting the stern to determine how much curve, if any, will be in the cants as they rise from the chine to the deck line; in that event, the waterlines are laid down and faired in plan view for proof. Each cant is then projected as a diagonal would be, and templates are made of each. If you build a round stern, you will generally find that the designer provides enough detail on the plans to give you a good start in the lofting. Cant B illustrates the expansion to true dimensions.

Stern Plate Template for a Round Stern

Depending on "yard practice," the final template for the stern plate will either be lifted off the vessel directly, or the stern will be expanded on the floor of the loft and the template made there. The latter is the best method, especially for a complex stern using cant frames, for if any doubt exists about its correctness, the template can easily be fitted to the vessel in a fraction of the time required to make the template in place.

To loft this template it is necessary to erect two *set lines* perpendicular to the centerline of the stern of the vessel, which will later be used to lay down the true girth of those set lines. The centerline of the stern in profile must also be extended downward, and the cants, where they intersect the chine and the deck line, must be projected back perpendicular to the centerline. It is now possible to construct the set lines in plan. To do this, first erect a perpendicular on the half-breadth plan from station AP (the after perpendicular) to the point where each of the cants intersects the deck; do the same from frame 18 over to the point where each of the cants intersects the chine. Having done this, measure the length of each line you projected, from the profile centerline to where it intersects the deck line, and mark these lines a, b, c, d, e, and f. Transferring these lengths to the half-breadth plan, lay them off forward from the AP along the perpendiculars previously erected, and mark their end points. A fair curve drawn through these points will give the plan projection of the upper set line. Now follow the same steps to project the lower set line, finding the lengths of u, v, w, x, y, and z from the profile; lay these off along the perpendiculars in the half-breadth plan from frame 18, marking the end points as before. A fair curve drawn through these points represents the lower set line.

You may now establish the true girth of each set line by springing a batten around it and then measuring the straightened batten. Take a slender batten and bend it to the curve of the set line, scribing it at the centerline and each cant frame, as well as at frame 17 and the plate end. Straighten it and lay it down on the profile set line; this will allow you to transfer the true girth distance between each mark. Transfer the girths for both set lines. At each mark you transfer, erect a perpendicular downward from the set line. Next, extend a, b, c, d, e, and f on the profile until they intersect these perpendiculars, line "a" intersecting the perpendicular from girth "a", and so forth; do the same for u, v, w, x, y, and z. Fair lines drawn through the two series of intersections will describe the upper and lower edges of the expanded stern plate from the centerline of the vessel. A straight line connecting the extreme end points describes the seam (butt) of the plate. If everything looks like Figure 44 (with allowance made for differences in design, of course), you have successfully gotten through a tricky bit of lofting and can proceed to make and mark the expanded stern template.

As with all templates, diagonal bracing is needed to keep the stern template from going out of true. After marking the lower set line on it, you are now ready to transfer the template to the actual stern for cutting. Both are shown in Figure 44 as the expanded stern plate layout. After you have scribed the correct shape, you must scribe the locations of the cant frames and frame 17 on the plate. The set line, too, must be transferred and permanently marked on the plate, for pulling must be done along this line to wrap the plate around the hull.

It helps to know how this stern plate is applied in order to gain a better understanding of its lofting. Rather than having to cover this in another chapter, it will suffice to say here that once the stern plate is cut, ground, and marked, it is lifted into place and carefully positioned so that the centerline of the plate matches the centerline of the vessel. Pad eyes—sometimes several of them—are welded just below the deck line, on the inside of the plate along the set line. With come-alongs secured to opposing pad eyes and sometimes, in the initial stages, to the hull structure itself, the plate is gradually wrapped around, forming the stern of the hull. It is tack welded as it comes to bear on the chine and deck pipe (if one exists), and to each of the cant frames. Finally, when it has been brought all the way home, it is tack welded to frame 17. Both sides are worked at the same time. Since considerable pressure is exerted on this plate in the process of bending, it is desirable not to use the hull itself for pulling, as it could be twisted out of alignment. This caution does not preclude using numerous clamps to help the come-alongs.

Yards equipped with bending rolls can preroll these plates to a partially correct curvature. However, a round stern is usually neither cylindrical nor conical in shape, but a combination of the two; a fairer stern is therefore achieved by not rolling.

Raking Transoms

Figure 45 shows an expanded transom. Its projection is covered in most standard texts on lofting. It is important to remember that the radius is the line of expansion and that the lines must be relofted perpendicular to this radius; otherwise, the stern will be false. This type of stern is purely cylindrical. The expanded shape is normally shown on the lines plan but must be proved on the mold loft floor.

Sterns Without Lofting

Some builders omit fitting the stern until all of the remainder of the plating is in place. Whether it be flat or cylindrical, they slip the stern in and scribe it to the existing plating rather than depend on lofting. This method can and does work; however, by knowing how to use (and by using) the mold loft, you can save much time and labor. Indeed, many designers provide full offsets for an expanded transom, which has always been my practice.

Lofting at first appears to be a mystery and, admittedly, it is difficult to describe in simple terms every facet of the subject. Nor is there any reason to, since you, as an individual builder, need not clutter your mind with obscurities you may never use nor consider in your lifetime. Watching a builder loft a vessel would certainly clarify some of the more intricate procedures described in this chapter. Alternatively, if an exercise is needed, it would be possible to gather a few small wooden splines or plastic drafting battens, some pins, a straightedge, and a sheet of soft pine or particle board painted with flat white paint, and then lay down the lofting grid for your proposed vessel to the same scale as the drawings or a bit larger. Using the information given on the Lines and Offsets Plan, you can reproduce this drawing as it would appear on the mold loft floor full size. You will discover that doing anything in miniature is much more difficult than doing it full size. It must be remembered that much of the drawing done by designers is with very specialized weights, splines, and

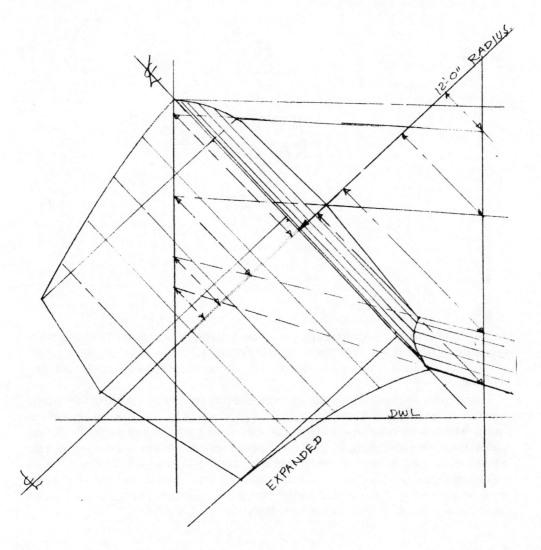

Figure 45. *An expanded transom.*

curves, and many of these curves are developed by the designer and are not available to anyone else: they are tools of his trade.

Lofting is but one of the many skills required of a boatbuilder, and for the first-time builder it is beneficial to acquire this skill. For some reason, most first-time builders have a fear of lofting; however, as with everything else, understanding conquers fear which then, in turn, leads to respect. Thus, understanding lofting makes it much easier for the novice builder to begin to cut and assemble his yardful of plates, bars, and assorted other material into a completed vessel.

8
▽
KEELS,
FRAMING,
AND
TANKS

Earlier chapters have discussed in general and in the specifics most of the aspects of constructing a steel hull, with the exceptions of keels, frames and framing methods, and tanks in their numerous variations. This chapter will round out the discussion.

The majority of vessels now building in steel are to stock plans, some of which may have been drawn many years ago and in all probability for a specific region of the world. The builder must, if at all possible, construct the vessel as originally drawn, unless there are compelling reasons to adapt the vessel for his locality or perhaps for a new function, such as conversion from a fishing vessel to a yacht or vice versa. In some instances the designer may be available for consultation and can offer some suggestions or give his approval for any proposed changes. In others, the builder must know enough to make sound modifications on his own.

KEELS AND COOLERS

The keel is the structural member most often changed, because of depth restrictions, availability of material, or other reasons. The change, when it must be made, is made with extreme caution, since in some hulls the keel constitutes the only major longitudinal strength member. This is especially true of sailing vessels, which often lack bulkheads, and are subject to racking in a seaway under a press of sail. The smaller vessels always need some external keel, centerboard, or combination of both in order to gain the lateral plane necessary to go to windward, and this, in turn, imparts much of the longitudinal strength necessary for the vessel to function at sea. Then proper framing in small sailing vessels will take care of most if not all of the racking strains.

Today few pure sailing vessels are built, as most incorporate auxiliary power. These normally have bulkheads installed to separate the engine compartment from the remainder of the vessel. Integral tanks also stiffen the structure. If an auxiliary is added, it may be necessary to reinforce the keel structure in way of the spars, and perhaps in the forward portion of the hull as well, in order to accept the thrust and other loads imposed by the spars when the vessel powers into a head sea. Under this condition, the compression load on the keel is about doubled, while the fore-and-aft loads on the deck at the partners are nearly three times the normal ones experienced by a pure sailing vessel. Thus the builder may also have to reinforce the deck by increasing the beam size and plating in way of the mast. If you plan to add auxiliary power without the knowledge and consent of the designer, you must take the increased loads into consideration and do the necessary reinforcing to the hull structure and keel in order to accept these added loads. Such alterations must be lofted and thoroughly checked before you start construction.

Modifications are also frequently made to power designs. In many instances, the builder of a power vessel finds it possible to utilize certain keel configurations formerly used only in sailing vessels. This is especially true with regard to keel cooling arrangements.

Figure 46 shows several common types of keel construction, the simplest being the bar keel, which has survived from the earliest days of metal construction. In early construction it formed a perfect connection between the two halves of a riveted vessel, and builders still use it today in many of the welded power vessels. Note that the welded style extends farther inside the hull than the riveted keel. When using the bar keel, a builder must take care lest it begin to wander from a straight line during framing; after the bottom plates are tacked in place, this danger no longer exists. The welding of plating to the bar keel is complicated by quench effects; in cold weather you should warm or heat the keel prior to welding and, if possible, for some hours afterwards, so as to normalize the metal (100 degrees Fahrenheit is plenty for this). The lower corners of bar keels—and all keels—should be slightly rounded in order to hold paint. Some builders weld a round bar to the bottom of the bar, but this is a poor substitute for the bulb bar that is, or was, used in Europe. A variation of the bar keel is the double bar keel, which divides near amidships, one bar continuing aft to the stern and the other running downward to form the skeg. A filler plate of lighter metal is used between the two bars.

In some vessels that ground out frequently or need to maintain a minimum draft, the keel is often inverted and sited inside the hull. In riveted structures this is accomplished with angles riveted in one direction to a spacer plate on top of a horizontal keel plate, and in the other to a vertical, center keel plate. The spacer is usually the same thickness as the shell plating. A top plate is also riveted to the center vertical keel via angles, in effect making the keel structure a built-up I-beam. The frames (floors) are in turn riveted to the top and bottom keel plates. In welded construction, you could duplicate the riveted structure by omitting the riveting flanges (angles) and welding a T-bar directly to the shell or keel plate. Contrast the simple, clean structure that welding permits with the complexity of riveted structures in these two keel sections.

A still better structure is made by using an I-beam to advantage, as shown, and this

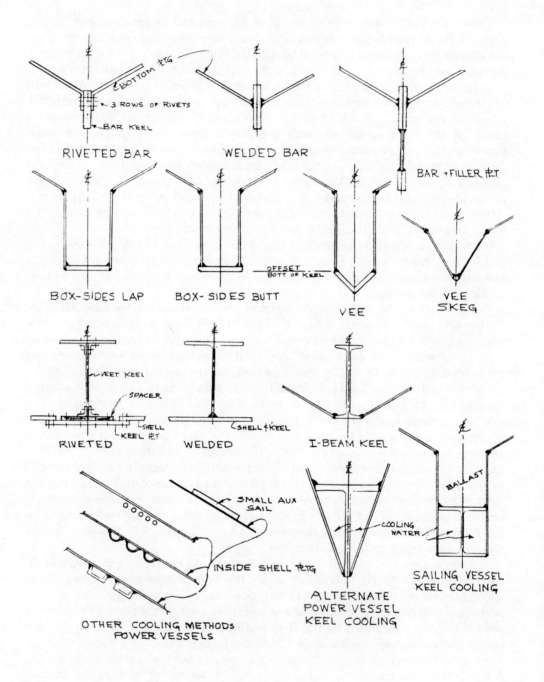

Figure 46. *Several common keel constructions.*

is an excellent way to make a small flat keel, especially when there is deadrise in the bottom.

Sailing vessels usually have box keels, and the two most common ways of constructing these are shown. In the first instance, the keel sides lap the keel plate, with the weld forming the bottom edges of the box. In the second instance, the side plates of the keel butt on top of the keel plate, set in by just the depth necessary to form the weld. The former is best when construction allows the keel bottom and side plates to be laid down and welded up before framing commences. The weld can be ground smooth and the whole edge rounded. This method also gives the greatest internal room for ballast or tankage. In the latter construction, the keel is laid down all at once and the welds are then made in the flat position, which is the quickest method of constructing the keel because framing and plating work can go on at the same time. It does not give as nice an edge on a sailing keel, and there is an internal loss in volume if the same keel plate width is used. In both types of construction the inside edge will be welded continuously as far as is practicable.

When drydocked, the bar keel has the advantage over the other types already discussed, in that you need not move the keel blocks supporting the vessel in order to paint the part of the keel edge resting on the blocks, for it is usually an inch or less in width. The total unpainted area comes to less than one-half square foot. Vessels having box or plate keels would use the same three to five blocks that the bar keel needs for support, each block about 12 inches wide. However, they would probably have one square foot of unpaintable surface at each block, meaning 3 to 5 square feet of bottom all told to foul between drydockings. Painters customarily skip the area in way of the blocks and hope on the next haulout to have different block locations. In some waters this may not cause a problem, but in the tropics it should be avoided due to the rapid fouling, which not only harms the sailing qualities but causes a loss of speed and a greater fuel consumption.

Another way to eliminate the need of a double haulout to shift blocks or a double lift in a traveling hoist would be to make the bottom of the keel out of a heavy angle. This construction retains the box keel and allows side plates to be easily fitted atop the keel when in the upright position, making for a better and easier weld than on the normal box keel. When angle is used on an existing sailing vessel design in lieu of the flat-bottom box keel, the upper edge of the angle is always sited at the bottom offset of the original keel. In other words, the angle is added to the existing depth of keel, replacing the original heavy flat bar bottom plate, with no other dimensional changes. This modification adds little in the way of lateral resistance, but it lessens the vessel's total resistance to forward motion.

Coolers

The automotive-type engines—the high-speed diesels—usually require freshwater cooling. This is often efficiently accomplished with a heat exchanger that uses raw seawater to cool the freshwater coils. However, in many areas this plan can lead to problems if there is a great deal of silt or sand in the water; sargasso weed, conch grass, eel grass, and the like will also plug up the strainers and ruin the pump impellers. This means some sort of closed system will probably work better—for example, an external heat exchanger consisting of several tubes suspended close to the bottom of the hull. Unfortunately, the latter system, too, causes a difficult maintenance problem in seawater, especially in the tropics, with their prolific marine growth. Even though the tubes themselves will resist fouling, being made of cupronickel, the shell plating under them will prove remarkably difficult to maintain. The alternatives to tubes are half pipes welded to the outside of the bottom plating, or channels used in lieu of the half pipes. Maintenance then becomes quite straightforward. This system works well on power vessels, where the pipes and channels can more or less be aligned with the path of least resistance, but it is unworkable on a sailing vessel, which will make a certain amount of leeway while sailing. Since her leeway and her speed along the course steered both vary with conditions, the angle of their resultant vector will also vary, and it is impossible to align the pipe and channels in the path of least resistance.

In sailing vessels, a thin box welded to the inside of the bottom shell can meet the cooling needs of small engines, but this method is very inefficient because it exposes less cooling area than do external channels or split pipe. The more efficient method is to use a wide-flange I-beam for a combined keel bottom and keel cooler. Cool water is drawn from one side of the web, sent through the engine and the exhaust water-cooled silencer, then returned to the opposite side of the web, where it starts its journey down that side of the web to a hole at the after or forward end and back up the opposite side again to the engine. Keel-cooled engines use a dry exhaust whenever possible. Unless this type of keel was part of the original design, the builder usually adds it below what would otherwise have been the keel bottom, so as not to raise the center of gravity of the ballast; however, the weight of this keel plus all the coolant contributes by itself to ballast, since there is no free surface in this closed-loop type of cooler. The coolant, regardless of the waters in which the vessel will operate, always consists partially of antifreeze, because of its rust-inhibiting qualities. You can often use this same type of keel on a power vessel by shaping the ends for minimum resistance.

A variant of the I-beam keel cooler is the V keel or skeg formed by using a T-bar for the keel and closing in the sides to form water passages. This plan suits some power vessels quite well if their engines are not too large. Do not confuse this keel with the one formed with a V, using a solid round bar at the bottom as in the construction of a chine. The latter, so-called Vee Skeg construction is often employed to lower an engine installation, and more or less resembles a pod added below, but integral with, the hull proper.

Before deciding on a particular keel or external cooling arrangement, always consult the engine manufacturer to determine the amount of cooling necessary. Be sure, though, that the manufacturer doesn't calculate cooling capacity based on the speed of the vessel, as the capacity in that case will be too small when the vessel runs aground (using full power attempting to get off) or when it is trawling or towing. It is always better to have more cooling capacity than necessary rather than too little. I prefer basing my cooling estimates on a seawater temperature of 80 degrees Fahrenheit, about right for tropical lagoons. If an auxiliary generator will be installed during construction or later, one should make due allowance for its cooling when sizing the system.

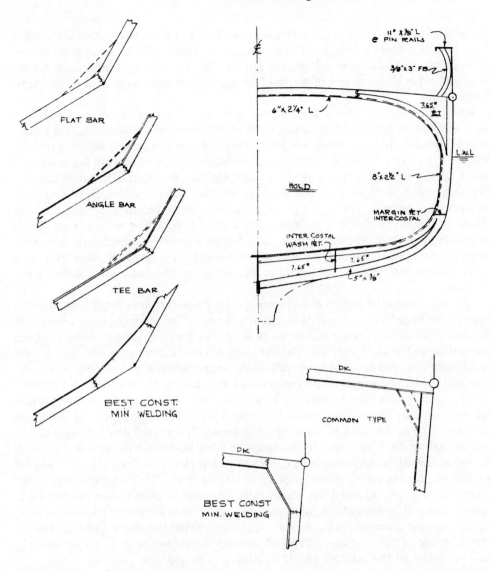

Figure 47. *Frames can be constructed of flat bar, angle bar, or Tees. Gussets at a chine or at the deck can be attached to the frames or integral with them. The half-section of a round-bottom vessel shows an intercostal wash plate, an intercostal margin plate, and a bulwark stanchion construction that is useful when the bulwark height is 30 inches or more.*

FRAMES

Frames take the form of flat bars, angles, or Tees. These are indicated on Figure 47. Sometimes gussets will be used at the chine and deck; I have shown these using dashed lines. They are usually of the same material as the frames. Also shown is a better method of accomplishing the same task, one that involves a minimum amount of welding and maintenance. Here, the gussets become integral parts of the frame; they can often be made out of whole channels if the frames were split channels to begin with.

It would be difficult to say anything definitive about which frame shapes are the best and easiest to use; the pros and cons of any given style always depend on the hull in question. In small sizes, weight and ease of maintenance sometimes require the use of flat bar. There is nothing more miserable than trying to paint the inside of a small angle you can't possibly see to inspect. On the other hand, the angle frame is not only much stronger than the flat bar, but also quite rigid, which reduces the setup time in framing. The minimum dimension for angle frames is two and one-half times the depth of the longitudinals they will be notched to accept, so there is generally no difficulty in painting unless the flanges exceed one-third the depth of the angle. T-bars are seldom used for transverse framing except in the case of a deep web frame, when they become more or less necessary to ensure the stability of the section.

In some vessels the angle frames forming the topsides are split lengthwise near the turn of the bilge to form a radius at this stress point. The inner portions of the split frames continue over to form the tops of the floors; the remaining portions are then carried down the shell plating as flat bar frames. The gaps between are filled in with solid plate in way of any tanks, and with plate having lightening holes elsewhere. Any longitudinal girders are usually intercostal (that is, inserted between frames without notching) with this type of framing. In a sailing vessel, with its deeper keel, these frames normally stop at the tops of the deep floors. This same type of splitting can also be done at the deck to form hanging knees. The splits must be made at the neutral axis of the T-bar, close to the flange, or it will be difficult to bend. Note that an intercostal wash plate, sometimes called a "swash plate," is fitted tight to the hold ceiling and up from the bottom a couple of inches or so. This keeps the bilge water from sloshing around when the vessel rolls. The margin plate is also intercostal in many hulls and normally fits tight to the shell, which then keeps the bilge water from splashing over onto the cargo. Incidentally, I have taken the opportunity to show in the drawing of this section a type of bulwark stanchion which can be used to advantage when the bulwark height is 30 inches or greater.

DOUBLE BOTTOMS

Small steel vessels do not usually have double bottoms. With less than 4 feet of height between the bottoms, such a vessel is difficult to construct and even worse to maintain unless numerous cover plates are used to permit access to all areas. In any vessel that uses a double bottom for fuel, smaller cover plates must also be fitted for washing out and to permit pumping air in during any gas-freeing operation necessitated by bottom damage.

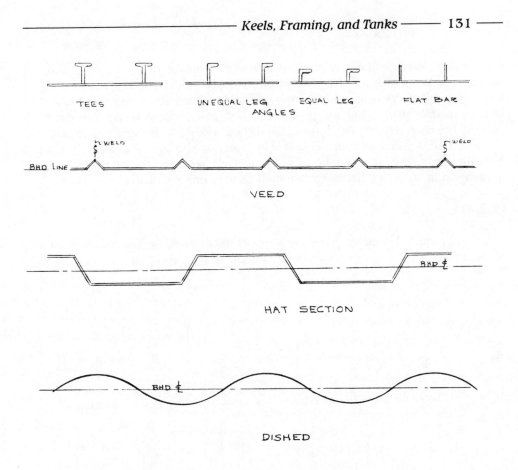

Figure 48. *Several configurations for steel bulkheads, viewed from above.*

BULKHEADS

Figure 48 shows the various bulkhead constructions used on vessels large enough to accommodate their weight. In many vessels it is better to use wooden bulkheads attached to the steel frames. Wooden bulkheads are easy to make watertight, and can easily partition the separated compartments—for example an engine room and an accommodation cabin on yachts, or the engine room and the fish hold on fishing vessels—without additional framing. Some of the advantages of steel construction are lost with wooden bulkheads, such as the effectiveness of the bulkhead as a fire break, tank ending, or contributor to structural rigidity.

Tees offer the strongest method of reinforcing bulkheads, and T-bar frames are the easiest to paint. Tees are also very useful for joinery work, simplifying it immensely. (This subject is explored in Volume 2 of *Steel Boatbuilding*.) Angles offer the next strongest method of reinforcing, but the angles are very difficult to paint if equal-legged. Flat bars are not very strong and require supporting chocks at more frequent intervals than would either Tees or angles. When saving weight is essential, the bulkhead itself can be Veed if a brake press is available. However, it would make no sense to form such a bulkhead by continuously welding each Vee using angles and plate. When Veed in wide panels, a bulkhead forms an exceptionally rigid structure while presenting few problems when you scribe it to receive the shell plating. The deep U or hat-section and the dished bulkheads are seen mostly in barge construction. Again, this construction is very strong and light and, with the proper forming equipment, also economical. In vessels with rapidly changing shapes, scribing to fit such bulkheads to the shell can try one's patience.

PILLARS

Pillars are required in many vessels to support deck beams or girders, and in some, such as fishing vessels, are not as objectionable as they would be in either a cargo

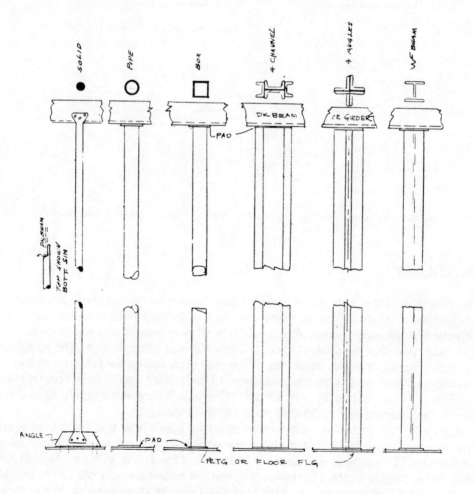

Figure 49. *Six common pillar shapes.*

vessel or a yacht. It is occasionally possible to omit them by fitting one or more girders longitudinally. Pillars are usually sited at every fifth frame in a transversely framed vessel, preferably, though not always, on the centerline. Figure 49 indicates several pillar shapes commonly used. The solid rounds are the heaviest and used to be generally favored in riveted construction. Pipe is now accepted as better to use in a hold, since it weighs less for the same compression load. The wide-flange I-beam has advantages when the hold must be compartmented, as in fishing vessels and some small bulk cargo vessels. The box beam is fine for yachts. The pillar made up of four channels is seldom used because of its weight, but does simplify installation of pen boards. The four angles together make a strong pillar. This style was widely used in riveted construction, but is not favored in welded construction. The success of any standing pillar depends on fixing the ends with adequate bracketing. All pillars require pads on the top and bottom.

BRACKETS

Figure 50 shows some details of brackets and some rules proportioning them. Brackets come in more styles than it makes any sense to discuss, but by studying the bracketing of a longitudinal girder we can arrive at principles to cover most instances. These longitudinal girders are unusual features, being most frequently used when pillars or columns would be objectionable in a hold. They are discontinuous in the length of the vessel, occupying only the hold area and ending on a bulkhead. In this situation, longitudinals must be continued forward and aft of the hold girder; these must have a depth at least equalling that of the transverse web-frame deck beam, and must be bracketed to the bulkhead as shown. All flanges must have either chocks or anti-trip brackets (which prevent the flanges from twisting or collapsing under pressure), and these are also shown. The column supporting the girder and attaching to the bulkhead must also have at least the same depth as the transverse web deck beam, even though the normal vertical stiffeners on the bulkhead would be smaller.

Long columns, pillars, mooring bitts, towing bitts, and other load-bearing members will either require bracketing to the deck or hold, or else to a girder or beam. Where a bracket is required in the hold, or to the shell or a deck, a doubler (pad or backing plate) will be used. The doubler should be 2 inches wider than the flange width of the bracket and 1 inch longer than the bracket to the bulkhead.

Widely spaced deck beams, which essentially are part of the web frames and are connected only by longitudinals, have a definite maximum spacing, beyond which each longitudinal requires bracketing to a beam. Figure 50 shows the maximum allowable unsupported length of deck longitudinals for seven normal depths used in vessels up to 80 feet in length. Vessels carrying cargo on deck need beams spaced closer together than vessels not carrying deck cargo. In general interisland trade, the unsupported length decreases for normal deck loads. Unusual deck loads, such as engines and automobiles, require special reinforcing and closing of these beams, but miscellaneous cargoes such as lumber and barrels of fuel do not concentrate enough weight per square foot of deck area to require reinforcing.

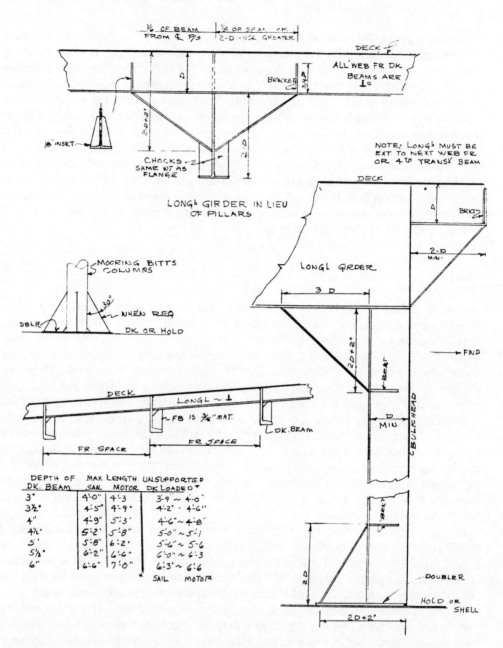

Figure 50. Top: *A longitudinal girder viewed in cross section, showing bracketing to a web-frame deck beam. Chocks or anti-trip brackets on the flanges of the girder and deck beam are also shown.* Right: *A longitudinal extending forward from the hold's forward bulkhead is bracketed to the bulkhead. The column supporting the girder end attaches to the bulkhead and is bracketed top and bottom.* Left: *A doubler plate is required when a mooring bitt is bracketed to a deck or hold.* Bottom left: *Maximum spacing for deck beams of different depths. If the maximum is exceeded, longitudinals must be bracketed to the deck beams as shown.*

TANKS

Water and fuel tanks need to be carefully thought out, not only by the designer but by the builder. It seems that most builders go ahead and increase the capacity without consulting the designer, since the change only involves a bit more weight. Remember, however, that along with all the other things on a boat that get tumbled and tossed in every conceivable direction and probably simultaneously, one must contend with the free surface effect of liquids stored in the tanks, and be sure to consider how they may affect the stability of the vessel.

When a tank is completely full there is no free surface effect, so the contents of the tank then effectively become ballast. This is why keel coolers may help stability. Regardless of the roll or pitch there is no shifting of weight. If the tank is slack, however, the liquid has a surface that will be independent to that of the vessel, remaining parallel to the external water surface and thus forming a wedge of fluid from the high side to the low side of the vessel, the thrust of which is downward through its center of gravity and not upward through its center of buoyancy. The liquid causes a rise in the vessel's virtual center of gravity equal to the moment of inertia of the free surface multiplied by the weight of the liquid per cubic foot and divided by the weight of the vessel in pounds. The depth and volume of the tank are independent of the surface area: a parallel-sided tank has the same effect on stability, whether it be one-quarter or three-quarters full, at least at normal angles of inclination (heel). At large angles of inclination, the amount of fluid in the tank would have a direct bearing on the amount of free surface, which could increase dramatically. Boiled down to its practical implications, all this theory goes to show is that in any vessel, tanks must be sized in proportion to the vessel's displacement. The surface area of the tank must be kept as small as possible, and when an increase in volume is required, alterations must be reasoned out and not done willy-nilly.

Figure 51 shows several types of tanks that are commonly used. The narrow vertical tank is one of the most satisfactory, because large volume can be obtained with the minimum of surface area. This type of tank is especially suited to fishing and cargo vessels, long-distance motor yachts, and auxiliary sailing vessels needing high capacity in the minimum space. Indicated on the drawing is a transverse frame within the narrow tank. Because of the need for gas-freeing the tank in the event that hull damage makes work in it necessary, the frame itself is mitered at the deck beam–side frame joint. It is also cut out in way of the pipe at the deck edge and the round bar at the chine. All Tees have exposed openings through the frame and must also have numerous holes drilled into their stems adjacent to the plating to assure proper drainage. There are generous snipes (cut-outs) in the frame at the bottom and top edges of the fore-and-aft bulkhead. If the tank is deep enough and stiffeners are required, they, too, should be sniped back, leaving large holes where they join the bulkhead. In short, all possible steps should be taken to eliminate places that could entrap fuel, the vapors from which could be ignited, causing an explosion.

Yachts, be they sail or power, often need space above their tankage for accommodations, and thus must use wide tanks with little depth. Such tanks must be fitted with baffles that restrict the liquids to the minimum space and slow down their movement when the vessel rolls. If just the corners of the baffles are sniped—the

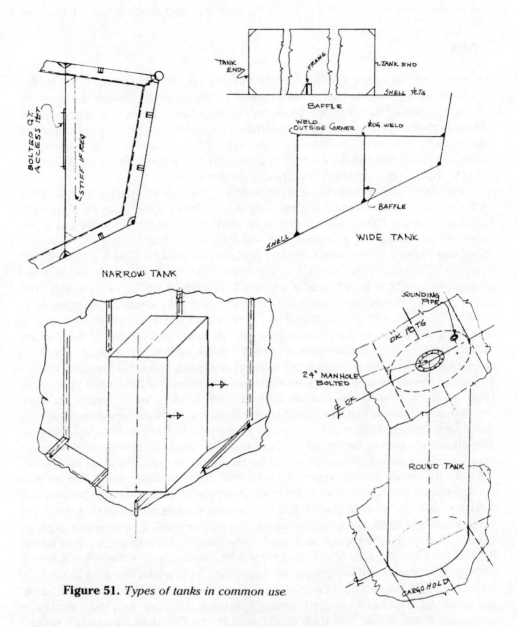

Figure 51. *Types of tanks in common use.*

upper corners to allow air to equalize along the top, and the bottom corners to equalize the liquid—the motion of the liquid surface will be restrained. If there is a frame in the tank, then the baffle is cut out in way of the frame as indicated.

Fitting baffles improves but does not cure the effects of free surface on wide tanks. An arrangement permitting a vertical tank, square and of small dimensions, has much to recommend it, especially if the tank is connected to and part of a bulkhead. In some sailing vessels, it was once found advantageous to use cylindrical tanks in the vertical position. These were located on the centerline, extended from the tops of the floors to the deck, and were large enough for a man to enter for cleaning. Being round, they required no framing, so they were easy to maintain, and there was a minimum of interference with the cargo. A sounding pipe was set into the deck and tank, extending down to within an inch of the bottom, with a striker plate fitted below the sounding pipe on the tank bottom.

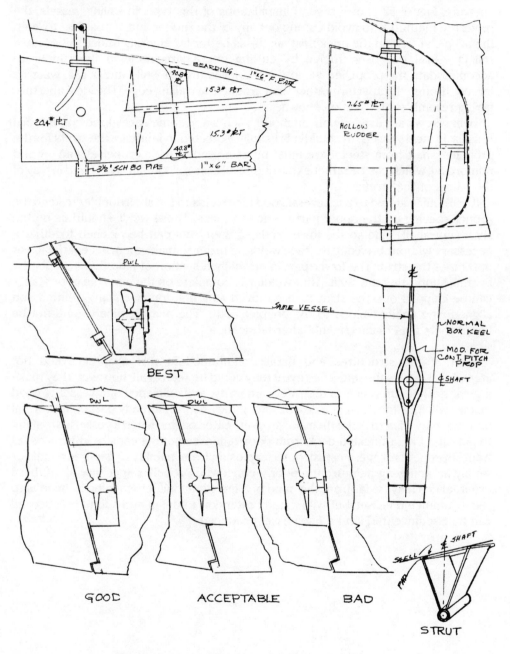

Figure 52. *Some single-engine propeller installations.*

APERTURES AND STRUTS

Most commercial vessels and auxiliary sailing vessels have but one engine, with its shaft on the centerline and the propeller protected by the hull structure in an aperture. Figure 52 shows several installations of this type. In sailing vessels, the preferred method is to avoid cutting out any of the rudder and, if possible, to keep the propeller behind the prick post, as this is better for steering under sail. Many a sailing vessel has been ruined by cutting out a large hole in the rudder to accommodate the propeller; when the rudder is turned while under sail, water is forced through the aperture rather than around the trailing edge. The ideal aperture fairing resembles the section shown.

Twin screws are used mainly on motor yachts and some specialized commercial vessels. In steel vessels, the builder is usually expected to fabricate the struts for the propeller shaft from steel. Care must be exercised in their proper alignment and reinforcing, which can be rather extensive. In all cases, a doubler is required in way of the palms of the struts.

It will suffice at first to use several good tack welds to the shell doubler to keep the proper spacing on the upper part of the strut legs. These welds should be on the shaft (not shell) side so the lower ends of the struts can be pinched together if necessary without breaking the tack welds, in order to make them accept the lower portion of the strut. The lower part is normally a section of pipe that accepts the bearing supporting the shaft. After welding is complete on the pipe, the upper tacks can be chipped out, the strut then removed as a unit for machining, refitted and aligned, and finally welded to the doubler plate. The bearing pipe should not be bored to its final diameter until after fabrication.

Most of the structures and details mentioned in this chapter would not immediately strike the untrained eye if they could be seen at all; however, they make a great deal of difference to the safety, integrity, and efficiency of a vessel. A good builder will look for them in a design, and, if they are not already part of his normal practice, may wish to make them so. An overheated engine when a vessel is straining to get off a bar, a buckled deck from poor reinforcement, a capsize in heavy seas from improper tankage, a catastrophic explosion from inability to gas-free a tank, or simply an annoying helm from a poorly conceived propeller aperture: all of these eventualities may be far from the mind of a first-time builder when he is anxious to see a completed vessel, but with careful attention to detail and sound practice, all can be circumvented, and a fine vessel produced.

9
▽

MAKING
THE
PARTS

In the previous chapters I have discussed steel boatbuilding in a general way, and also cited many specific construction details relevant to the building of small steel vessels. This sort of discussion could go on almost indefinitely, and to little purpose; the time has now come to put theory into practice and build a specific vessel. The advantage is mine, in that I can choose the one I want to build; however, in each stage of construction of this particular vessel, I shall digress when necessary to indicate different methods or problems associated with other types of vessels. Since the lofting of the Pinky has been covered in Chapter 7, I have chosen this design as the vessel to build.

I have owned several shipyards, and it would be much simpler for me to describe construction from that point of view only. However, I do not now own a shipyard and there will be a time in the not-too-distant future when I shall again build myself another vessel. When I do, I will face the same problems any other home builder faces. This is how I plan to proceed. As I outline the steps in this and the following chapters, you, the reader, are welcome to observe, but I must ask you not to help me unless I specifically invite you to do so. In this book, it is necessary that I build the vessel myself, for to do otherwise would imply that it could not be done by an individual. Also, in every yard I have owned and most yards in which I have worked, no visitors have been allowed during working hours. If you will observe what I am doing and listen well, you should have no problem in following my procedure for building this vessel. It is well to remember that each vessel is an individual and must be treated as such. Regardless of how many vessels you build, steel boatbuilding is a learning process and not an assembly line.

First of all, a building site must be selected. Since I now live in the tropics where the palm trees grow, I will build out of doors; to build indoors would add an additional expense for just one vessel. I would opt for a shed if one were available but, since one probably won't be, I will have to build in a field or lot with reasonable rental. The building site must be oriented north-south or east-west, because orienting the axis of the keel north-south makes compass correction easier. East-west would also be acceptable, but if at all possible, we want to avoid the intercardinal points, because of the difficulty of correcting a vessel's permanent magnetism with quadrantal spheres (often called "the Admiral's balls") which are inferior to the more powerful fore-and-aft or athwartship magnets. It would be nice to have electric power available, but this is not mandatory. If some shade can be had from a large oak tree, so much the better; a few pines or palms would also do nicely. Lacking any of the above, I will still need some sort of shade from the sun, for which I think I'll choose the same screen cloth the nurseries use. This will of course be a temporary shelter, and the covering will be supported by pipe frames. I can probably get around any local building restrictions, since my shelter is a greenhouse of sorts, and I am only "growing" a boat. Just to avoid any problems, however, I will also check with the neighbors to see if they have any objections, explaining that I plan to keep reasonable hours and that, for the most part, there will be no more noise than if I were building a house.

Under this temporary shelter I will lay down the mold loft over a framework built about 8 inches off the ground, using well-driven stakes to support the loft framework; I could also use concrete blocks for support, with a bit of mortar to keep the loft from capsizing. The framework to support the loft will be made of 2 x 4s and, if needed, some 2 x 6s spaced about 16 inches apart. From the plans, I note that ⅜-inch plywood is required not only for laminating the cabintops, but also for the shelving and berth bottoms, so I make the loft floor from the best grade of ⅜-inch marine ply, free of voids, knots, and rough laminates. The floor will ultimately be incorporated in the vessel. Half lengths, full widths, and full heights will be lofted, as shown in Figure 36 (Chapter 7), using 16 feet by 28 feet for the loft, or 14 sheets of ply.

Next I will need to obtain a shed (generally called "the shack"). I could build one, but I think I would rather buy one of the small prefabs and sell it when I am through, or, if some kindly person helps out here and there, maybe just give it away when I have no further use for it. This shack should be about 16 inches off the ground, with two concrete blocks under each corner and one in the middle to keep the floor from sagging. If the prefab comes without a floor, I will lay the cheapest exterior grade of plywood as the floor—¾ inch thick will do. The shack need not measure more than eight feet square.

I already own some power tools, namely, two ⅜-inch drills, a ½-inch drill, a slow-speed disk sander, a vibrator sander, a sabersaw, a portable router, and a small, self-contained airless sprayer, all electric. My present stock of hand woodworking tools is already extensive, and I have plenty of the hammers and mauls used in steel building. I will have to buy an oxygen-acetylene cutting torch with three different tip sizes plus a heat ring or tip, 100 feet of dual hose, regulators, striker, tip cleaners, and goggles. (I don't recommend looking for a bargain here; the outfit will more than pay its way.) A welding machine, of course, will also be necessary. If electric power is available—fine. If not, a gasoline-driven self-contained machine can be purchased. An AC/DC machine of about 200 amps looks about right, for according to the plans, there will be some stainless steel and aluminum to weld. The Pinky measures about

50 feet over the rails, so 100 feet of electrode cable should reach wherever it has to go. To save money, I can make a ground from round bar inserted in garden hose for insulation.

Grinders will be necessary; a medium-speed sander-grinder and a small 3 ½-inch grinder will prove more versatile than one heavy-duty grinder. I will also need a vise, and it should be a good one, since it will be carried aboard the completed vessel. For clamps I would ideally choose the quick-acting, deep-throated bar type. A dozen of the 10-inch size I would consider the minimum, plus three pipe clamps to fit ¾-inch pipe, and a one-ton come-along or maybe two half-ton come-alongs. I would add to these items a couple of wooden shell, 4-inch, double blocks with beckets—roller bushed with hooks, and all ironwork galvanized—plus 150 feet of ½-inch Manila line for the blocks and at least 200 feet more for guys, chokers, and the like. The blocks will also go aboard the completed vessel. A couple of chipping hammers with wooden handles and six stainless steel wire brushes should round out the list of miscellaneous tool requirements.

So far, so good—now to the scrap yard to find a piece of 3-inch-thick steel about 12 inches by 24 inches, one 20-foot section of 2½-inch pipe, and some scrap angles (2 inch by 2 inch by ¼ inch) to make a stand for the anvil and any other stands and fixtures that might be needed. I might also try to find some scrap ⁵⁄₁₆-inch galvanized chain—20 to 30 feet of it—to avoid buying it at the hardware store, and I will certainly look around for future reference because a scrap yard is as close to heaven as a boatbuilder can get on this earth.

Back at the site, everything that had to be ordered is coming (I hope) as needed, and not all at once. The screen roof has been set up, and the area beneath it cleaned up and reasonably leveled off. The roof should be at least 10 feet longer than the hull. I proceed to set up the mold loft and, at the same time, lay down some concrete blocks for the platen. The platen will be 10 feet by 20 feet, or the size of the two 7.65-pound keel side (deadwood) plates for the Pinky. Obviously, this thin material will require more supports than the plywood, so I'll make the frame level and about 8 inches (or one block) high, in spite of the convenience of greater height. After all, I'll only use it once.

By now the shack should have arrived. I'll select a good site for it, well clear of the hull—about twice the Pinky's beam—if there is enough land available. On the side of the shack I'll construct a hanger for the oxyacetylene hose (see Figure 53). As the new tools arrive, they will go in the shed on shelves and in boxes and bins. A small desk or workbench will be needed for the plans, catalogs, and other paperwork. Near the shack I'll dig a hole and set a stout fence pole in concrete, to hold up the oxygen and acetylene bottles.

The material for the hull should now be ordered, if it has not been ordered already. The ideal delivery time is the day before it is needed. When the plywood arrives, I'll nail it to the mold loft frame using twopenny galvanized common nails (a couple of pounds will be more than enough for this and the patterns). I will use as few nails as possible, and since this wood is going to be reused, I will avoid monkey faces. When the plywood is secured, it receives two coats of flat white paint. Now is the time to select the paint to be used as a final finish, ascertaining that it will be compatible with the flat paint undercoating. Since some of these sheets will have to be sanded to be

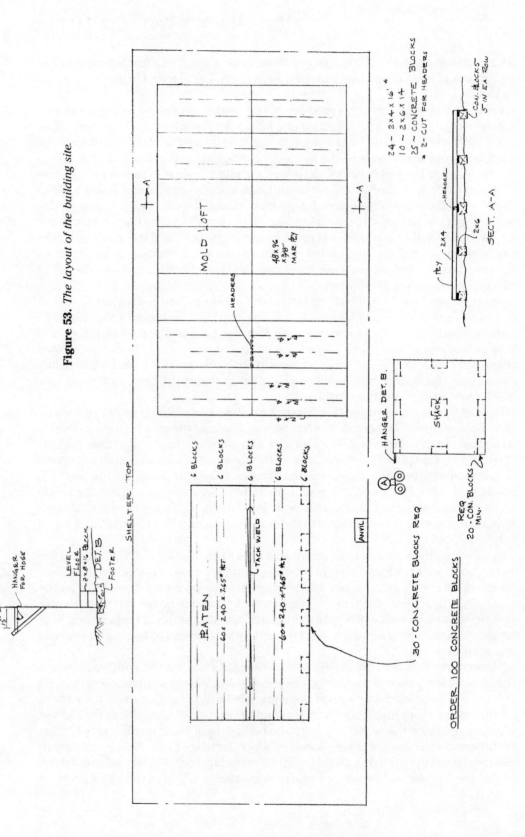

Figure 53. *The layout of the building site.*

reused as a glued laminate, the use of a sealer is not recommended in this case.

Figure 53 shows how the site is laid out. Note the ease of movement it allows, and the convenience of the shack to both the loft and the platen. Also note the material list of 2 x 4s, 2 x 6s, and concrete blocks required to set things up. The extra blocks are "just in case," but will also prove handy to elevate the frame material when cutting. Never cut over the loft or the platen.

It is time now to loft the vessel, as described in Chapter 7.

Once the lofting is completed, I can make the patterns and assemble the parts. First, I will make and assemble all the frames. In Figure 76 (the Shell Expansion, Scantlings, and Details Plan), there are two options for the detail of the main deck edge: 2-inch Schedule 80 pipe below the deck; or a fender rail. I do not intend to fish the vessel, so the clear drainage ensured by the pipe joint is not important; on the other hand, I wouldn't want to void the possibility of some day reselling the vessel as a yacht, and the fender might detract from its yacht potential, since it would destroy the fine finish on other yachts should they raft, which they are wont to do. Besides, I'm lazy and don't wish to spend the time making this rail when I could be doing something else. Therefore, as a builder, I will exercise my option and select a bisected pipe joint. (All three of these styles are illustrated in Chapter 4.)

The choice of one style or another of deck edge will determine whether and how the frames must be notched out in the way of it, and making frames is what we are now about to do. With a marking stick about 10 feet long and 2 inches wide, made from ¼-inch marine ply, transfer the measurements of each frame from the mold loft to the platen; lay out both halves (port and starboard) of the frame and, with a sharpened soapstone, connect all the offsets in their proper sequence, to indicate the outline of the frame. Now return to the mold loft and recheck each of the offsets. If satisfied, return to the platen and repeat the procedure. If everything checks, then and only then, centerpunch each offset intersection into the platen, marking also the height of the deck edge on the centerline.

The next step is to determine the height of the deck centerline at each frame. The half-breadth of frame 7, the midship frame, is 6–0–0, and Note 4 on the Lines Plan (Figure 30) calls for 1 inch of height per foot of half-breadth as the camber of the deck. To the deck-edge height previously marked on the centerline at frame 7, add 6 inches and centerpunch it in. This procedure will be followed on every frame and every bulkhead, taking into account the differences of half-breadth.

Some prefer to make each frame as they lay it down. My own preference is to complete the layout and then make the frames, so I now lay down frames 5, 4, 2, and 1, double-check them, and punch them into the platen, then do the same for the afterbody as shown in Figure 40, which finalizes frames 9, 10, 11, 12, 13, 14, the after perpendicular (AP), and the transom (T). Note that I have opted to change bulkhead frame 12, specified on the plans, to just plain frame 12, in case I decide to alter the interior arrangement. The option on the plans is to use either frame 12 or frame 13 as a bulkhead. This will be impossible to do in steel; however, since there is no tankage there and very little in the way of stress at these frames, a proper wooden bulkhead could replace the steel one with almost the same strength, and would also be lighter. Once again, I have exercised a builder's option, and since I am also the designer of this vessel, I have the designer's approval.

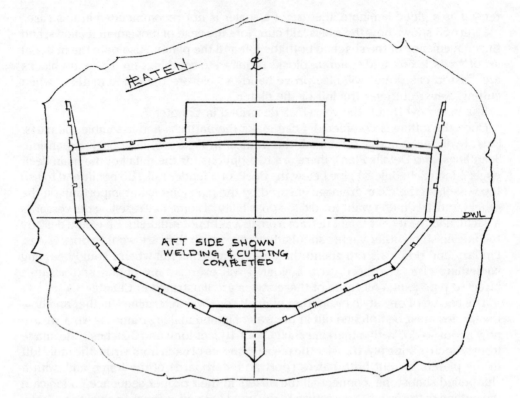

Above: Figure 54. *Frame 7 of the Pinky laid down on the platen.* **Below: Figure 55.** *Method of deriving the deck camber for the great beam template.*

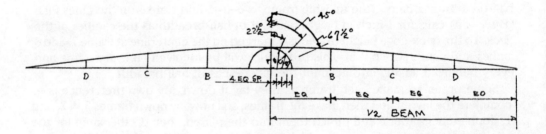

Figure 54 shows frame 7 laid down on the platen. You can see that the change in the deck edge has been made, and the bulwark stanchion modified to suit. A great beam pattern can now be made, using station 7 as the great beam. This template will be used for the other frames as well, thus assuring me of a uniform curvature to the deck and the same camber on all frames. The curve is derived as shown in Figure 55.

From the construction sections, you will note that a cargo hatch ends on frame 7. The pattern is on hand and, with the other parts of frame 7 in place, is now cut from the appropriate plate, ground, fitted, and tacked in place.

Figure 56, the Construction Sections and Details Plan, shows every frame in the hull, and will aid in assembling the frames. You can see that in this design all frames have a separate floor, rather than just carrying on down to the centerline, which would be perfectly acceptable in yachts. Since this is a commercial vessel, her tonnage will be measured to the top of a floor that must not only have a flange, but also must be a distinct element of the frame, and must touch the shell. While adding these floors will not make a great difference to the design, every little bit helps, for in some countries the light dues and harbor fees are based on gross tons.

By the way, some designers indicate only one or two frame sections, the idea being that if you've seen one, you've seen them all. If the designer does this, a builder should then make a drawing of *all* frames, as some peculiar things can happen from one to the other, and he has enough to think about without some costly surprises.

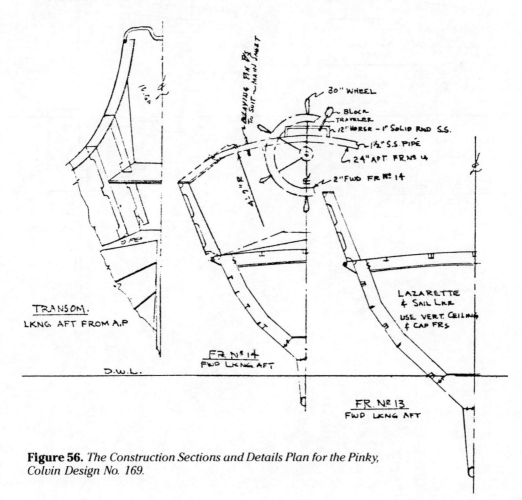

Figure 56. *The Construction Sections and Details Plan for the Pinky, Colvin Design No. 169.*

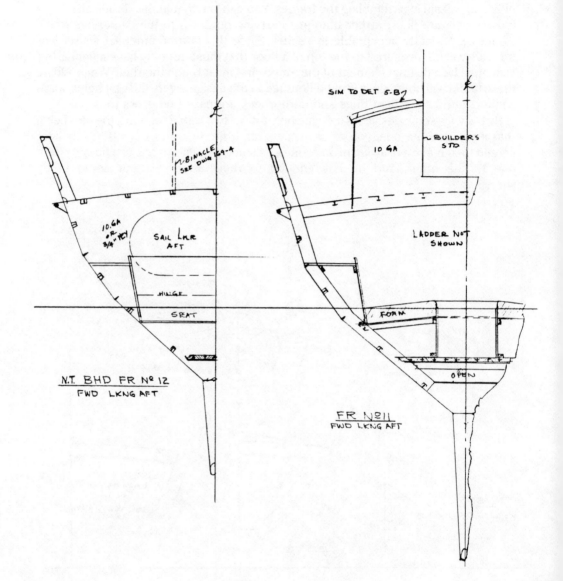

SIM TO DET 5-B

10 GA

BUILDERS STD

BINACLE
SEE DWG 169-A

10.GA
OR
3/4" WD

SAIL LKR
AFT

HINGE

SEAT

LADDER NOT
SHOWN

FORM

OPEN

N.T. BHD FR Nº 12
FWD LKNG AFT

FR Nº 11
FWD LKNG AFT

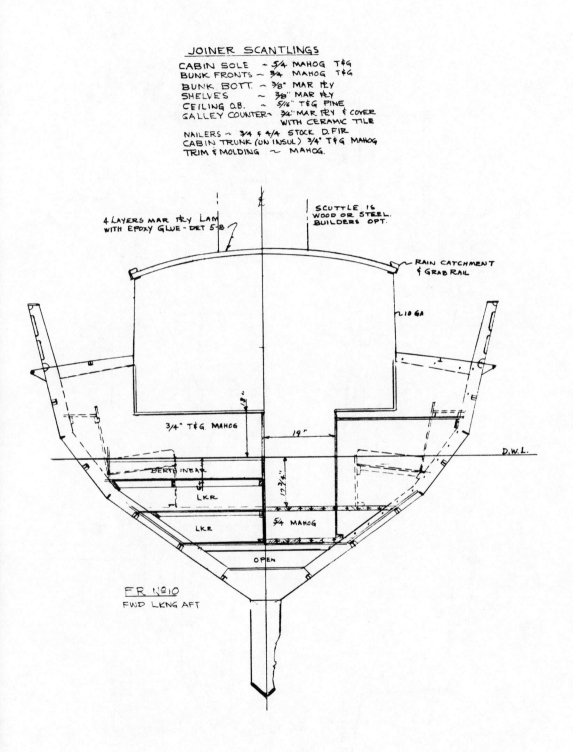

JOINER SCANTLINGS

CABIN SOLE ~ 5/4 MAHOG T&G
BUNK FRONTS ~ 3/4 MAHOG T&G
BUNK BOTT. ~ 3/8" MAR PLY
SHELVES ~ 3/8" MAR PLY
CEILING O.B. ~ 5/16" T&G PINE
GALLEY COUNTER~ 3/4" MAR PLY & COVER
WITH CERAMIC TILE
NAILERS ~ 3/4 & 4/4 STOCK D.FIR
CABIN TRUNK (UN INSUL) 3/4" T&G MAHOG
TRIM & MOLDING ~ MAHOG.

4 LAYERS MAR PLY LAM
WITH EPOXY GLUE - DET 5-B

SCUTTLE IS
WOOD OR STEEL.
BUILDERS OPT.

RAIN CATCHMENT
& GRAB RAIL

10 GA

3/4" T&G. MAHOG

19"

D.W.L.

BERTH NEAR

LKR

12 3/4"

5/4 MAHOG

LKR

OPEN

FR. Nº 10
FWD LKNG AFT

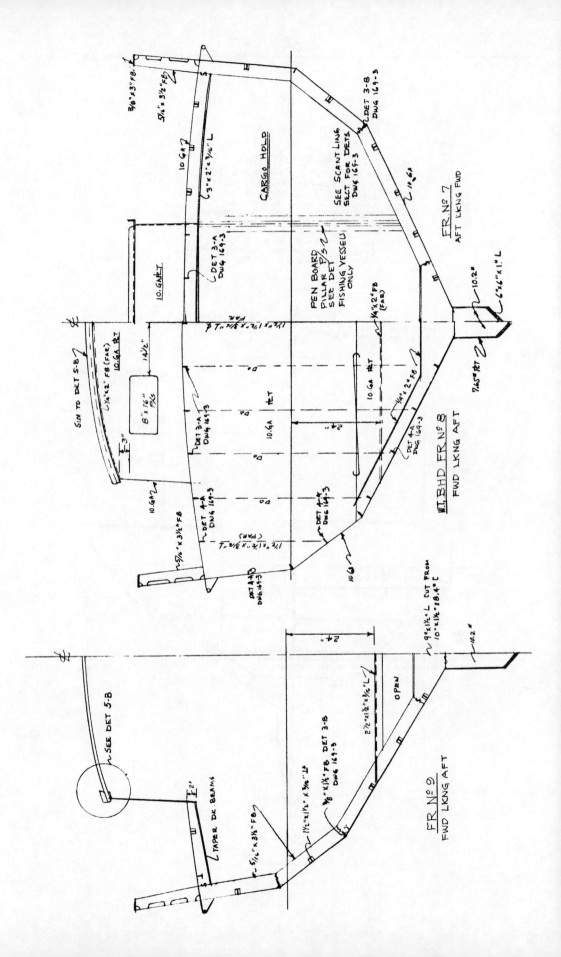

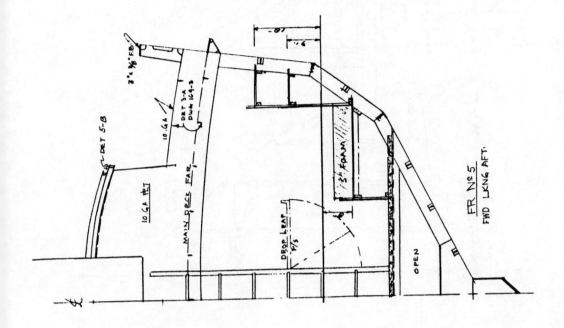

FR Nº 5
FWD LKNG AFT.

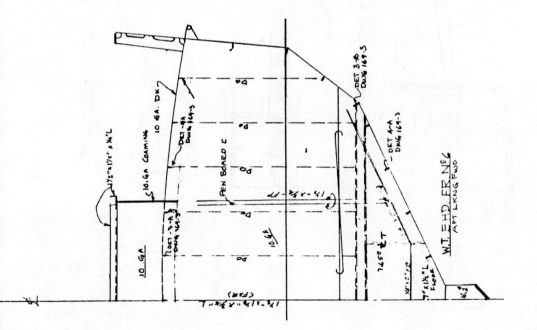

WT. BHD. FR Nº 6
AFT LKNG FWD

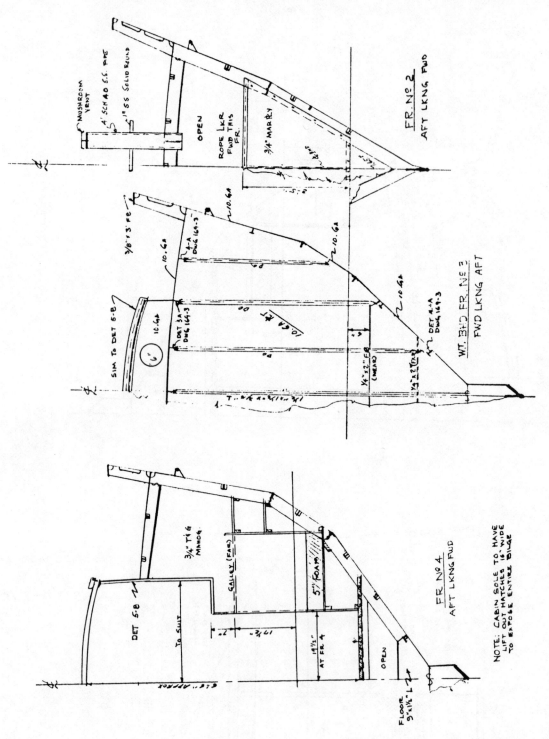

NOTE: CABIN SOLE TO HAVE
LIFT OUT HATCHES 16" WIDE
TO EXPOSE ENTIRE BILGE

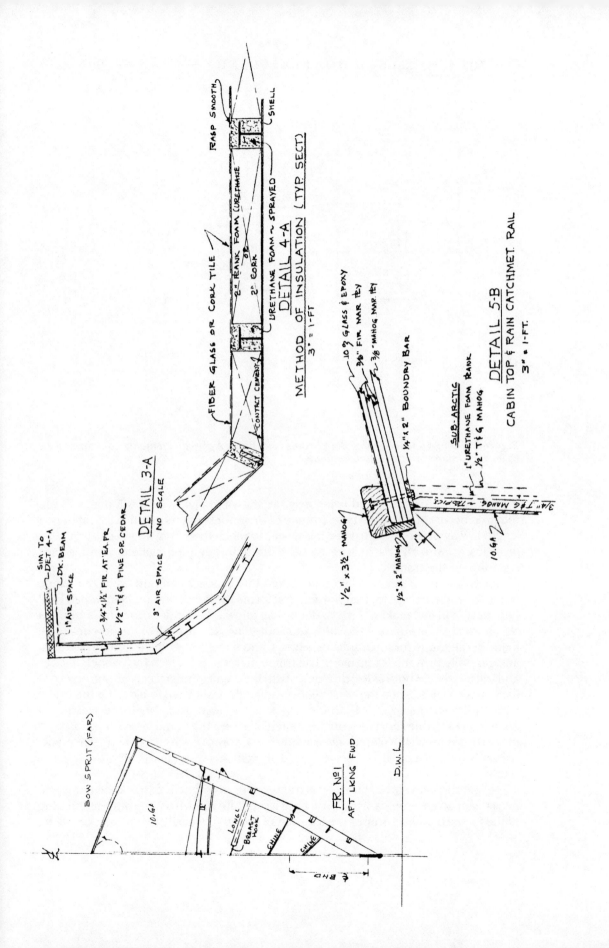

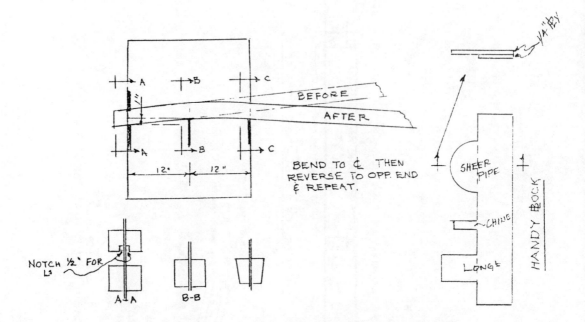

Figure 57. Left: *A jig for bending deck beams cold.* Right: *A plywood template for marking the sheer pipe, chine, and hull longitudinals.*

Deck beams are bent cold using a jig, as shown in Figure 57. I will make all the required beams at the same time. In spite of their not being required in a continuous length in way of the cabin trunks, it is easier to make them this way because it later provides a more rigid structure to bend the gunwale pipe against, and also for squaring up the frames.

Finally, the deck beam is laid and tacked into place. I can now weld the whole frame together, except for that portion that forms the bulwark stanchion, which I will only tack in place, making sure to deduct an allowance for deck thickness from its height. Next I centerpunch the DWL and centerline, scribe in all of the notches to be made in the frame for longitudinals, chines, and sheer pipe, chip off the tack welds, and carefully turn the frame over. The frame material is 5/16-inch by 3½-inch flat bar and will be welded both sides; therefore, with the small grinder, I carefully groove out each of the welds. Since the deck beam is an angle, I will have to block up the frame with short lengths of 2 x 4 scraps adjacent to each weld. Once the welding is complete, I add one short tack on the stanchions, turn the frame over again, and then move the frame off the platen edge slightly in the way of each cut that must be made. As each hole is cut, it is best to grind it right away to finish all work on the frame.

I repeat this same procedure for all frames and, as completed, stack them upright, deck beam down. Frames 5 and 7 will go in a separate stack from the others. On some of the forward and aft frames the location of the DWL will either not exist or will be too low to be of any use. On these frames, I boldly strike in a new one at some distance above the DWL and mark it—for example, "the +12-inch WL" or "the +24-inch WL"—whatever it happens to be.

After the frames, the bulkheads are the next to be made. I will use the existing patterns, modified for the change in gunwale, remembering not to make one for frame 12. The welding of the bulkheads is done in the same manner as for the frames, except that the plate(s) needed for each bulkhead will be laid on the platen after cutting, with the centerline and DWL in proper alignment, and tacked down so that the deep floor and bulwark stanchions can be added. I make the first welds in the way of stiffeners and grind them smooth, that is, flush with the plate. Then I tack all bulkhead stiffeners in place and trim the ends as indicated. I use a ³⁄₁₆-inch, 1½-inch, 12-inch staggered spacing (³⁄₁₆-inch fillet, 1½-inch weld length, and 12 inches between weld centers, with welds staggered on opposite sides), as indicated in Table 9 (Chapter 5). The next heavier listed plate from the table is used for welding, since the bulkhead is both 10-gauge and 7.65-pound plate, and not ⅛-inch or 11-gauge plate. As the stiffeners are welded, they must remain square to the plate.

With the stiffeners attached, the notches are scribed on the bulkhead edges and (assuming a bulkhead cut from two plates) an intermediate 1½- or 2-inch weld is made on the plate seam between each of the longitudinal bulkhead stiffeners. A small plywood template can be worked up, similar to that shown in Figure 57 to speed up the marking for the sheer pipe, chine, and hull longitudinals. The bulkhead is now chipped loose and turned over, and several short tack welds made, about 2 to 3 inches in length, skipping at least 2 feet between welds. When this is done, I return to the opposite edge and do it again, but this time midway between the previous welds, and then return and do it yet again. It is now time to turn the bulkhead over and do the same on that side, but each time a weld on the opposite side is encountered, a small cold chisel is used to make sure no flux or slag remains in the joint. Let me say now, so I won't have to repeat it again, that *always*, prior to welding, the area to be welded *will be wire-brushed and the seam chipped out to sound metal*. I now complete all welding on this side, using the step-back procedure as shown in Figure 58, with the direction of weld deposit opposite to the direction of travel from weld to weld. The notches may now be cut, prior to turning the bulkhead over to finish the welds on the opposite side. At this time, I transfer the centerline to this side at the top and bottom, marking and centerpunching it. I do the same for the waterline, for the stiffening side of a bulkhead obscures all measurements.

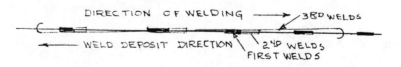

Figure 58. *A schematic drawing of the step-back welding sequence.*

If the welding has been done properly and in the right sequence, the bulkhead should lie flat. If it exhibits a small amount of transverse warpage, I can rectify this later, but it is always better to work more slowly and do it right and keep it flat. I will use a ³⁄₃₂-inch, 7014 rod in the flat position, at about 110 amps AC. With all the bulkheads made, bulkheads 6 and 8 are set aside with frames 5 and 7, and the remainder are stacked with the other frames.

It remains for me to bend the stem. For the most part, the stem is straight, which will make the jig for bending it a simple one. I can make several cleats out of leftover framing scraps, cut and ground in the shape of a flattened L (Figure 59). The long legs want to be 1½ inches in height, as the stem bar must rest well above the platen to minimize distortion in the platen due to excess heat. With these cleats welded to the platen, the bar is welded to the vertical leg of the first L, at what would correspond to frame 3. Now, with the two come-alongs attached at one end to the edge of the platen, and at the other end to the stem bar, pressure is applied. Now apply some heat to the stem's lower edge, in order to stretch the edge a bit at a time. (Bending cold is out of the question on this thin platen.) When the tension eases on the come-alongs, I go over and give a bit more pull, and keep this up until the bar comes home to all of the clips. Letting the bar cool, I then ease off on the come-alongs. If there is no change in shape, then all is well and the stem bar can be picked up. If there is a lateral bow in the material, this will have to be hammered out on the anvil in order to make the bar come straight.

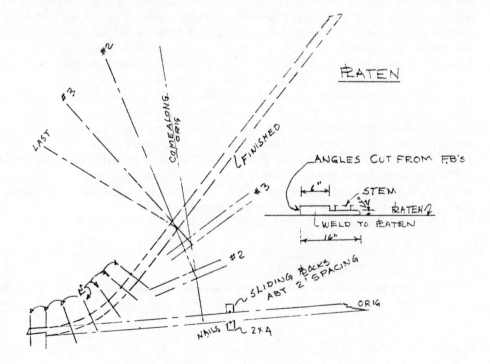

Figure 59. *Bending the stem on the platen.*

Bending done, the lower notch can be cut and the DWL marked, along with frames 2 and 1, the forward perpendicular (FP), the chines, and any other marks on the stem pattern. If the billet (clipper bow) is to be used (and using it will make the Pinky more salable as a yacht at some future date), it will be welded on at this time, using a weld similar to a B-48 type. With this completed, I will next add the 1-inch solid round stem facer bar. Since the stem is only ½ inch thick, it must be elevated ¼ inch above the platen so that the round will meet in the proper place. This round extends to cover the lower edge of the billet, and because the billet is thinner than the stem, it will have to be shimmed even farther underneath to assure its proper height and alignment with the bar. The stem facer bar should already have been bent separately to the proper curves, perhaps not exactly, but very close, in order to minimize the clamping pressure. The weld and stem preparation is detailed on Figure 76. The amount of welding done at this time varies with the preference of individual builders. Since the assembly is lying flat at the moment, it will be easier to complete now than after it has been set up. Using an E-7018 rod of ⅛ inch diameter (DCEP), I will skip weld using no more than one-third of the electrode. Spacing these first welds about 15 inches apart, I then turn the stem assembly over, reinsert the spacing blocks, and repeat—only this time it is permissible to go back to the opposite end and add some intermediate welds before turning the stem over again. Keep turning it from side to side, and keep the welds short and well spaced. If welding is done properly, the stem assembly should not warp. Lay the pattern on it as a check and, if all is well, place the assembly upright.

The platen can now be cleaned up, and all the pieces to be cut from it laid out, scribed, and cut at this time, which eliminates the platen. Remove the concrete blocks and clean up the area. Small pointed scraps of steel should be cut off or the ends bent back on themselves; otherwise, sooner or later, someone will stab himself and spill blood all over the place. By the way, it would be wise to get a tetanus shot prior to working with steel. The shot hurts only for a day or so, and is a small price to pay for peace of mind.

A few more things remain to be done before dismantling the mold loft, the first of which is to lay down the true length of the keel angle, and its true slope (drag), since the lofting was done at half-length. Then I will mark in each frame station along the lofting, and next lay up the angle itself on the loft, with one side flat and the other elevated. At that point I will centerpunch the frame lines into the toes of the angle, plus a three dot pattern (·: or :·) to indicate on which side the frame goes. I'll also scribe in on the elevated flange the taper that exists from frame 10 to the after end. Now the keel can be removed, the taper marked on the opposite leg, and the whole cut and ground. The cut is made square to the leg of the angle.

Now the angle is turned so that the actual bottom of the keel faces up, and its whole length is rounded slightly. I commence by grinding a flat edge, parallel with the ground and ⅛ to 3/16 inch wide or whatever is scribed, doing this with the grinding wheel kept at a very low angle so as not to gouge the keel. Next, with the sanding disk and 80-grit paper, I round off the ground edge. One must keep sighting what has already been done, and try to retain the same radius throughout. Now a slower speed flex-backed sander and 120-grit paper are used to polish the keel. This is not to impress the fish but to provide a good paint edge.

The pieces already made and stacked all over the place should be checked once more against the patterns. The plans should be thoroughly checked to determine if anything else could be lifted from the mold loft floor, for now is the time to do it. When satisfied of no further need, I can take the loft up, selecting an area near the shack and laying down six concrete blocks to support the plywood well clear of the ground. The blocks are laid in pairs, and a 2 x 4 is placed across the pairs so that there will be support at each end in the center. As I remove each sheet, I'll pull all the nails, then stack the sheets with the paint side down on the first sheet and paint side up on the second sheet, and so forth, so that paint faces paint throughout the stack. This, of course, assumes that the sheets were dry prior to stacking. If there is any doubt, I'll stack them with lattice strips between sheets to allow air to circulate. The top should have 2 x 4s laid across it, and the whole should be covered with a tarp. The patterns that have no further use should be taken apart, the nails removed, the pieces sorted by size, and the collection stacked clear of the ground on a few concrete blocks on the other side of the shack. All 2 x 4 material should be knocked apart, the nails removed, and the wood stacked on the opposite side of the building area, again on several concrete blocks.

Hopefully the rest of the steel has arrived and that kindly driver left behind some of his skids and separator wood. Whatever is not being used at the moment should also be stacked near the 2 x 4s on blocks, for this is a free treasure.

At this point, there is still not much to show for all the work I've done. All those parts, and it still doesn't look like a boat—in fact, it looks more like a nightmare of funny upside-down shapes. But I know that the progress I've made is very real, and I am satisfied.

After each major stage in building, take time to clean and rake the area. This will get rid of anything that might cause one to trip, stumble, or fall. Also, it usually yields some lost tools. While this cleanup may seem unimportant, there are builders who do it daily. Steel boatbuilding is considered heavy industry, so when you are building your own vessel, I hope you will remember this need for orderly cleanliness.

10

$\bigtriangledown$

THE
BUILDING WAYS
AND
BASIC SETUP

Now that the area is clean, it is time for me to set up the building ways. The first item of business is to determine where the centerline of the vessel will be. With this decided, a couple of 2 x 4s about 3 feet long should be sharpened up and driven into the ground—one at each extremity of the shelter (or 10 feet more than the overall length of the vessel). The tops of the stakes should stand about 18 inches above the ground, and each should have an eightpenny nail driven into the top. A string is tied off between the two stakes, with a line level fitted at the middle. Whichever end is high, that stake is driven down until the string is level.

Next I must decide which frame will serve as the master. The designer used frame 7; however, a bulkhead would be preferable, so bulkhead frame 8 is selected instead. Looking at the site and the location of the shack, I try to visualize the vessel for the convenience of moving around it, and having done so, I drive a stake close to but not touching the string. This will mark the approximate location of bulkhead frame 8. I must now establish a perpendicular to the centerline at this point, which I accomplish by first driving a small stake exactly 12 feet away from the first, toward the bow and directly below the centerline of the string. A nail is driven into its top, right on the spot that reads 12 feet, and the end of a steel tape is hooked to the nail and walked back toward the stake at frame 8, but about 9 feet out from the centerline. After making a small clear area on the ground, I scribe a short arc with a knife blade at the 15-foot mark on the measuring tape, repeating the process on the other side. Then I measure out exactly 9 feet either side of the centerline, and where the tape intersects the 15-foot arc, I again drive stakes, one on either side. A line strung between these two stakes ensures that bulkhead frame 8 squares with the centerline.

At this time, I select a good, straight 2 x 4, at least 12 feet and preferably 14 feet

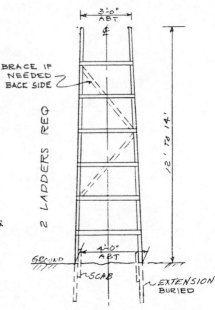

Figure 60. *The construction of the two end ladders.*

long. Also required will be five good stakes, a small shovel, and a maul. After nailing the stakes to the 2 x 4 with their tops flush to one of its edges, I dig five holes to match the stake locations. The holes should be deep and large enough to permit some driving of each stake and to allow lining up the clear edge of the 2 x 4 parallel to the cross-string. The height above the ground doesn't matter, but 8 inches is a good clearance. The centerline string need not coincide exactly with the middle of the 2 x 4, but the top of the 2 x 4 must be level. Once satisfied, I clean any loose dirt from the holes and fill them with concrete. Once the concrete sets, my cross spall is completed.

Ladders to go at either end of the vessel will be made from the pile of 2 x 4s that remain from the mold loft. Four straight ones are needed, and 12 to 14 feet would be a good length for the unburied part of the ladders; the portions to be buried can be scabbed on if necessary. Figure 60 shows their construction. The rung spacing makes little difference, but the rungs must be parallel to each other. As for strength, the rungs will later support scaffolding, and should be built accordingly.

After making the ladders, I construct a workbench about 8 feet long, using 2 x 6s for the top. This I locate near the shack, with room all around to work. The legs should be buried, and the top should be level in all directions. The vise should be mounted at one corner, preferably on its own steel plate made from some 7.65-pound scrap. The plate should be bolted to the table and a lug welded to it so that it can be grounded when I wish to weld on the table.

At the same time the ladder and bench are being made, it would be wise to make a sheers (Figure 61), which will make many of the jobs easier. This should be made of 4 x 4 material, with legs at least 16 feet long and of as clear a stock as possible, because the lifts required are such that one would not want them to fail.

Now back to the scrap yard to find some heavy channels (12-inch by 5-inch by 35-

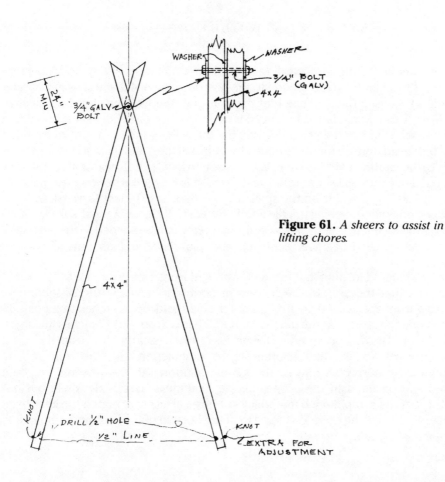

WASHER

WASHER

3/4" BOLT
(GALV)

4X4

24"
MIN

3/4" GALV
BOLT

Figure 61. *A sheers to assist in lifting chores.*

4"X4"

KNOT

DRILL ½" HOLE

½" LINE

KNOT

EXTRA FOR
ADJUSTMENT

pound) or I-beams (12-inch by 8-inch by 40-pound) to support the hull during construction. Three pieces will be required, the longest about 5 feet and the shortest about 3 feet, plus some scrap ⅜-inch plate or, better yet, say, ⅜-inch by 8-inch flat bar—4 feet will do. I'll look around some more before leaving, as it helps to know what the place has to offer should a need arise later.

The end ladders are set up next. The forward one should stand about 28 feet forward of the cross spall, and the after one about 25 feet aft of the spall. Holes for the ladder legs are dug, so that when the ladder is set up, its centerline will be exactly aligned with the keel centerline string. The bracing for the ladder had best face away from the hull; two braces for each leg are put up, one near the top and one about halfway up. These can be splayed a bit in order to improve their support. The ladder must be plumb, and, as stressed before, the rungs must be level. Furthermore, I'll need to make sure the rungs of the aft ladder are at the same heights as the rungs of the forward ladder. Once everything is checked and found satisfactory, cement is poured in the holes for the ladder legs and the support bracing. I can now release the keel string from the stakes and transfer it to one of the rungs, checking, of course, that the line is level.

Before setting up the keel I will have to set up the three support I-beams, first making sure that the keel bottom, when laid, will rest high enough above the ground to permit welding along the bearding line. When a builder is sitting on a concrete block, a total height from the ground to the bearding line of 4 feet will be about right for comfort, considering the need for room to pull the welding shield up clear of one's eyes. This means that at bulkhead frame 8 the bottom of the keel should rest about 33 inches above the ground. Using the Lines Plan, I measure down from the keel at bulkhead frame 8 the scale equivalent to 33 inches, and draw a line parallel to the DWL from stations 3 to 11. There is no reason to locate the I-beams at any precise place, but since they will support the vessel until it is finished, it seems reasonable to locate one aft, say 8 feet from the spall, and another, say, 14 feet forward, with the third one somewhere between. I dig a hole for each of them; in most soils, a 2-foot depth should be enough. If the soil is soft, a flat plate can be welded to the bottom of each I-beam. Each I-beam is centered and plumbed, and its hole filled with concrete.

From the Lines Plan, note that the keel is straight from frames 3 to 11, a distance of 26 feet, and that the drag is 22½ inches, or about 19 inches in the 22-foot span. Measuring from the centerline string, I determine the drop in inches to a point 33 inches above the ground at the master station. To this drop, I add 7 inches and mark the aft I-beam. The drop at the after I-beam, less 19 inches, is the drop from the string at the forward I-beam, and another string connecting these extreme points determines the correct height of the middle support. All the I-beams are then checked and trimmed to the proper height. Exactness here is desirable but not critical. From the scrap ⅜-inch material, I cut three cleats that match the keel angle (see Figure 62), making them V-shaped to fit the bottom of the keel, and weld one to the aftermost I-beam.

Figure 62. *A cleat notched to receive the Pinky's keel.*

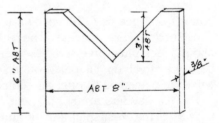

Figure 63 shows the plan view of the building site up to this point, including the steel storage rack and details of how other material should be stored. Figure 64 shows a profile of the same building site, looking at the ladders and the three I-beams cut and ready for the keel.

Now the keel is moved approximately into position, so that spall 8 and the mark on the keel at station 8 are close. The keel will have to be rolled into position, and then elevated enough to clear the cross spall as it is brought alongside the three I-beams. The keel weighs about 900 pounds, and it is not fragile, so it is prized up until it is even with the middle support I-beam, that is, about three concrete blocks high. It is not necessary to lift both ends at the same time. A small hydraulic jack would speed up

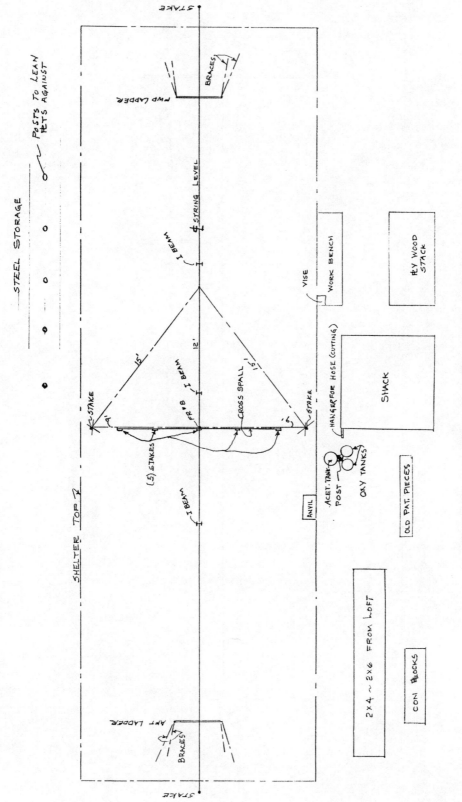

Figure 63. *An overhead view of the building site.*

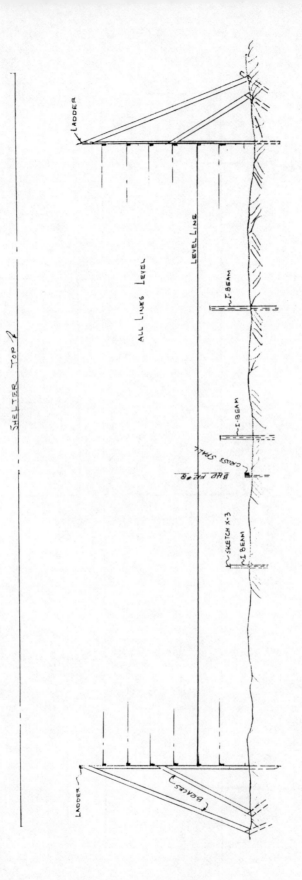

Figure 64. *Side view of the building site.*

the work, but this is an even better time to utilize sheers. Lacking the sheers, the method of raising the keel and getting it in place is as follows. Each time the keel rises a bit on the jack, a block of wood is shoved under it, then it is jacked a bit more until there is enough room for another block. One should always use a piece of wood atop the jack, or it will slide on the steel keel. Once the keel is high enough, it must be eased over by swinging the aft end sideways until the center of the keel lies above or rests on the center I-beam. The forward end must be restrained from moving; a loop of chain around the forward I-beam and the keel will suffice. When the keel is over the center support, and the flanges of the I-beam are clear, two short 2 x 4s are clamped onto the flanges so they extend upward about 8 inches. Now that the worst is over, the blocks from the aft end of the keel are removed to the level of the top chock welded to the I-beam. The keel is prized around until it touches the forward I-beam, then lifted and blocked until it is level with the top of the I-beam. If all has gone well, a small gap will exist over the center I-beam, which should be padded to protect the keel. The aft end is now prized over until the heel of the keel rests over the V-chock and the rest of its length over the centers of the other I-beams. The keel is levered upright using a 6-foot piece of 2 x 4 clamped to its elevated face, until it can be seated in the aft V-chock; at the same time, it should have come off the pad on the middle I-beam. Now it is moved either forward or aft to align the bulkhead 8 marks on the keel with the cross spall. One can do this with a come-along on the end of the keel, pulling from the nearest I-beam.

The keel must be elevated to the proper slope. Starting at frame 11, I measure the depth from the level line to the throat (inside of the angle); then I move forward. The keel stops before frame 3, so I make an extension by clamping a piece of leftover framing material with one edge resting in the throat. This piece should be long enough that at least 2 feet is housed in the keel, to ensure a straight extension. I clamp well, then measure out and find frame 3, remembering to use the *slope* of the keel length and not the horizontal frame space. Now I elevate this point until it is exactly 22½ inches higher than frame 11, place the V-chock on the forward I-beam, snug to the keel, then clamp it. I remeasure the depth at frame 11; it is probably slightly different now, especially if the forward end had to go up very much. Taking one-half the difference between the original and new measurements, I lower the forward end by that much. Then I remeasure and readjust until the keel is correct, weld the forward chock to the I-beam, and then clamp in the middle V-chock to its I-beam. In a keel this heavy, and positioned as it is, one should find neither hog nor sag between the two supports, but it is best to check to make sure. At frame 7, the exact center between frames 3 and 11, I must determine whether the difference in elevation compared to frame 11 exactly equals 11¼ inches (half the total keel drag of 22½ inches). If it does, then I may weld the V-chock at the middle I-beam; however, if it is more or less, the keel will have to be adjusted at the middle I-beam. When I am satisfied, I weld the V-chock to the I-beam. A final check is now made to be sure that the marks for bulkhead frame 8 align with the face of the cross spall; the keel is adjusted forward or aft until the marks align. Then, and only then, I weld the keel to the V-chocks. Needless to say, at all times checks must be made to assure that the centerline of the keel coincides with the centering level line, and no welding may be done before it lines up.

This may seem unnecessarily complicated, and it *would* be if I had a nice level concrete slab to work on, or planned to purchase a heavy, wide-flange base-beam that could easily be leveled. But such a beam would represent a ton of steel to be purchased that would not end up in the actual vessel. When you elect to build on open land, you must start by getting level and square with the world. Once you've done this, everything else is easy. Most amateurs are prone to hurry up to this point, but mistakes made now will require many extra hours to rectify later. A builder must always firmly grasp three basic axioms: first, *because something is possibly possible, it does not follow that it is necessarily necessary*; second, *don't worry that the sun has gone down—it will be back up tomorrow*; third (although we have all been told, "Don't just stand there, do something"), *stand there, don't do just something*.

Note that I have so far made no reference to the designed waterline or DWL: this is because there was no way of establishing it until now. The keel first had to be set and locked into place, independent of everything except a level line and a cross spall square to it. The DWL must now be established. Since we have a level line already in position, this becomes a simple question of how far up or down the existing level must go. The keel is now laid and I cannot reach the bottom of it anymore. Even if I could, the keel bottom is no longer accurate since I rounded it off, so I must use the inside of the keel for measuring. The throat of the angle is rounded but has no offset yet. I must, then, determine just how much of a deduction to make from the original bottom of the keel (used for offsets on the plans) to the inside throat of the angle. The procedure is to measure a piece of leftover (unrounded) keel and deduct its thickness at the throat from the lofted offset given to the bottom of the keel from the DWL at frame 11; this will give the true DWL offset from the keel throat. Instead of adding a rung in the end ladders, it is best to mark the DWL on vertical sticks that cover all the rungs. Just any old sticks will *not* do, as it will be necessary to use a DWL string offset a bit to one side or the other to allow room for setting up the stem and the sternpost. The stem facer bar is 1 inch in diameter, and the sternpost is a 2-inch Schedule 80 pipe with an outside diameter of 2⅜ inches, or a half-diameter of 1³⁄₁₆ inches, plus ³⁄₁₆ inch for the thickness of the keel side plating (deadwood); this gives a total of 1⅜ inches that the centerline string will have to be offset at the DWL to avoid fouling it on actual pieces of the keel assembly. (The thought has possibly occurred to you that this will not work when the deadwood plating is in place, but that is in the future. Remember that the centerline bulkhead stiffeners also require a ¾-inch offset to clear their flanges from the centerline.) The sticks must therefore measure 1⅜ inches wide. They are nailed in place, and the DWL is marked across them. The string is stretched between uprights and checked for level. The depth at frame 11 is also checked—is it in agreement with the corrected offset?

One more offset is needed, from the DWL to the top of the cross spall. This is found by standing a stick on end close to the keel and on top of the cross spall. A level is moved up the stick until it just touches the underside of the string; the stick is marked and the measurement ascertained. I write this measurement on the Lines Plan and on bulkhead frame 8. Before proceeding any further, with a marking pen, I write a large *S* on the right and a large *P* on the left after face of the forward ladder; now on the stern ladder's forward face, I mark a large *P* on my right and a large *S* on my left. I don't mean to make fun of anyone's intelligence, but when building a vessel, one can easily confuse port and starboard. It is not uncommon to take a measurement facing aft on one side of a bulkhead, say to the right of the centerline, then go to the opposite side of the bulkhead and transfer that dimension to the right again, which of course puts the measurement to the wrong side of the centerline.

With the keel set up, a first-time builder usually wants to see how the vessel is going to look, so many go ahead and set up the stem and sternpost. On Figure 65, these have been indicated as dashed lines. Personally, I consider it a useless exercise at this time, a lot of extra work, and of no immediate use. Nevertheless, for those who can't wait, here's how to do it. You will need to erect the sheers before transferring the DWL to the offset position, and if the sheers has not already been made, it must be made now.

Gently lean the sheers against the after face of the forward ladder, legs spread. Take a small length of chain, shackle the ends together after passing them through the Vee formed at the top of the sheers, rig the twofold purchase, hook the block to the chain, and mouse the hook. Bring the stem assembly alongside the keel in approximately correct position, but slightly athwart the centerline, with the billet on the opposite side of the centerline string from the base of the stem. Make an eye on each end of two 30-foot lines and cast the eyes over the head of the sheers. Lead one guy line forward and the other aft; the after line must lead to the same side as the DWL string. Move the feet of the sheers about 5 feet aft of the forward ladder, and dig a hole about 6 inches deep for each foot. Take the after guy and lead it in its proper direction; about 6 feet off the centerline, and near the end of the guy's scope, drive a 2 x 4 stake leaning at a slight angle away from the sheers. Now use the guy to pull the sheers into a nearly upright position, and tie it off temporarily to the stake. The forward guy wants to be set out about 6 feet to the opposite side of the centerline, where another stake is driven in, also leaning away from the sheers. Secure the forward guy with a bit of slack, as the head of the sheers should fall a bit aft, say about a foot from the vertical. Now tighten up the after guy. At or near the forward perpendicular (FP) mark on the stem, take a choker (a large loop of line, cable, or chain), pass it around the stem at this point, and hook it to the lower block; then hoist away. As it goes up, guide the stem between the legs of the sheers and walk the lower portion over to the keel on the ground, until the billet clears the forward ladder.

Now the stem must be brought up to where you can slide it in place, since it is notched to fit over the keel, and the stem facer bar fits under the keel. Heave up or ease off on the fall until the keel notch lines up. To send it home will require a come-along; secure a clamp athwart the stem bar at the bottom, then hook the ratchet to the clamp and the end hook to the forward I-beam, and take up the slack. Bring the stem home by easing on the falls of the purchase as you tighten the come-along. If there is too much pressure and the stem just will not slip in, the choker may have to be repositioned. If the hook is large enough, this can often be accomplished by passing another line through the lower block hook and around the stem, farther up. If this does not work, clamp a 2 x 6 across the insides of the sheer legs and against the stem face, slacken the falls, and readjust the choker. (*Never* use steel clamped against steel as a working support unless you want sliding or slipping.)

When you have the heel of the stem seated, check the DWL. It is extremely doubtful that it will be found exactly right, since it strikes the stem about 6 feet away from the connection just made. Take up or ease off on the fall until the DWL of the stem bar matches that of the string. When it does, spike a 2 x 6 to the forward ladder, after cutting a round notch about 1 inch deep for the stem bar, and rasp it to the approximate slope of the stem. Before nailing, center the notch to match the centerline of the hull. At the DWL we can make one further check. The stem is of ½-inch by 3-inch bar, so its half-siding is ¼ inch; the centerline string has been offset 1⅜ inches. Thus the gap from the stem to the string must be 1⅛ inches. If it is not, then the lower portion of the stem must be pulled one way or the other, and only a minute amount will cause a large movement at the DWL. When all is correct, tack weld the stem to the keel in two places *only*. Leave the sheer legs where they are.

The sternpost is light enough to manhandle, so all you need is a 2 x 4 about 8 feet long. In one end, cut a deep notch the same diameter as the sternpost; about 4 inches forward of the frame 11 marks, clamp a short 2 x 4 athwart the keel. Now put the heel of the sternpost into the keel, orienting its axis with that of the vessel, and lift it up; at the same time, prop the notched 2 x 4 at about shoulder height to support it. Nail a couple of temporary braces to the 2 x 4 to keep it from falling sideways. Next, adjust the bottom of the sternpost to its proper position in the fore-and-aft direction. By direct measurement from the plans, it may be determined that the after side of the post meets the DWL approximately 5 feet 6½ inches aft of frame 11. Mark frame 11 on the centerline string using a small piece of electrician's tape; then, at the 5-foot 6½-inch mark, place another small piece of tape. Elevate or lower the notched 2 x 4 until the edge of the tape and the DWL mark in the pipe align. The exact intersection may be a bit forward or aft of the mark, as any dimensions measured from a print are suspect. When they are in line, drive a stake against the bottom of the 2 x 4 to prevent its kicking out. Find two more permanent braces, a couple of stakes, and a small piece of ³⁄₁₆-inch steel. Move the sternpost athwartship until the piece of steel will just pass between the pipe and the string; secure the braces and stake them down. Make two tack welds at the heel of the sternpost and tack weld a small piece of steel above the 2 x 4 brace to keep it from climbing. The final adjustment of the sternpost comes much later. The DWL string may now be taken down.

Move the sheer legs aft to just forward of the cross spall, gradually walking the legs aft and adjusting the tension on the guys to prevent the sheers from falling. About 2 feet forward of the cross spalls, dig holes about 1 foot deep to match the feet of the sheer legs, and move the legs into them. Tighten up the foot rope of the sheers to keep the legs from spreading, and let the head of the sheers fall aft until the hook on the falls is about 3 inches forward of the cross spall. Now bring bulkhead 8 to the keel, with the top edge facing forward. The Scantling Plan calls for bulkhead stiffeners to face aft, except on fishing vessels, so they will be up. Rather than lift from the centerline of the bulkhead, it would be better to bridle off and lift from the cabin ports. Halving 8 feet or so of chain, about four links down fit a shackle with at least the same diameter as the chain link. On the last link of each leg of the now-formed bridle, shackle on a ⅜-inch slip-eye hook. Hook the bight of bridle to the moving block of the falls and mouse it. Pass the slip hooks under the bulkhead from forward, and hook them into the port and starboard ports, taking up the slack. Before starting the lift, shackle another chain around the keel just forward of the center I-beam, hook a come-along to it, ratchet end down, mouse its hook, and pay out about 6 feet of

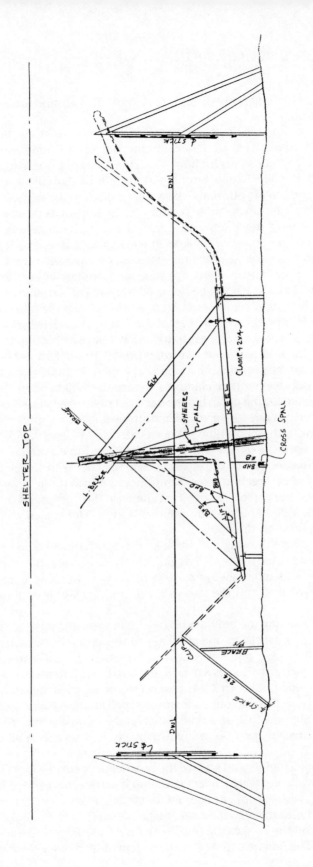

Figure 65. *The building site with the keel in place. The stem and sternpost are indicated by dashed lines.*

chain. Then lead the after guy forward, and also make it fast around the keel forward of the forward I-beam.

Now the lift can commence. It goes rather easy at first, but since the bulkhead weighs close to 800 pounds, it gets tougher, and the four-to-one purchase makes the final lift more than 200 pounds plus friction. When the going gets too tough, stop and secure the fall—now it is time to use the come-along. With a short piece of line, stand on the keel, and, at the top of your reach, tie a rolling hitch to the fall and secure the free end of the come-along close up; then ratchet it up. Repeat as often as required, tying off the fall, moving the hitch and come-along, and ratcheting away. The bulkhead need not be lifted clear of the keel. It will suffice just to drag it along until the bulkhead is almost upright, at which time you will clamp a short 2 x 4 across the keel so the bottom of the bulkhead will not slide aft. Continue lifting the bulkhead; when it is almost vertical, the fall will be doing all the work. Too much of a pull now will send the sheer legs toppling forward, so it is time to take the after guy aft and secure it under and around the keel, just aft of the last I-beam. The bulkhead is now brought gently to the vertical, or at least to the point where its bottom lines up with the punch marks on the keel. Since this is an *after* frame, the after face of the floor lies against the mark. Move the previously clamped 2 x 4 up to the bulkhead and reclamp it securely to the keel; use another clamp to secure the bulkhead to the 2 x 4.

The angles purchased for the cabin beams have not been used yet, so two of them may now be employed. Set one forward and one aft, resting their upper ends atop the cabin plate on or near the centerline. The elevated leg of each angle faces the centerline, with the opposite leg resting on the plate. Let the elevated ends extend upward as much as needed to rest the lower ends in the keel, with sufficient room to move a foot or so in either direction. Now clamp short 2 x 4s to the keel, just touching each of the angles; pull the angle legs together, and weld the undersides of the angles to the bulkhead with a good tack weld of about ¾ inch. The angles will brace the bulkhead in the fore-and-aft direction.

Figure 65 is a composite drawing indicating all that has happened up to this stage of construction, including the method of rigging the sheer legs and the bracing of the bulkhead. The sheer legs must always slope a bit toward the load being lifted. In future illustrations I will not draw the sheers in position, for it only confuses a small drawing.

The worst part of erecting the bulkhead is over. Now you just have to secure and align it. Use two more 2 x 4s; clamp one vertically to the after face of each side of the bulkhead, between the upper and lower chines. Note that the butts should rest on the cross spall; if they will not, there is a twist in the bulkhead. If there is a twist, gently pull the bulkhead around until both 2 x 4s rest on the cross spall. Again, a couple of short 2 x 4s will be needed. Clamp one to the cross spall in the vertical position, then clamp the bulkhead support to it, and repeat this on the opposite side. You need no longer fear that the master frame is going any place. It is secure in all directions except up.

It is time now to level, plumb, and square the bulkhead. First, a 12-foot (or longer) 2 x 4 (the best one available) will be needed. Clamp it across the forward face of the bulkhead at the DWL, with the upper edge just touching the line. The 2 x 4 wants to be centered. Drill three holes through the 2 x 4 and bulkhead (¼-inch is all right, but ⁵⁄₁₆-inch is better), and bolt the 2 x 4 to the bulkhead. Check to make sure that the holes clear any stiffeners. The bulkhead may now be plumbed by moving the fore-and-aft

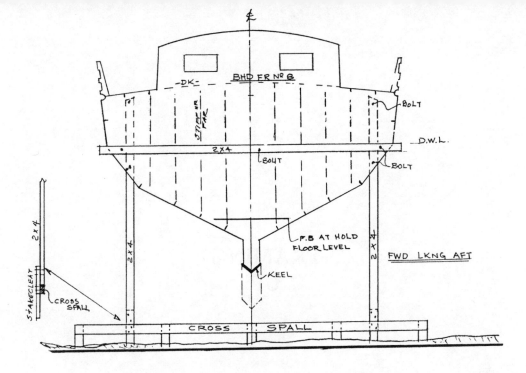

Figure 66. *Bulkhead 8 of the Pinky in position.*

angle bars, making sure to reclamp the blocks that cross the keel near their butts. Leveling comes next, and is accomplished by adjusting the 2 x 4 supports. No welding should be done at this time. Now check to see if the DWL is at the right height. The offset to the cross spall was marked on the bulkhead earlier, but may have been rubbed off; luckily, it was also marked on the Lines Drawing. There are now three possibilities for the DWL offset: too high, too low, or just right. The latter possibility would be pure luck. Of the other possibilities, too low is the better, unless the error is drastic; too high means that the bulkhead must be lifted and the surplus metal ground off. Once the DWL has been adjusted, the keel marks are checked; if these are correct, a final check should be made on the plumbness, which should now be exact. If it is not, check not only that the DWL is level athwartships, but also that it is still at the correct height. Finally, make a short tack weld between the throat of the keel and the bulkhead.

The bulkhead is now level and plumb to the vessel, but not necessarily square throughout its width, as it may have a slight bow. You can correct this later; at this time, the 2 x 4 uprights should be bolted to the bulkhead and the cross spall. The tops of these 2 x 4s should terminate at least 4 inches below deck level. Where the uprights meet the cross spall, drive in two stakes on the after side of the spall. These stakes should also be bolted to the cross spall and the support legs. These supports will be the last items removed when plating. The finished bulkhead, as erected, is shown in Figure 66.

At this stage, you can consider the vessel set up and ready for framing. As mentioned before, the inclusion of the stem or sternpost is really immaterial for quite some time, and setting them up now creates a lot of unnecessary work, but you now have some idea of how the vessel will look (in profile, at least).

11

$\triangledown$

FRAMING
UP

I have described the building of the Pinky through Chapters 9 and 10 in the first person, for three main reasons. First, I want it to be understood that the vessel can be built by a lone individual. Second, I do not wish to impose my methods and procedures on every present and future builder who reads this book. Were I to say, "Now you should position this," or "Next you will need to weld that," the reader might suppose that it can be done my way and my way alone. I do not believe that. While I do know that the procedures I'm outlining in this and in the second volume of *Steel Boatbuilding* will result, with care and some ability, in a fine vessel, I do not know that an alternative procedure, perhaps even one for which the tools or materials do not yet exist, could not create a vessel just as fine or finer, and with less work. Finally, the procedures I'm describing are tailored to the Pinky whose construction is detailed here. For another vessel, one or more of the steps in the building process, or the sequence in which they're arranged, might well vary.

For these reasons, I have given you, the reader, the role of observer, surveying the building site from a good vantage point and watching what I do with a critical eye. I want to continue that arrangement as I push ahead in the building process, but the use of the first person is often awkward and would soon grow tedious, and I want to avoid that. Please understand, therefore, when I write "Grind off the weld" or "Weld the after brace" (as I do in the next paragraph), that it is myself I am directing, and not you.

BEGINNING THE FRAMING

The vessel may now be framed up by starting with the existing bulkhead frame 8 and working forward. After checking once more that the bulkhead is indeed plumb, grind off the weld on the forward brace at the cabintop and weld the after brace onto the keel, then move the sheers forward of bulkhead frame 6 and set up to lift that bulkhead. Bulkhead frame 6 will be longer from bottom to top than the space between bulkhead frames 6 and 8, so the lift will have to be made somewhat across the vessel.

There is no good place on the frame to hook into; therefore, a flat bar should be welded about a foot below the deck level to the bulkhead stiffeners. This bar can be of leftover framing stock, and must extend outward from the centerline stiffener to the second stiffener, port and starboard. The welds on the bottom of the flat bar should be at least 1 inch long; for the weld to the top of the bar, only a good, sound tack is needed. This bulkhead, according to Figure 76, will have the stiffeners on the forward side, and since it is a forward frame, the forward face will lie against (and will become) the frame line. Therefore, with the stiffeners facing down, place the slip hooks 12 inches out from the centerline, hooks facing aft under the bottom of the flat bar, and commence the lift.

When the bulkhead reaches the vertical position, clamp a piece of 2 x 4 athwart the keel on the after side of the bulkhead, and clamp the bulkhead to the 2 x 4. Take another 12-foot piece of 2 x 4 and bolt it along the DWL of the bulkhead, just as on bulkhead 8. Then level the bulkhead athwartships and on the forward face clamp vertical 2 x 4s, port and starboard, also as on bulkhead 8, but do not bolt them. If the ground is soft, mount these legs on concrete blocks laid on their flat sides. Check the bulkhead to make sure it is vertical (close will do). Cut a piece 6 feet 6 inches long from one of the T-bars eventually intended for longitudinals in the deck, and lay it on top of the hatch coaming that forms part of bulkhead 6, keeping one edge of the flange on the centerline. The other end will be welded to bulkhead 8, with the same edge on the centerline; however, the Tee must be leveled prior to welding on bulkhead 8. For now, return to bulkhead 6, plumb the bulkhead, and tack the Tee to it.

Frame 7 is now offered up. This being the midship frame, the builder could set it correctly on either side of the frame mark. However, to prevent the deck beam angle from landing on the hatchway, frame 7 should have its forward face on the frame line. The frame is not heavy, so it may be tilted against bulkhead 8 for the moment to keep it from toppling over. Place the deep floor into the keel, and then secure a piece of line to the Tee, just forward of where frame 7 will stand. Clamp a block of 2 x 4 to the keel at the frame mark, and push the frame upright. When the frame is approximately in position, pass the tail of the rope under the hatch plate and back over the frame, and secure it to hold the frame up. Bolt another 2 x 4 across the frame so that the waterline marks are flush with the top of the 2 x 4. Level the waterline, fit short legs, and clamp them to the 2 x 4; also clamp the keel portion of the frame in the correct place, but do not weld.

Before frame 5 can be offered up, the sheers must be moved forward. It is not a heavy frame, but the use of the twofold purchase will be welcome. Like frame 7, frame 5 will also have its forward face on the frame line, with a block clamped to the keel and the frame clamped to the block. As with all the other frames and bulkheads, a 2 x 4 will be bolted across the DWL on the face opposite the stiffeners. Vertical braces will extend to just below the deck level, outboard of the lower chine.

SQUARING THE FRAMES

Now it is time to string the DWL again (remember that it was taken down temporarily in Chapter 10). First, in each bulkhead, mark and drill a ¼-inch hole exactly 1⅜ inches off the centerline either to port or starboard—whichever way the vertical sticks are offset on the ladders—and exactly ¼ inch above the DWL. Thread a piano wire through the holes and over the 2 x 4s that were used for marking the DWL at the bulkheads and frames. At the end ladders, secure this wire exactly ¼ inch above the DWL marks on the offset side. At one of the ladders, affix the end of the wire to a small eye-and-eye turnbuckle and tighten it. The idea is not to pull the ladders together, but to minimize the sag in the wire. Before tightening, insert the line level just forward of frame 7. If all is well, the wire will be level and will not touch either of the drilled holes.

Frame 7 is now ready to plumb, using another 6-foot 6-inch length of T-bar. This time let the Tee rest on bulkhead 6 as well as frame 7, and butt it against bulkhead 8. Since the first Tee is already lined up to one side of the centerline, line the second up on the opposite side of the centerline and tack weld it to bulkhead 8, frame 7, and bulkhead 6, making certain that the DWL remains level. Then secure frame 5 to bulkhead 6 with a short piece of T-bar from the centerline of the companion opening sill to the forward face of the hatch coaming; this piece should be level prior to tacking. Also check the DWL of frame 5 for level. When all frames are level and plumb, try to slip a small piece of ¼-inch plywood under the wire at each frame and bulkhead at the DWL 2 x 4. Should it refuse to fit, then that particular frame or bulkhead is too high, and if daylight can be seen, that particular one is too low. Bulkhead frame 8 is absolutely correct; therefore, adjust all others in relation to it. Again, correctness is an ideal seldom obtained by luck (and *never* absolutely achieved). Lows can be shimmed, while highs must be cut. The amounts involved usually come to mere fractions of an inch. One must be certain before shimming or cutting that the keel marks are checked first, since a fraction forward here will put the frame high, and a fraction aft will put it low. The distance from the DWL wire to the centerline of the frame must also be checked to verify that the frame or bulkhead remains exactly centered on the vessel. In general, the four checks to each frame or bulkhead are *square* to the centerline, *plumb* with the world, *level* with the world, and *centered* on the keel line. Once satisfied that each of them is level, plumb, and centered, tack weld frame 5, bulkhead 6, and frame 7 to the throat of the keel.

With three checks done, there is still one to go: the frames to the centerline must be squared, which is the same as making them parallel to bulkhead 8. Do this first at the DWL. Rip a 2 x 4 at least 10 feet long into four equal thicknesses, 1½ inches wide. To both port and starboard, lay one strip lengthwise on top of the protruding sections of the DWL 2 x 4s and nail it to the 2 x 4 on bulkhead 8. Note the keel marks: from the *after* face of bulkhead 8 to the *forward* face of frame 7 is a frame space, that is, 3 feet 3 inches. Mark this distance on each strip, then bring the forward face of frame 7 to this mark on one side. Repeat for the opposite side, nailing each side in turn. The forward face of bulkhead 6 is also on the frame line, so it, too, will be exactly 3 feet 3 inches forward of frame 7. And again, the forward face of frame 5 is also on the frame line, and therefore exactly 3 feet 3 inches forward of bulkhead 6. When all have been nailed, the DWL at each station should prove square to the centerline of the vessel, since all stations are now parallel to bulkhead frame 8, which is the master station. Check once more for level and plumb on frame 7, bulkhead 6, and frame 5, adjusting where necessary.

The correct distance between the forward face of bulkhead frame 8 and the after face of frame 5 is exactly 9 feet 9 inches less the thicknesses of the bulkheads, which in this instance are both 10-gauge. This gauge measures $\frac{5}{32}$ inch, which, times two, equals $\frac{5}{16}$ inch; therefore, the true measurement between bulkheads is 9 feet $8\frac{11}{16}$ inches. Two 2 x 4s are cut to this length; at the same time, four 4-inch-long pieces of bar scrap from the framing will be required to make some support clips. At 2 feet 10 inches off the centerline, port and starboard, tack two clips to bulkhead 8, with their tops 3 feet 9 inches above the DWL, the clips lying horizontal and having the tacks on their undersides. Do the same on frame 5. Now place one of the two 2 x 4s on each pair of clips, fore and aft, after marking on each the correct distance of frame 7 and bulkhead 6 from bulkhead 8. Clamp the 2 x 4s in place, making sure that their respective bulkheads fit snug against their ends. Bulkhead frame 8 must now be checked to assure that it is bowed neither forward nor aft. If it is, it will have to be sprung in the opposite direction. When it is absolutely true, then frame 5 will also be absolutely square with bulkhead 8, at 2 feet 10 inches off the centerline.

MARKING AND CUTTING THE FIRST DECK LONGITUDINALS

Using one of the remaining strips cut from the 2 x 4, cut it about 9 feet 8 inches long and lay it on the deck so that it parallels the longitudinal cutouts or marks at 3 feet 0 inches off the centerline. At frame 7, clamp it into place; at bulkhead 8, it will need to be elevated with the aid of a short pipe clamp; at frame 5, it will need to be depressed a bit; it should rest without pressure on frame 6. Measure and mark how much length the strip lacks to reach frame 5; also mark the bevel that the bottom of the strip makes against the vertical portion of the frame. Do the same at bulkhead 8, and mark the intersection at bulkhead 6. Using a length of T-bar ordered for the deck longitudinals, cut two Tees to the length obtained on the measuring stick, and bevel their ends. Figure 76 indicates the use of Detail 3-A at the ends and Detail 4-A at bulkhead 6—these details are drawn on the same plan—and the Tees must be prepared accordingly. When finished, fit them into place, and when assured of the correct height, tack weld them to bulkhead 8, clamp them at frame 7, let them seat at bulkhead 6, and weld them at frame 5. From each frame mark on the fore-and-aft 2 x 4s connecting bulkhead 8 and frame 5, drop a plumb and adjust the frame forward or aft as required, correcting any bow that may be present; then tack the longitudinals in place. All frames should prove square at 3 feet off the centerline.

Now cut the five short longitudinals (on the centerline, and 12 and 24 inches off the centerline, port and starboard) between frame 7 and bulkhead 8. Both ends will be as shown in Detail 3-A of Figure 76; the measurement and the bevels of all five will be ascertained at the 3-foot longitudinal. When these are cut, install them by first welding to bulkhead 8 and then to frame 7. Similarly, cut the other five short longitudinals (the centerline, and 12 and 24 inches off the centerline) between frame

5 and bulkhead 6, measuring again at the 3-foot longitudinal and providing Detail 3-A
ends. Install them by first welding to bulkhead 6 and then to frame 5. The ten shorts
should not be cut at the same time, since the two sets have different lengths and
bevels. Finally, remove all temporary supports that were welded to the vessel above
deck level, except the 2 x 4s.

THE FIRST DECK PLATE

With these longitudinals in place, the first deck plate can be laid. From the plating
rack, select the 60-inch by 120-inch plate ordered for the deck, and lay it flat on
several concrete blocks. First, measure its true width and chalk in a centerline; next,
determine if one end is square to the centerline. The tolerances of steel are such that
the length and width ordered are only nominal, as is the actual thickness. The
sheared ends are also not always square with the sides, and so must be checked
whenever squareness is vital, as it is in this instance. If neither end of the plate
squares with the centerline, then alter the centerline, making it square with one end.
The stick used for measuring the longitudinals should now be laid upside down
against the hatch coamings on bulkhead 6 and frame 7 in order to determine the
actual length between frame 5 and bulkhead 8; at the same time, mark on it the aft
face of the coaming at frame 7, the forward face of the coaming at bulkhead 6, and the
distance from frame 7 to bulkhead 8. Measure off on the plate the true length, less ⅛
inch for clearance. Then lay the stick on the centerline of the plate. *Deduct* ¹⁄₁₆ inch
from the measurement between bulkhead 8 and frame 7 to allow for the correct
seam gap, and mark in the hatch coaming face on the plate; then *add* ¹⁄₁₆ inch at each
face *away* from the hatch, and mark these off as well. Back on the vessel, measure
athwartship over the crown of the deck to determine the girth between each side of
the coaming, and add ¹⁄₁₆ inch per side. Return this measurement to the plate. From
the marks representing the hatch coamings, erect perpendiculars to the centerline
of the plate, and lay off one-half the girth distance on either side.

Next, square the plate end that is to be cut, and drill a ¼-inch hole at the centerline,
outside but adjacent to the cutting line; follow the same procedure at the hatch
opening, drilling two holes inside but adjacent to the centers of the forward and after
hatch lines. Cut the end off by starting at the middle and cutting about halfway to
each edge, then returning to the first side cut and cutting half of the remainder. Make
the last cut on each side from the edge of the plate toward the centerline. Chip off the
slag on the edge and grind smooth. Now cut the hatch openings. Starting, say, at the
aft end, cut from the centerline to the port corner, and then from the centerline to
the starboard corner. Cut the forward end in the same manner. The sides are cut
from the corners toward the middle, the cuts meeting halfway. Tap the cut-out plate
loose if it has not fallen out, chip the hatch opening clean of slag, and grind the edges
smooth.

The hatch opening has weakened the plate; therefore, in order to prevent its
buckling, clamp on a 2 x 4 along each edge and move the plate alongside the sheers,
aligned fore-and-aft. Hook the purchase to one corner of the hatchway and hoist
away, letting the plate slide up the leg of the sheers while guiding the other end of the

plate clear of the vessel. The plate weighs only about 200 pounds, so this will be awkward but not strenuous work. Once the plate clears frame 5, work the aft end over until it rests on one of the 2 x 4s clamped between frame 5 and bulkhead 8; then lower away, pulling the plate aft at the same time. The purpose is to get the plate canted across the deck so that it can be positioned. At this time, clamp an 8-foot piece of 2 x 4 athwartships, just aft of frame 7, to the underside of the longitudinal 2 x 4s. Jockey the plate aft and around until its forward end rests on the deck longitudinals and its centerline matches that of frame 5. Clamp another short 2 x 4 to the aft side of the hatch coaming near the centerline and just touching the suspended plate; remove the athwartship 2 x 4 and release the clamp on the short 2 x 4 supporting the plate; then, while one hand supports the plate, pull the top of it aft with the other hand until the plate rests on the longitudinals. If the plate rests on the coaming, it will be necessary to elevate the forward end a bit until it drops into place.

Once the plate is on deck, remove the clamped-on strengthening 2 x 4s from its edges, and align the centerline of the plate and the vessel at bulkhead 8 and also at frame 5. Return to bulkhead 8 and make sure there is a $\frac{1}{16}$-inch gap. With the plate resting firmly on the centerline longitudinal, tack the plate to the bulkhead. At the forward faces of frames 7 and 5, clamp 2 x 4s in the vertical position on the centerline, with their heels in the keel and also clamped to the floors.

The deck is now safe enough to walk on at bulkhead 8. Alternating port and starboard, check for the proper $\frac{1}{16}$-inch gap at each longitudinal and then tack weld. Starting at the centerline, do the same in the way of the hatch coaming at frame 7, making sure that a $\frac{1}{16}$-inch gap exists between the plate and the coaming; repeat this for bulkhead 6 and frame 5. The longitudinals must be tacked to the underside of the plate, and this should be done first at the centerline. To attempt to weld the plate without clamping is just asking for trouble; however, a 5-foot-wide plate is difficult to clamp, so it will be necessary to use a rolling clamp, which is simply a straight piece of deck beam angle laid athwart the plate midway in each frame bay. Hook a short pipe clamp near each end of the angle bar and also to the 3-feet off-centerline longitudinals. As the clamp on one end of the bar is tightened and the other clamp eased, the angle will roll toward the tightening side. When it bears on the longitudinal to be welded, snug up the appropriate clamp, then weld the longitudinal and the plating with about a 1½-inch segment. Repeat until all longitudinals are welded. There is no need to move from side to side while welding the underside of the plate to the longitudinals; just complete one side and then the other. The plate should also be welded about one inch in from its edge to each frame.

There remains one more task before moving on, namely, to make and install the hatch side coamings. If a pattern was made during lofting, check it against the vessel now; however, if no pattern exists, the coamings may be done by direct measurement. The top and bottom of the side coamings are straight and parallel, and the ends will be raked to match the plumb end coamings. These side pieces will be ⅛ inch less in length than the actual length of the hatch, since they butt the end coamings. Cut and fit them in place, maintaining the proper gaps. Put a good tack weld on the top, middle, and bottom of each corner.

Now check that the deck plate alongside the side coamings is straight. It should be,

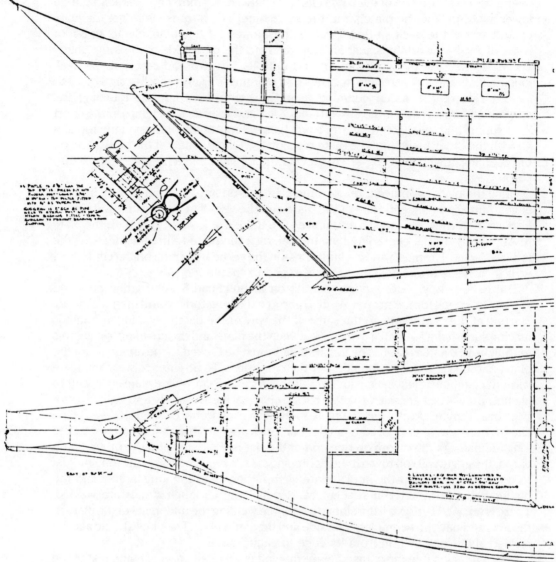

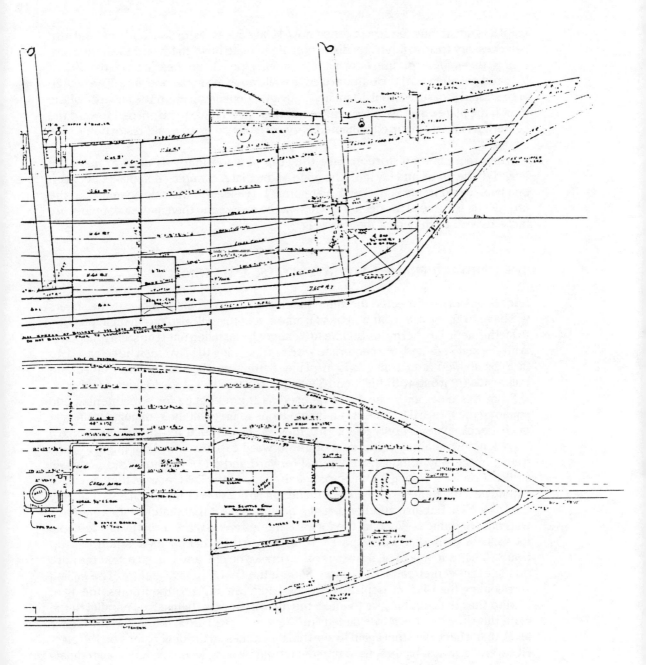

Figure 67. *The Construction Plan of the Pinky, Colvin Design No. 169.*

but if it is not, it must be straightened now. Heat causes distortion, and heat will also be necessary to straighten any distortion. If the plate bows in toward the centerline, clamp the middle of the bow with a small pipe clamp bearing on the 3-foot longitudinal, then heat the outboard edge while applying some pressure. The heated area should measure about 12 inches in length, depending upon the severity of the bow. If the plate bows away from the centerline, it will have to be pushed toward the centerline, and its inner edge heated very carefully so as to avoid distortion to the coaming.

When there is no distortion, take the strip of wood that was used to mark the length of the plate, and lay it on the edge of the plate, clamping it in place. Between bulkhead 6 and frame 7, the deck plate must be welded to the side coamings at the proper sheer curve of the deck. Tack first at the center and then make a couple more tacks toward each end of the coaming.

THE FORWARD FRAMES, LONGITUDINALS, AND CHINES

Had we not already erected the stem, the time to do so would be now, as the sheers will have to be moved to lift bulkhead frame 3, and this will also put them in position to lift the stem. Furthermore, bulkhead 3 cannot be installed until the stem is in place. With the stem erected, the centerline wire representing the DWL can be released, to be repositioned after frame 2 is in place. Setting up the rest of the frames and bulkheads (starting with bulkhead 3) simply repeats the steps followed earlier.

From this time on, frame 5 will be used as the reference for straightening and squaring the forward frames. It is advantageous to erect all the remaining frames at once, checking at first only to see that they are centered, level, and plumb. Place a 2 x 4 lengthwise along either side of the forward cabin trunk, clamping it to each frame. In the way of bulkhead 3, a nail forward and aft of the bulkhead plate will suffice. Continue bolting 2 x 4s across each frame at the DWL marks; they need not extend past the frames more than 24 inches on either side. Frame 2 will need not only the DWL 2 x 4, but also another one at a height above it that matches the reference waterline of frame 1. When all the forward frames are in place, drill the ¼-inch hole for the DWL centerline wire to pass through, as on the other bulkheads, and set it up again. Check and adjust all frames for the correct height, and make certain they are on the exact centerline of the vessel. Square the DWL 2 x 4s as before. The nailing strip joining the DWL crosspieces may be laid at an angle to the frames, toeing in toward the stem, but be sure to make the measurements themselves parallel to the centerline, to preserve a true dimension. Square frame 1 from frame 2 at the higher level, then check the stem again to see that it matches all the dimensions on the plan. Fit several athwartship braces to prevent it from twisting when the hull longitudinals and chines are added.

On the Construction Drawing, Figure 67, the deck longitudinals are shown with different lengths and details, since some end on frames, some pierce bulkheads, and so forth. Therefore, it is easier to fit all of them than to precut them. First, clamp the straightest 2 x 4 available, on edge, aft of and against frame 5. Four clamps will be required, one at each end and one at each side of the companionway. Make sure that the forward face of each frame is exactly 3 feet 3 inches forward of the last, excepting, of course, frame 1 (which is spaced at half this interval). The first longitudinal to fit is the outboard short one. When the centerline longitudinal is the only remaining one, lay it in its proper position, but on top of the beams and butting against the cabin at bulkhead 3; then obtain the bevel that will be required at the stem. Take a short piece of the same material the longitudinal was cut from and, making sure it is square on the end, slide it along the underside of the longitudinal until it touches the stem; then mark the longitudinal. The bevel will be applied from this point. With the bevel cut, fit the longitudinal to its slots, and weld it to the stem and all frames. Before proceeding further, check all work done forward of frame 5; also check all DWL measurements from bulkhead 8.

After the deck longitudinals are fitted, the upper chine can be fitted, starting at the stem and continuing as far aft as one bar will go. The chine is detailed in Figure 76, Detail 3-B, and more or less explains itself. The proper amount of welding is a tack weld to hold the chine bar at each frame. Bevel the bar to fit the stem first, and then tack it to the stem. Both sides will be brought home at the same time. The chine will run past frame 7, and, since the DWL 2 x 4s block the chine, it will be necessary to cut off enough of each of them to clear the chine slot. Therefore, a new spacing strip must be nailed to the DWL 2 x 4s inside the frames from bulkhead 6 to bulkhead 8 at this time, so that the original strip can be removed. Before removing the original strip, find a piece of scrap T-bar to weld on the inside of frame 5, butting against bulkhead 6; this bar will assure that the proper spacing is maintained. The projecting end of the DWL 2 x 4 need not be cut off on frame 5, since the chine will clear it.

When the upper chines have been tacked in, installation of the lower chines follows. Both sides will be worked at the same time, as with the upper chine. Again, check that the frames are still properly spaced.

The topside longitudinal Tees go in next. There are two acceptable ways of installing them. The more common way is to scribe the Tees to the correct bevel and weld them to the stem. At best, this always takes time, since the slightest mistake in the cut requires the end to be recut for a proper fit. The alternate method is to use a small breasthook, which will lie in the same plane as the stems of the Tees and extend aft far enough to allow the full depth of the Tees to be inset and welded without any cutting. This is a blessing later on, when the shell plating must be welded to the stem. Figure 68 shows a typical breasthook used for this type of construction.

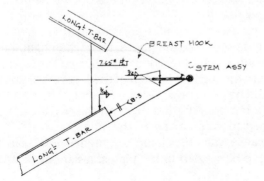

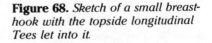

Figure 68. *Sketch of a small breasthook with the topside longitudinal Tees let into it.*

Reviewing Figures 76, 67, and 56, note that no special cuts occur in the topside longitudinals until bulkhead 6. This means the longitudinals will not have to be cut as per Detail 4-A until that point, and so may simply be clamped in place and tack welded to each frame and the breasthook, starting at the breasthook. When bulkhead 6 is reached, cut the longitudinal as per Detail 4-A and slip the longitudinal into its proper slot. When making such cuts in a longitudinal, always support the free end or it will droop. Bulkheads 3 and 8 utilize similar details, as indicated on the Expanded Shell Drawing.

THE KEEL SIDES

The upper portion of the vessel is now locked in place, and it is time to lock the bottom by adding keel sides and more longitudinals. The keel sides are now added, starting with the forefoot pieces, which extend from the stem to about midway between frame 5 and bulkhead 6. But before going further, check the floors to assure their proper spacing from bulkhead 6, and if the spacings are correct, weld the bottoms of the frames on their forward and after sides to the keel angle and the stem. Use a ⅛-inch rod for this (preferably an E-6010 or an E-7018), and DC welding, as deep penetration welds are now desired. Select one of the forefoot plates and set it in its proper position; elevate it above the keel bar by the thickness of a deck plate, clamp it to each frame, and then tack weld it to each frame, using only enough weld metal to keep it from falling off. *Do not* tack it to the stem. Now set the opposite plate in place, spaced above the keel by the same thickness as on the other side, and tack it to each frame. Cut a piece of 2 x 4 to a length exactly equal to the deep floor width at frame 5; at the aft ends of the plates, rest this block atop the keel bar and clamp the two plate ends together, squeezing them into exact alignment against the block. The outside edge of the keel must lie in the same plane as the keel sides. In case of misalignment, work a second clamp upward from the bottom of the keel using two short blocks, which will pull the keel sides one way or the other as a unit. Figure 69 indicates the method of doing this. When the alignment is correct, tack weld each side to the keel bar about 1 inch from the end, on the inside of the plate. Move the inner block about 12 inches forward, repeat the alignment, and tack. When a frame is reached, use a larger weld, welding down the frame and along the keel in a continuous weld, each leg being about 1½ inches in length. Continue this process toward the bow, until the end of the keel bar is reached. From this point forward, the keel tapers and the block is no longer useful.

At bulkhead 3, clamp the keel side plates to the bulkhead, drawing them in at the same time; use a clamp on the top and bottom of the plates, and, when tight, tack weld each plate to bulkhead 3 on the after face only, about 1 inch from the top and bottom. A small plate must be added to the top end of each of the forefoot plates to finish it off at the stem, and this should be done now. Using a ³⁄₃₂-inch rod, weld the plates with a B-3 weld (see Figure 6), but do not grind them on the outside at this time. The plates may now be clamped to frame 2 and to the stem.

Clamping at the stem is vexing, because when the clamp is tightened, it will slip. In order to prevent this, clips will have to be welded to the plates. A flat bar scrap is

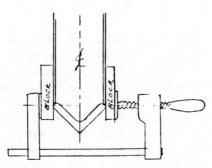

Figure 69. *Using a clamp and two blocks to adjust the alignment of the keel side plates over the keel bar.*

usually enough for the screw end of the clamp, but a small scrap of angle is required on the fixed end. After the plates have been brought home on the stem, check before welding that the stem has not been pulled out of alignment. If satisfied, tack weld the plates to the stem, alternating sides, placing the tacks at intervals of 6 inches or so.

Two more small plates must be added (one on either side) to complete the keel-forefoot-stem connection. Add these now, first tacking them to the main keel bar, and then tacking them along the stem bar where they twist upward to the forefoot plate. The forefoot plates will have to be moved in or out to make the joints at the plate edges. To move the forefoot plate in requires clamping; moving it out can be done with a block and a wedge on the inside of the keel.

The next pieces of plate extend the keel sides to just aft of frame 10, and they are now added in the same manner as the forefoot plates, only at this time the welding will stop at bulkhead 8. The butt joints where these plates meet the forefoot plates should be tacked in several short tacks, on the inside only.

THE AFTER FRAMES, LONGITUDINALS, AND CHINES

The sheers is now brought aft and set up to lift frames 9, 10, and 11 into place. At the same time, remove the angle brace that was required before to keep bulkhead 8 plumb. This bulkhead cannot move anymore, since it has been tied via plating and longitudinals directly to the stem. The after frames will be installed in the same way as the forward frames, having 2 x 4s bolted across their DWL marks. Release the centerline wire until these frames are in place, and then reset it, checking that the DWL marks are at the correct height and that the frames are centered. When squaring the DWL of these frames to bulkhead 8, locate the nailing strip inside all the frames, since the chines would otherwise interfere with it farther aft. Use a piece of T-bar to connect bulkhead 8 to frame 9. All other spacing strips may be of wood, in lengths long enough to space each frame. When everything lines up, frames 9 and 10 may be welded to the keel, and the keel sides secured to the frames as done previously. Frame 11 may also be welded to the keel. The remainder of the deck longitudinals are now added, except the two that are 3 feet off the centerline port and starboard.

Had the sternpost not already been set up, now would be the time to do it. The procedure would be as follows: Nail two straight 2 x 4s to the undersides of the DWL 2 x 4s on frames 10 and 11, extending aft about 7 feet, with their inboard edges exactly 1³⁄₁₆ inches off the centerline of the vessel. Now bring the sternpost into the slot formed by these 2 x 4s, orienting it so that its bottom, cut end rests on the keel and slips under frame 11. From the center of the top after edge, drop a plumb bob. This is the after perpendicular (AP), and it can be determined from the Lines Plan that this should fall exactly 8 feet 7 inches aft of frame 11; therefore, the end of the sternpost must be adjusted up or down until this measurement is obtained. When it is right, clamp the sternpost where it passes through the 2 x 4s. Check that the post is centered to the vessel by measuring to the centerline wire. When satisfied, add two braces aft, well staked into the ground, and then further brace these braces from side to side, anchoring them again to more stakes, also well driven into the ground. Weld the heel of the sternpost to the keel and to frame 11.

Since the sternpost has already been installed, it is only necessary to follow the alignment procedure as just outlined. It may be necessary to cut loose those original tacks securing the heel of the sternpost to the keel, since this is the first opportunity to ascertain the correctness both of the sternpost's slope and of its exact alignment to the DWL and to the centerline.

The 2 x 4s can now be removed and the wire released, so that the last three frames can be set in place. Move the sheers aft until it is clear of frame 14, and from it suspend a 2 x 4 that also rests on the sill of the companionway at frame 11. Now set into place frames 12, 13, and 14, bolting DWL 2 x 4s onto 12 and 13. Also on frame 13, bolt on a higher waterline marker to match the one that will be used on frame 14. These three frames attach to the sternpost, and their weight must therefore be borne by the suspended 2 x 4. A short length of line passed over it at each frame will do to support such a small amount of weight. Reset the centerline wire, then plumb, level, and true up each frame as before. The first longitudinal to install is the centerline, so it will now be beveled to fit the sternpost. Weld it first at frame 11, and tack it to all other frames. Lastly, weld this longitudinal to the sternpost, making sure that the post has not moved. Add the remaining longitudinals, working alternately from side to side.

The last of the lower keel sides are added and tack welded to the sternpost when the afterbody has been framed up. With the main plates fitted, add the last portion of the keel sides, which will end at the top of the sternpost. Weld to each frame as the welding sequence demands.

The upper chines are now added, followed by the lower chines. Where these meet the forward portions already in place, cut, bevel, and weld the pieces, being sure to maintain a fair curve in all directions. The topside longitudinals (one on either side) can then be set in place, ending at frame 14. As these longitudinals pass through the bulkhead at 8, it will be necessary to use Detail 4-A. When they meet the forward Tee, cut and fit the ends together. *Never* make a joint on a frame. The longitudinals between the upper and lower chines will not be laid in place until all plating on the bottom, sides, and deck has been completed, since this opening provides air, light, and access to the hull.

The bottom longitudinals can now be run in. Since the afterbody is the most straightforward part and will, after completion, aid in fairing the forebody, start at bulkhead 6, 3 feet 0 inches off the centerline. On the Shell Expansion, Figure 76, note that all bottom longitudinals terminate here and are cut as per Detail 3-A. In a small vessel like the Pinky, when the cargo hold bulkhead adjoins a potable water tank, it is best not to pierce the bulkhead at all, in order to avoid the chance of eventual contamination from bilge water from the cargo hold seeping through a pinhole in the weld joint that may have been bridged enough to withstand a pressure test during construction. As with any tank that will always contain a liquid and cannot readily be inspected or maintained, prudence dictates the elimination of any penetration through bulkheads, except where absolutely unavoidable. Detail 3-A prevents this and permits a continuous weld between bulkhead and shell on the cargo hold side. The Detail 4-A cut, used elsewhere when a longitudinal passes through a bulkhead, is otherwise a good, safe, watertight welding detail. The 3-feet-0-inches longitudinal terminates on frame 13, 5 inches below the lower chine. There is no need to stop exactly on this frame, and a couple of inches more make the Tee easier to clamp. At this time only a good tack weld is needed at each frame.

Next, install the longitudinal at 2 feet 0 inches off the centerline. Again, look at the Expanded Shell Drawing, Figure 76, and note that aft of frame 11 there is a fair diminish in section, and that the 2-feet 0-inches longitudinal is abandoned. Like the previous longitudinal, this one also terminates on a frame and may, for convenience in clamping, also pass through the frame an inch or so.

Before running in the lower longitudinal, weld the inside of the keel to the keel side plates from the sternpost to frame 9, or even a bit forward. Also weld up the inside of the plates, up to frame 13 on the sternpost, for one can stand alongside the keel in a more comfortable position now than would be possible after the bottom plates are on. Exercise caution while welding, lest the keel begin to warp due to excessive heat. If the back-step method of welding is used, and the welds are spaced about 18 inches apart, there is little likelihood of this happening. Both sides (port and starboard) of the keel are welded in the same area at the same time. The keel, being vastly thicker than the keel sides, will require that most of the weld be directed toward it. An E-7018, $\frac{1}{8}$-inch rod would be a good one to use, on DC power. The butt joint in the keel side plates between frames 10 and 11 should also be done now, but the electrode diameter should be reduced to $\frac{3}{32}$ inch. Use a downhand pass in short increments. A couple of 2 x 4s clamped to the outside of the joint will help restrain it, should it wish to walk away during welding. Once this welding is done, clean out the frame bays of all slag and debris, as they are now more or less watertight. Now fit the lowermost longitudinal to the vessel. Since it is more than 20 feet from bulkhead 6 to frame 14, the Tee will have to be lengthened. This should be done at the aft end.

I have assumed throughout that, prior to tacking in any longitudinal, a check was made to assure that the frame is straight and still parallel to bulkhead 8. Nevertheless, I should perhaps stress the importance of this again before more longitudinals are added. The last longitudinal is the short one that extends from bulkhead 6 to frame 9, and each end will be as per Detail 3-A.

THE WATER TANK AND FORWARD BOTTOM LONGITUDINALS

Before the forward longitudinals can be fitted, it is necessary to install the water tank and its fore-and-aft divisions. This will require four nominal 1 x 6s (actually ¾ inch by 5½ inches), each at least 14 feet long. Rather than use just any old pieces of lumber, use a grade and type that can later be cut up and used for cleats and nailers for the interior joinerwork. Clamp one 1 x 6 on either side, its center located 15 inches off the centerline, starting just aft of bulkhead 8 and extending to just forward of frame 4. Site the other two planks between the 2-foot and 3-foot longitudinals. Now fit the 15-inches-off-centerline water tank bulkheads in place, and if there are any irregularities in their bottoms, scribe them to the 1 x 6s and grind off any surplus. Tack weld the tank bulkheads to bulkhead 6.

The keel and keel side plates must now be welded on the inside from bulkhead 6 about 24 inches forward, and the bulkhead must be welded to the keel side plates. This is necessary because, according to the plans, a 7.65-pound 8-inch-wide plate forms the tank bottom, so access to weld the bulkhead to the keel side would be restricted later on, as would any other welding underneath this plate. Also at this time, weld the butt joint between the forefoot plate and the after keel side plates, on the inside only. Fit the 8-inch-wide plate to the keel after welding is completed, and tack it in place so that its bottom lies just fractionally below the bearding line.

The forward tank bulkhead is now offered up, and will rest on the planks and against the 15-inch bulkheads; it must be centered, and then its top may be leveled. Bring the 15-inch bulkheads square to bulkhead 6, and tack them to the forward tank bulkhead. (Carpenters' squares are useless in metal boat- and shipbuilding, unless modified by cutting off the outside corner; otherwise, the welds will always prevent them from squaring two plates. Figure 70 shows this modification. Tack the forward water tank bulkhead to the 8-inch bottom plate. At the end of the bulkhead, cut a piece of scrap T-bar, long enough to span from its top edge to bulkhead 6, and tack it to both when the two are parallel. Do not remove the planks, but do clamp onto the after lower edge of the forward tank bulkhead a 2 x 4 on edge, from each 15-inch bulkhead outboard to the end of the forward bulkhead to prevent it from being pulled out of shape when fitting the longitudinals.

The longitudinals at 2 feet off the centerline will be the first forward bottom longitudinals installed, and will end on frame 2. Starting at the forward water tank bulkhead, bend one in place, and by sighting along one of the planks, check that it has a fair curve. If it does not, remove it and bend in whatever curve is needed; then tack weld it to each frame. The opposite one is fitted the same way, then the 3-foot longitudinals, and lastly, the longitudinals at 1 foot. The planks around the tank may now be removed and stored, and the area cleaned up.

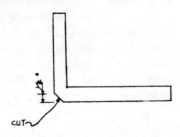

Figure 70. *Modification of a carpenter's square, enabling it to clear a weld when two plates are squared.*

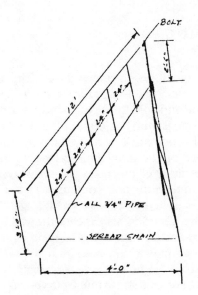

Figure 71. *An A-frame ladder to support scaffolding planks.*

THE GUNWALE PIPES

Because of all the longitudinals, the hull is now rigid and will resist the strains imposed when the gunwale pipes are bent on. For this job, scaffolding is required. Four metal A-frame ladders can be made using pipe, hinged at the top to fold and having rungs on both sides, since this will permit the scaffolding planks to be slid through either ladder for moving the other. The scaffolding planks must be of wood at least 12 inches wide and 2 inches thick; in spite of the weight, oak is the best to use, of clear stock and not less than 16 feet long. Rough stock, not milled, is best, because the rough surface gives better footing. In some localities these ladders can be rented, as can the scaffolding. If they are available, a couple of extra pairs would eliminate having to move the scaffolding in most instances. Figure 71 indicates the approximate size and construction of these ladders.

The pipe for the deck edge comes in 21-foot lengths, and since two lengths will not quite gird each side, a third short piece will have to be added. The stern has less curve near the end than the bow, so the extra will be added there, making two joints per side. The pipe is 2-inch Schedule 80 with an inside diameter almost the same as the outside diameter of a 1½-inch pipe, so a few feet of the 1½-inch size will also be needed.

At frame 7, loop lengths of chain around the frame and over the longitudinals at 3 feet off center, port and starboard. The loops should be roughly 4 feet long, or long enough to extend about 2 feet past the edge of the deck at frame 7. Then clamp a 16-foot length of 2 x 4 across the vessel on this frame, about 12 inches below the deck edge. At frame 5 and again at bulkhead 3, also clamp on a 2 x 4 (these need not be as long). Pass up a length of pipe, port and starboard, and slip it through the loops of chain at frame 7. With the pipes more or less resting on the other 2 x 4s, push them forward or aft so the forward ends are approximately in line with the stem, lifting each to rest in the notch cut for it at frame 1. A short length of line will be sufficient to secure the pipes to the frame at this time. The after ends of the pipes must now be raised or lowered until their forward ends, without using pressure, are in line with their final resting place on the stem. Secure a line to one of the pipes about 12 inches aft of the forward end, then loop it over the other pipe and return it twice. This becomes part of a Spanish windlass to bring home and hold the pipes to the stem, but first pull them as close together as possible by snugging up the loops of the line. Now secure the tail of the line and insert a piece of broomstick or a chipping hammer handle. Wind the two pipes together until they rest on the stem, then scribe the pipes and cut each of them so that the cusp of the resulting ellipse rests precisely on the scribe mark on the stem. Clean off the slag from the cuts and continue to wind in, until both pipes touch the stem. It may be necessary to roll the pipes a bit to get the tops and bottoms snug. After checking that the bearding also meets the vertical center of each pipe, make a substantial weld, top and bottom, securing each pipe to the stem, and remove the Spanish windlass. About midway between frames 4 and 5, hook a come-along to the two pipes, from side to side under the deck framing, and tighten. The pipes must be pulled to the vessel wherever there is much curve—*never* pull the vessel to the pipes.

As the pipes come together at frame 1, make sure they rest in the slots, and temporarily clamp them to the frame. If the pipes try to jump out and fall or rise, clamp a short length of wood to the frame to prevent this. When the pipes arrive at frame 2, repeat the procedure used at frame 1. Continue to pull the pipes together until they are seated in their notches at bulkhead 3. Returning to frame 1, weld the pipes to the frame on the after side only, and move the clamps to bulkhead 3. If two come-alongs are available, set up the second one just forward of bulkhead 6 and take up a strain, doing the major pulling from there. When the pipes seat in frame 4, weld frame 2. The pipes will now not only have to come toward the centerline, but will also need to be lifted to enter the notches. This can be done by utilizing the outer main deck longitudinal. Now, with a 2 x 4, prize the pipes into position. The pipes are elevated at their after ends to at least deck level, and then snugged up. Since there will be very little pressure on the pipes at this time, the vessel itself may be used to assist in pulling the pipes into place. Short pipe clamps are best for clamping, since their ends can be turned in whatever direction is desired. With one clamp to the outermost deck longitudinal, near the frame, bring the pipe into the notch, prizing upward as necessary, and when it is almost home, use another clamp at the throat of the deck beam and frame to seat it. Continue in this manner until all but one frame has been fitted with this length of pipe, and then weld the pipes to each frame on the after side only.

Cut two pieces of the 1½-inch pipe, 8 inches long, insert their ends into the 2-inch pipes about halfway, and use one small tack on the tops to hold them in place. Remove all the other crosspieces that held the pipes up forward, and clamp them in aft. For the present, they must be located at heights that will permit a fair continuation to the ends of the forward pipes. Lay up the next sections of pipe and insert the stubs of the 1½-inch pipes into their forward ends, leaving a gap of at least ⅛ inch between the after and forward pipes. Find a straight piece of deck beam angle, about 3 feet long, and clamp it to one of the joints just formed, with the Vee encasing the joint. Use four clamps to hold it in position, and make a finished weld as far as possible; do the same on the other pipe. When the first weld has cooled, reverse the angle and repeat for the rest of the joint. The pipes are now ready to be brought into

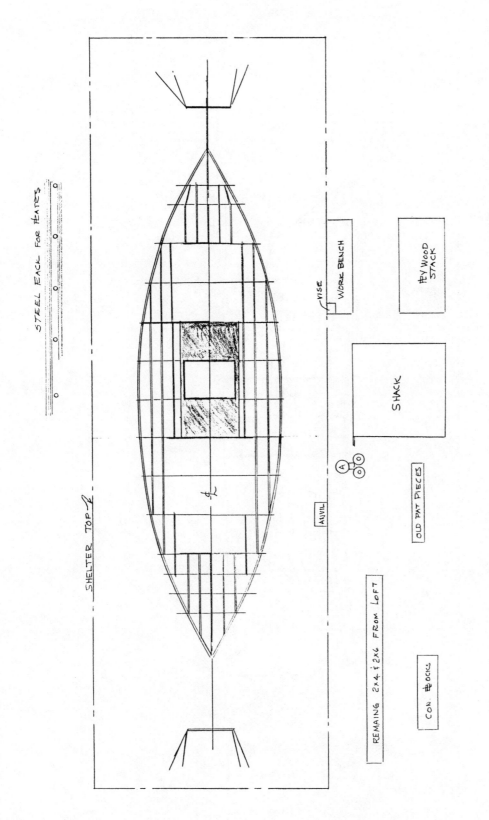

Figure 72. *A bird's-eye view of the building site, showing what has been accomplished on the Pinky to this point.*

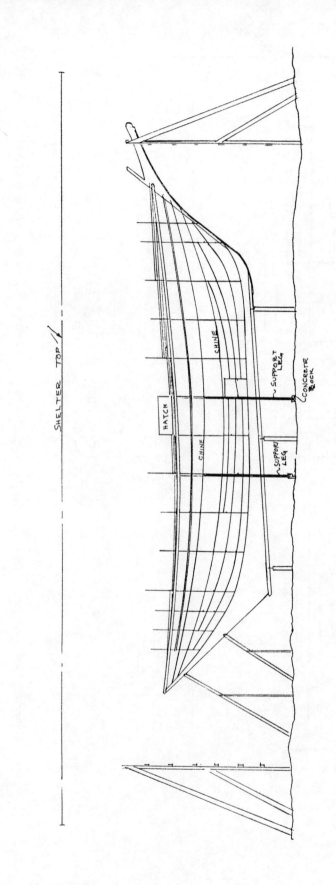

SHELTER TOP

HATCH

CHINE

CHINE

SUPPORT LEG

SUPPORT LEG

CONCRETE BLOCK

Figure 73. *Side view of the building site.*

place aft. The same procedure will be used as in the forebody, except that the pipes aft of bulkhead 8 will be continually rising. It will be advantageous to raise them a bit at a time, as needed, by inserting additional 2 x 4s atop the previous ones and reclamping, that is, by leap-frogging. As the last frame comes home, it will be necessary to add some more pipe to reach the stern. This is done in the same manner as before. Finally, fit the Spanish windlass to the pipes, bring them to the sternpost, and scribe them. In this instance, however, the pipe stands one-half its diameter above the top of the sternpost, since the deck edge detail was changed. This will mean scribing the pipes to meet each other above, and the post below. When this multiple cut is achieved, the pipe is welded to the sternpost.

The framing is now finished and the vessel is ready to plate. As usual, the last order of business is to clean up all around the vessel, and also to move the sheers out of the way. Figure 72 shows from above what has been accomplished so far; Figure 73 shows the same stage of construction in side view.

You have borne with me in setting up the Pinky. In many designs for steel construction, there are no steel bulkheads. The cabin trunks may land between frames. Hatches (such as cargo hatches), skylights, and other deck structures also land between frames. There is no foredeck or quarterdeck—in other words, the main deck is continuous from bow to stern. For any design, it is mandatory to work from a master station, as has been described. Once the master station is in position and secured, however, all the frames forward and all the frames aft may be propped up on the keel in such a way that, once the centerline wire at the DWL has been positioned, it need not be moved, and all of the frames may be slipped into their proper positions. The sequence remains the same in that a section near the master station must have a deck plate to lock this portion of the hull into position.

12
▽

PLATING

In describing the setup of the Pinky, I have frequently referred to Figure 76, containing the Shell Expansion Plan, the Midship Scantling Section, and Details and Notes. I mentioned in Chapter 1 that, in round-bottom construction, such a drawing would be mandatory and that the information shown on it would be derived from a half-model on which the various plates were laid off. When the information from a plating model is transferred to a Shell Expansion Plan, the forward and after ends of the plates are referenced to frames. The reason for this is that only the transverse widths of the plates can be accurately measured directly off the drawing, fore-and-aft distances being distorted by the method of presentation. It is impossible to project accurately on the drawing board the continuous changes in longitudinal girth for the whole hull. Individual plates that are true in all dimensions *can* be developed from the Lines Plan, and the loftsman will sometimes take the time to develop them. However, it is faster and therefore less expensive to make a pattern directly from the vessel itself as it is built, and one can then ignore the slight discrepancies that creep in during construction. If there ever was a perfectly built vessel, accurate to the merest fraction of a millimeter no matter where measured, she was never launched. The Expanded Shell Plating Drawing is for guidance *only*. A builder may be more or less assured that if the plates as laid out on the drawing have been developed from a model, and if he follows the sight edges of the plating, there is a good chance of the plates at least lying on the frames without his having to resort to arbitrary slitting. In other words, there is less "by guess and by golly" when using a model or a drawing based on a model.

Figure 74 shows the expanded shell plating of a 40-foot schooner with longitudinal and transverse framing, as well as bow and stern views indicating how the plating would look on the hull. Figure 75 shows the expanded shell plating of a 45-foot ketch, transversely framed and having a 122.4-pound keel plate, 3 inches thick. Weld details are shown, as is her tank arrangement. Both of these plans were developed from plating models. By contrast, the expanded shell plating for the Pinky Schooner has been developed directly from the Lines Plan without the use of a model, so that except for the first plate applied, the fore-and-aft locations of the plates can only be given as approximations. The object is to best utilize the available plate sizes, with more attention paid to widths than lengths. This is the approach generally used on flat-bottom, V-bottom, and multi-chine hulls.

PLATING THE BOTTOM

In general, plating is added to the framed hull in a sequence that helps make the work easier for the builder, planned especially with an eye to convenience of access and movement. The first plate to be affixed to the hull of the Pinky is the 60-inch by 192-inch bottom plate that starts 3 inches aft of frame 4 and continues aft almost to frame 9. Always remember that a plate *never* butts on a frame or a longitudinal.

The first task is to make an accurate pattern that will be used to cut the plate. On this first plate, the object is to avoid cutting the ends of the plate, and to cut *only* the edges, unless leaving a manufactured end (as the plate came from the mill) would create a problem, such as making a butt cross a frame diagonally or land inside a tank in an unweldable position. Also, on the first plate, it is desirable to make the pattern a few inches longer than the plate, so as to be able to orient the pattern to the best advantage. Figure 77 shows how the finished pattern will look and lie on the plate. A note on the scribing of patterns: use a block of wood whenever possible to mark the line along the keel, and not a pair of dividers or scribers. Once the pattern is laid on the plate, any irregularities can be smoothed out with a long batten; however, this does not relieve one of the duty to accurately transfer what is on the vessel to the pattern.

After cutting and grinding, the plate must be worked over to the vessel. This is best done by laying a plank or two on the ground and placing a few pieces of pipe on them so the plate will roll. It will help to use the three keel supports as anchors to pull from. Once the plate is near the vessel, some thought must be given to how it will be lifted in place and gotten under the vessel, since the legs supporting the frames are in the way but must not be moved. The plate is not heavy, weighing less than 400 pounds, but it is as limp as a wet noodle.

There are several ways to lift this plate. First, lifting pads can be welded to the plate, and come-alongs attached to them and to a deck longitudinal. This method has the following disadvantages: you must weld to the plate; more than one come-along will be needed; several extra lift pads will be required, aside from the original ones; and finally, the pads will have to be burned off and the area around them ground clean. Good practice on thin plates calls for using the minimum amount of welding, as each weld causes a small expansion of the plate and thus some distortion. A second method is to affix clips to the keel side plates, either by clamping or by welding them on, to which a timber can be fastened to make a supporting ledge about the same length as the plate; the plate edge is then elevated onto the ledge,

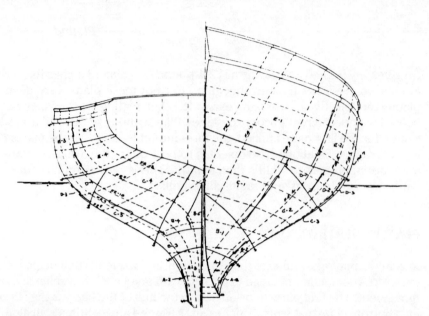

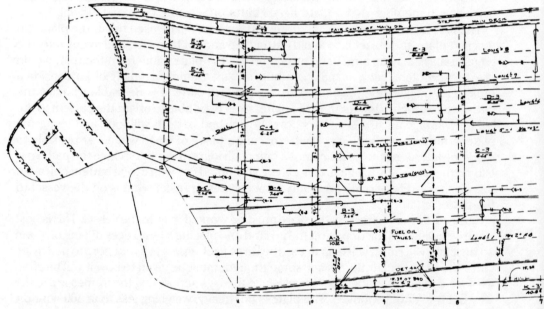

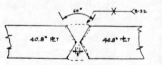

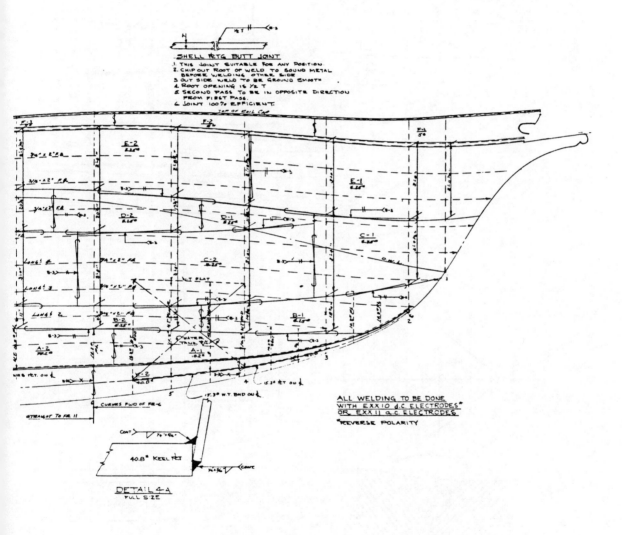

Figure 74. *The Shell Expansion Plan of a 40-foot schooner.*

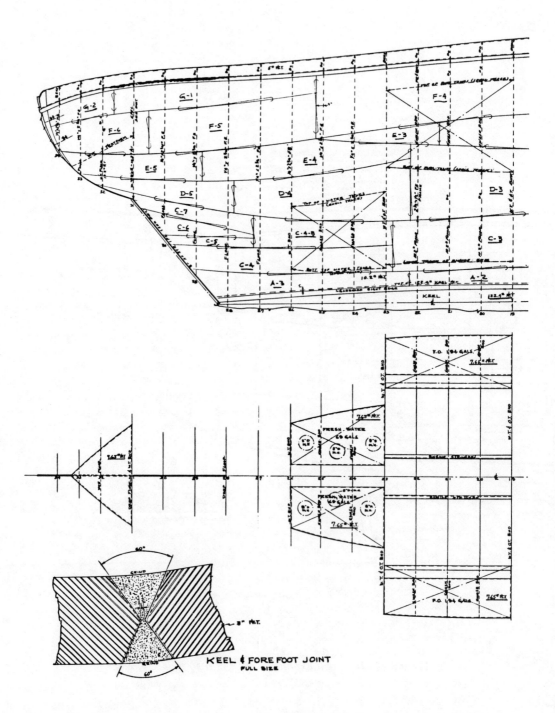

KEEL & FORE FOOT JOINT
FULL SIZE

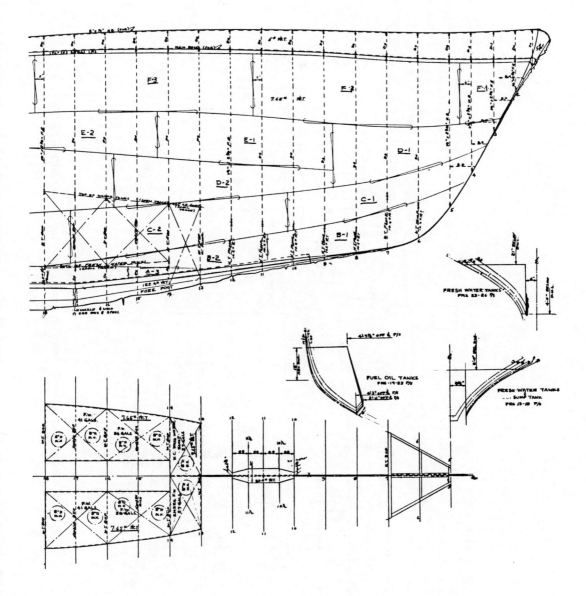

Figure 75. *The expanded shell plating of a 45-foot ketch.*

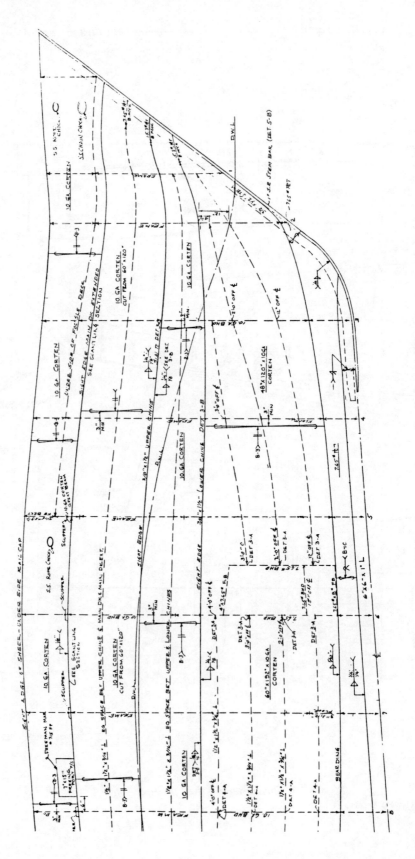
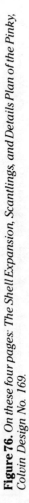

Figure 76. *On these four pages: The Shell Expansion, Scantlings, and Details Plan of the Pinky, Colvin Design No. 169.*

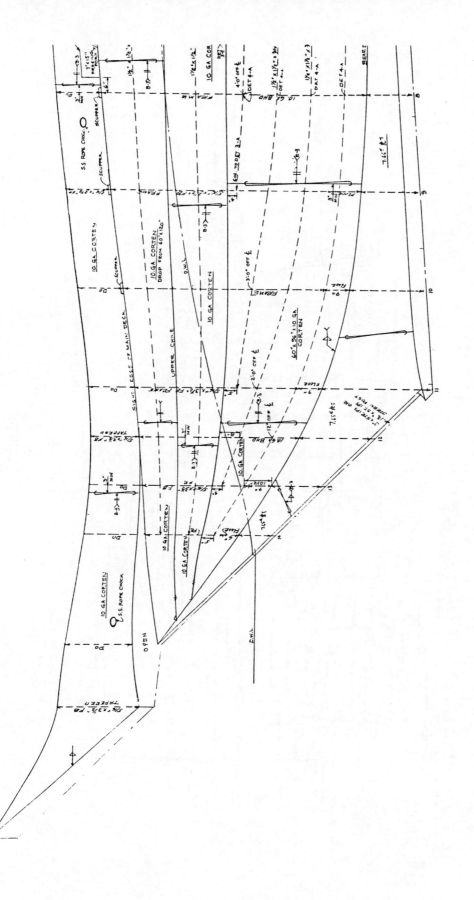

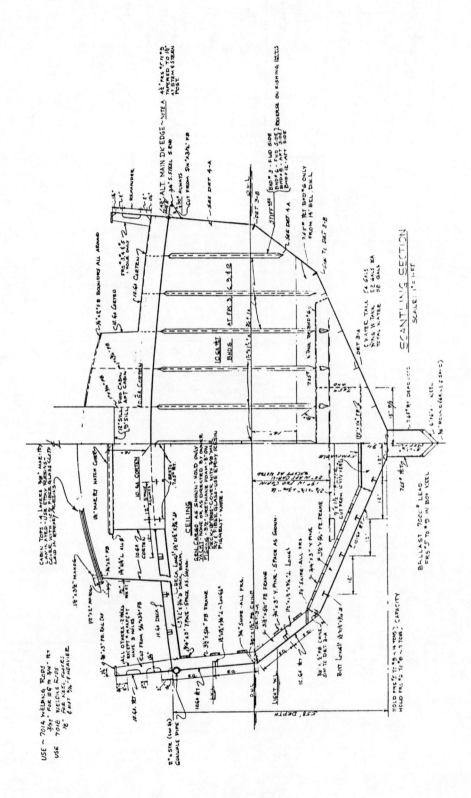

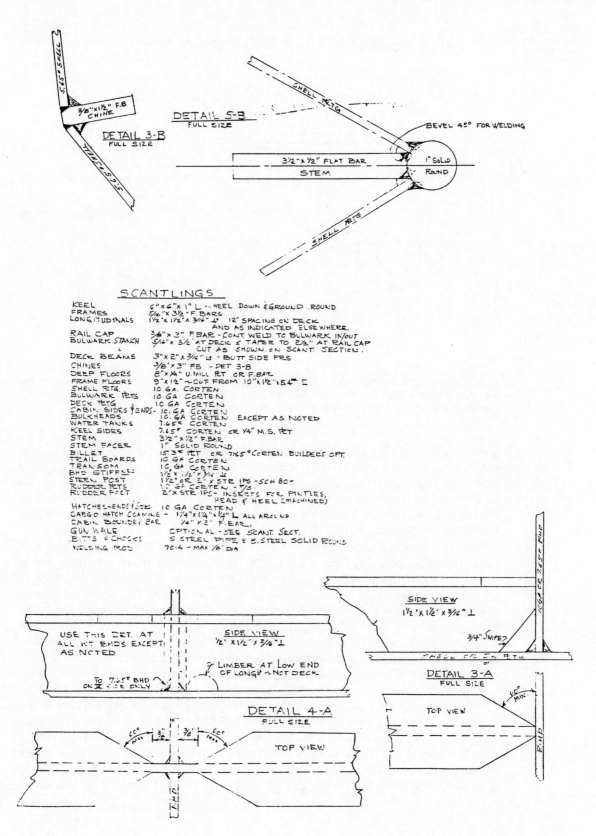

DETAIL 3-B
FULL SIZE

3/8"x1½" F.B.
CHINE

DETAIL S-B
FULL SIZE

SHELL PLTG

BEVEL 45° FOR WELDING

3½" x ½" FLAT BAR
STEM

1" SOLID
ROUND

SHELL PLTG

SCANTLINGS

KEEL   6"x6"x 1" L ~ HEEL DOWN & GROUND ROUND
FRAMES   5/16"x 3½" F. BARS
LONGITUDINALS   1½"x 1½"x 3/16" L   12" SPACING ON DECK
                                   AND AS INDICATED ELSEWHERE.
RAIL CAP   3/8"x 3" F.BAR - CONT. WELD TO BULWARK IN/OUT
BULWARK STANCH 5/16"x 3½" AT DECK & TAPER TO 2½" AT RAIL CAP
                                   CUT AS SHOWN ON SCANT. SECTION.
DECK BEAMS   3"x 2"x 3/16" L - BUTT SIDE FRS
CHINES   3/8"x 3" FB - DET 3-B
DEEP FLOORS   8"x ¼" U.MILL PLT OR F.BAR
FRAME FLOORS   9"x ½" ~ CUT FROM 10"x½"x84" C
SHELL PLTG.   10 GA. CORTEN
BULWARK PLTS   10 GA CORTEN
DECK PLTG   10 GA CORTEN
CABIN SIDES & ENDS 10 GA CORTEN
BULKHEADS   10 GA CORTEN EXCEPT AS NOTED
WATER TANKS   7.65# CORTEN
KEEL SIDES   7.65# CORTEN OR ¼" M.S. PLT
STEM   3½"x ½" F.BAR
STEM FACER   1" SOLID ROUND
BILLET   15.3# PLT OR 7.65# CORTEN BUILDERS OPT.
TRAIL BOARDS   10 GA CORTEN
TRANSOM   10 GA CORTEN
BHD STIFFNRS   ½"x ½"x 3/16" L
STERN POST   1½" OR 2"x STR IPS -SCH 80-
RUDDER PLTS   10 GA CORTEN - 7/8.
RUDDER POST   2"x STR IPS ~ INSERTS FOR PINTLES,
                                   HEAD & HEEL (MACHINED)

HATCHES ~ ENDS & SIDES 10 GA CORTEN
CARGO HATCH COAMING - 1/4"x 1¼"x ¼" L ALL AROUND
CABIN BOUNDARY BAR   ¼" x 2" F.BAR
GUN WALE   OPTIONAL - SEE SCANT. SECT.
BITTS & CHOCKS S.STEEL PIPE & S.STEEL SOLID ROUND
WELDING ROD   7014 - MAX 1/8" DIA

USE THIS DET. AT
ALL WT. BHDS EXCEPT
AS NOTED

TO 7.65# BHD
ON II SIDE ONLY

SIDE VIEW
½"x 1½"x 3/16" L

LIMBER AT LOW END
OF LONGL ~ NOT DECK

DETAIL 4-A
FULL SIZE

TOP VIEW

SIDE VIEW
1½"x 1½"x 3/16" L

¾" SNIPE?

SHELL OR 7.65 PLTG

DETAIL 3-A
FULL SIZE

TOP VIEW

E.HD

60°
MIN

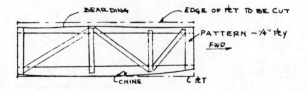

Figure 77. *The first plate-cutting pattern for the Pinky lying on the plate.*

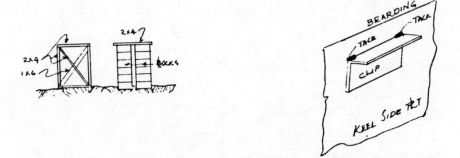

Left: Figure 78. *Two methods of building a support for the first plate when working it into position.* **Right: Figure 79.** *One of the clips tacked to the Pinky's keel side plate to support the inboard edge of the first plate when it is pulled into approximate position.*

and the outboard edge lifted using come-alongs. Next, the inboard edge is prized up until it touches the frame, at which time a few tacks to the keel will prevent the plate from dropping; finally, the outboard end can be lifted and secured to the frame. This method works best with heavier plating on vessels having very little fore-and-aft curvature to the bottom. Using this method, one must often cut loose the tacks at the keel after the final lift, should the plate not be snug against the frame.

Probably the most satisfactory method, especially when one is working alone, is either to build supporting frames approximately 3 inches below the bearding line in the way of each frame, or else to use concrete blocks with a 2 x 4 across their tops to come close to the height of the bearding in, say, three places. The supports, if used, need not be as wide as the plate; 3 feet long would be fine for the Pinky. Supports, having the advantage of light weight and easy portability, can be moved under the plate and from side to side. Unfortunately, they will be needed only once, so the time and material needed to build them must be considered. The concrete blocks already on hand would therefore seem to offer a good substitute. Figure 78 shows both methods.

Before bringing the plate under the hull and elevating it, weld a series of clips to the keel sides directly below each frame and bulkhead, and also midway between stations, setting them about 1½ inches below the bearding and parallel to it. Make the clips from scrap pieces of deck beam angle, cut in about 3-inch lengths. When welding to the keel sides, use a very short tack on each corner of the clip, on the top edge only; the long leg of the clip should face down. Figure 79 shows these clips.

With clips in place, work the plate under the hull to its approximate position and near, but not directly under, the keel. At either bulkhead 6 or frame 7, hook the come-along onto the hatch coaming, about 12 inches off the centerline, and if a second come-along is available, hook it to the longitudinal at 4 feet off the centerline. Lacking the come-along, one can use the twofold purchase instead. Hook the plate at both edges and lift. It will be impractical to make the complete lift all at once, since the bearding is about 4 feet above the ground, so lift the plate up about 2 feet, secure it, and clamp at the forward end of the plate near its center. Then, directly overhead, lay a 2 x 4 athwart the deck longitudinals, pass a line over it, and make it fast to the clamp. Lift and heave the plate end up until it is about level with the middle of the plate, and do the same at the aft end. Now continue the lift with the come-alongs, and when the plate nears the proper height, build up two columns of concrete block. After making the final bit of lift, slip in one or more 2 x 4s over the blocks and ease off until the plate rests on the 2 x 4s. Bring up the ends as before, but this time, about 2 feet in toward the centerline, build another pair of columns of concrete block, lay a 2 x 4 across, and rest the plate on it. Check that the columns are stable, and then release the come-along that was hooked onto the hatch coaming.

The inboard edge of the plate must now be pulled in toward the keel, but not closer than the edges of the clips, making sure the inboard edge is elevated so that it rests above every clip. This is done by adding shims on each of the 2 x 4s on the columns. If the plate hangs below any intermediate clips, then a 2 x 4 can be clamped to the keel near the clips in question, and the plate pushed upward (using the 2 x 4s) until it clears the clips. Using one or more pipe clamps sited near a frame and hooked to the keel side plate, ease the bottom plate toward the centerline until it touches the keel. The forward edge of the plate is the controlling reference, and must line up 3 inches from frame 4; move the plate forward or aft as needed to achieve this measurement.

The outer (upper) edge of the plate must now be lifted up to meet the chine bar. Move the clamps outboard as far as possible, but well clear of the chine, and set them up again. At the center of the outer edge of the plate, on the plate's outer side, clamp a short 2 x 4 lengthwise (one clamp), hook in either the come-along or purchase, and hoist the plate up as far as possible. Do the same at the ends. At this time the plate will be close enough that C-clamps can be used to seat the plate along its outboard edge. To provide a landing for the C-clamps, one must use short lengths of 2 x 4 resting on the chine and on top of at least one longitudinal. Initially, the C-

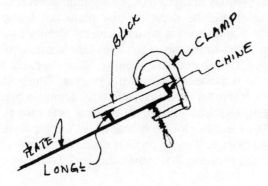
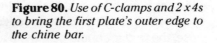

Figure 80. *Use of C-clamps and 2 x 4s to bring the first plate's outer edge to the chine bar.*

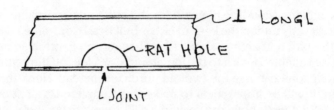

Figure 81. *A rat hole in a longitudinal in way of a butt joint in the plating.*

clamps will only be used to take the weight of the plate, so that the outboard hook of the purchase or come-along can be released.

At the forward edge of the plate on the 12-inches-off-centerline longitudinal, clamp the plate firmly to the longitudinal, but not so firmly that the plate will be unable to slide a bit. The forward edge must exactly meet the same mark from which the pattern was started. Now drive a wooden wedge at each of the clips—drive the ones at the frames hard, and follow up on the in-between clips until the plate is at the bearding. Wedging must begin at the forward end of the plate, and the wedges are all driven from the forward side of the clips so as to progressively smooth and lengthen the plate against the hull. If there is a gap between the plate and the bearding at the frames, the plate must be pulled closer to the centerline before hardening up on the wedges. When the plate comes home against the keel side plates, tighten the clamp to the forward inboard longitudinal, and then add clamps to the remaining longitudinals. Then, starting forward, bring the outer edge of the plate snug to the chine bar. If the number of available clamps is limited, use one near each frame or bulkhead until some of the others already in use become available. The aft end of the plate need only be clamped to the middle longitudinal at this time.

Prior to any welding, mark and cut in each longitudinal at the ends of the plate a ½- to ¾-inch-diameter half-hole (known as a "rat hole"), in order that the butt weld may be welded in its entirety. The plate should be dropped a bit so that it will not be scarred while the cuts are being made. This will be done at every butt joint in the vessel.

Tack welding of the plate to the hull may now commence, assuming that the plate fits the hull. The first weld is to the bearding, about 1 inch aft of the forward edge. At approximately 12-inch intervals, tack the edge of the plate to the bearding, as far as frame 5. The plate may not be found absolutely snug to all the longitudinals and to frame 5, and in any case, no welding should be done on any plate not firmly restrained from movement. The method employed is to use several shores that almost touch the plate, and to drive a wedge toward the centerline of the vessel until the plate bears firmly against all framing. The object here is not to lift the vessel (it can be done if you are careless), but to remove any sag in the plating. Figure 81 indicates how this would look. *Only one* frame bay is shored at a time. Should a gap occur which, in the builder's judgment, requires excessive wedging pressure to close, the wedge should be moved a bit, to another location near the offending area, and another attempt should be made to close it. If the gap still remains after several attempts, then it is best to ignore it for the present; that longitudinal will have to be

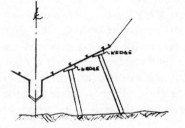

Figure 82. *Using shores and wedges to anchor a plate and remove any sag from it prior to welding.*

stretched later on. A gap on a frame or bulkhead cannot occur unless the longitudinal is set too low, and this must be corrected before proceeding by chipping away the tack weld and cutting the notch deeper.

When the longitudinal and transverse members of the bay fay against the plate, make a last check of the chine bar to assure its correctness. Then, working from the inboard edge of the plate outboard and from forward aft, tack weld the plate to all longitudinals. These tacks need not exceed ½ inch, and their spacing is immaterial, as they will be ignored when the final welding commences. When the chine is reached, tack weld the plate to the chine bar on the outside of the hull at approximately 6-inch intervals. Use this same sequence in each frame bay until the after end of the plate is reached. The last tack should not be closer than 1 inch to the end.

Now drive out the wedges between the clips and the plate. By hammering the upper flanges of the clips upward, one can break them away from the hull. Grind off the tack welds from both the hull and the clips, and set up the clips and blocks on the opposite side of the hull. Installation of the corresponding plate on the opposite side simply repeats the steps for the first plate. The pattern must be dismantled and refitted on the opposite side. Never assume that the two sides of a vessel are identical, for they seldom are, and an approximate fit is not close enough. Always aim for exactness. In a wooden vessel, you could have gaps like a picket fence and still caulk them, but welding rod and caulking cotton are two different things. The second plate will not be as easy as the first plate, because it is now necessary to climb in and out of the vessel to make adjustments and inspections previously done from the outside.

With the first two plates in place, the forward and after bottom plates can be added. The aft plates (two to a side) are the easiest to do, since the hull of a pinky presents no particular problems in the afterbody. Make the pattern for the first plate (which will be cut from a 60-inch by 96-inch plate). The butt joint must match the already-installed plate, but with the usual ¹⁄₁₆-inch gap between plates when the new one is set in place. Neglect this gap for the moment, however. Weld in the clips on the keel sides as was done previously for the other plates. Also cut several pieces of flat bar, 8 inches long. Align one of these with each longitudinal in the way of the joint between plates, then tack weld all of them to the outside of the already-fitted plate, projecting beyond its edge by about 3 inches so as to form clips to hold the new plate in position against the framing.

When scribing the plate for cutting, if at all possible retain the manufactured edge for the butt joint; cut and grind the other edges. Resetting the concrete blocks to elevate the plate will not be necessary now, because the clips will take their place. Lift the plate as before, but this time allow the forward end to droop a bit. The object is to elevate the plate until it will slide into the slot made by the clip extension at each longitudinal. Since the clips extend aft 3 inches, there will still be room for a C-clamp at each longitudinal, ahead of the plate, to hold it flush with the longitudinals. For clamping, one long 2 x 4 that spans all the longitudinals is easier to work with than several short 2 x 4s, each spanning just a pair of longitudinals. Use a similar 2 x 4 to clamp the after end of the plate.

At frame 10, under the hull but nearer the chine than the bearding, use a shore of the right length and wedge the plate snug against the frame. With a long pipe clamp, hook the lowest longitudinal and the outboard (upper) edge of the plate, and slowly ease the plate toward the centerline, making adjustments to the other clamps as necessary. Just before the plate meets the clips on the deadwood, the inboard hook must be released. This can be quite dangerous if the plate should slip; therefore, use several more temporary shores long enough to support the plate clear of the clips, then clamp the chine snugly and release the inboard lifting hook. *Never get under a loose plate.* At the chine, take up some more on the pipe clamp. (Two clamps are best, as the plate should go in evenly and not one end at a time.) Once the plate touches the keel, there is little danger of its falling, so the forward clamps can be released and the plate prized forward until it touches the forward plate. Drive the wedge at frame 9 snug, then snug up all the other wedges in turn; finally, snug up the clamps along the chine. The gap is now formed at the butt joint and all wedges are driven home. When tack welding this plate, follow the same procedure as before. Do not weld closer than 1 inch to the butt joint, and do not weld the butt joint itself. Make the pattern for the opposite plate, fit the plate in place, and tack weld to the vessel.

One of the DWL 2 x 4s is in the way of further plating and can now be removed in its entirety. Anytime a 2 x 4 interferes, remove it; if 2 x 4s are *not* in the way, let them remain until they are. The flat bar clips are repositioned to the aft end of the last plate fitted. Clips to the keel sides are tacked in place, and the aftermost plate fitted to the hull. Because of the curvature of the bearding, care must be exercised here, as an error of any magnitude in this area becomes greatly exaggerated. The tack weld spacing will be closed up to 4-inch intervals along the bearding. Note, though, that any extensive welding before both sides are on and even will pull the sternpost out of alignment. Prudence therefore dictates short weld increments at this stage.

PLATING THE FOREFOOT

The forward bottom plates are an area of doubt in all straight-framed vessels, especially those with a deep forefoot. The fastest way to determine whether there will be a problem is to offer up to the forefoot a solid sheet of ¼-inch ply that will be cut up for patterns. The question is: "Will it be necessary to strip-plate this area, or will one plate go on smooth?" Clamp the plywood sheet as close to the bearding as possible and also to the stem bar. The ply will naturally climb, but, unless the tendency is drastic, it need not be cut on this edge. At the frames and longitudinals, drill several holes and insert J-bolts or hanger bolts with the threaded ends outside the hull. Use generous washers under the nuts, and begin to tighten the bolts. At the areas where the ply will not snug, insert another bolt and tighten up. If the ply lies fair without buckling, then the steel plate will lie fair also. If there are buckles or the ply will not come home, however, the forebody will have to be strip-plated. In that case, it is necessary to determine how wide a strip will lie fair at the bearding line and also connect to the stem, as the worst twist will occur in this area. The first attempt for this size vessel would be an 18-inch strip. Cut it to fit the bearding, and then reduce its width until it will lie fair on all frames. Record the final, usable width, since all other strips used upward from this garboard plate will use the same dimension.

Assuming that strip-plating is required, make the pattern for the garboard and cut it from a plate; always use a manufactured edge for its *upper edge*. With both garboard plates in place and tacked, measure up and find the length of the next plate, taking into consideration that it will be longer than the garboard because of the stem. A pattern is not required for this, since the plate is small and light and can easily be clamped in place. The second plate will lap over the lower plate ¼ inch at both the stem and the after end. Let the middle fall where it will, since this is the amount of compound curvature in the plate. Securely clamp it in place, and mark the stem and stern cutoff lines. Also mark the first and last 8 inches of the lap on the inner face of the plate if the plate is to remain lapped; otherwise, mark the whole overlap, using the upper edge of the lower plate as the marking line.

There are two ways of treating the strip-plating. One is to let the plates lap as in a riveted structure, cutting only enough at each end to bring them flush with the aft plate and the stem. The other is to cut the entire edge of the second plate to match the first, so that the plating is flush with the lower plate. With 7.65-pound plating or lighter, the lapping method has many advantages. There will be less heat due to cutting—therefore less distortion—and the inside weld will be downhand at an angle, which is not only easy to see but makes for a perfect weld joint. Furthermore, the weld need not be completed until the final weld sequence is started. On the other hand, the outside weld will all be overhead and away from the centerline and therefore, at times, will require an awkward position for welding. The flush method involves a long cut on a narrow plate, and in spite of diligence, there will be a tendency for the plate to edgeset. It is then necessary to correct this set before the plate can be tacked to the vessel. Also, the seams will have to be continuously welded to at least a few inches aft of frame 2 as they are applied, since the area forward of this will be virtually inaccessible for welding once all the plates are on. (Welding is difficult in the bows of all vessels.) The advantage of the flush method is that it leaves the outside level, so the outside weld will be easier to make. At the beginning, the lap plates are quicker to assemble and the fitting almost nil; at the end,

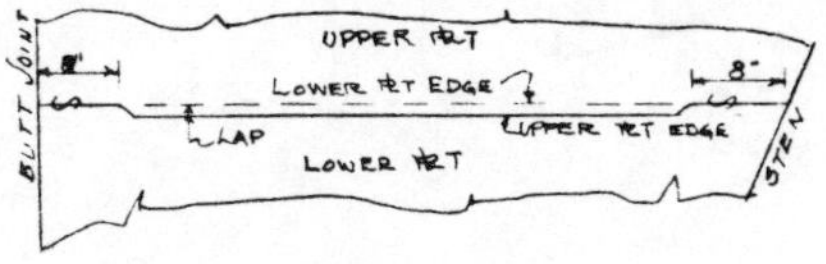

Figure 83. *The cuts on the ends of a lap plate.*

the welding is difficult. Thus, in actual sister vessels of this pinky design built at the same time, the difference in labor was nonexistent. The lap plating, however, has more strength. Figure 83 shows the cuts on the ends of a lap plate.

Whichever method is used, continue plating upward to the chine, tack welding to all the framing members. Transverse frames are welded on the aft side in the forebody and the forward side in the afterbody.

PLATING THE TOPSIDES

Now that the bottom is on, the topsides will be plated next, starting at the bow and continuing without skipping any plates. To each frame or bulkhead in the way of any plate to be offered up, clamp a short 2 x 4 and cant the outboard end upward to accept the lower edge of the plate. It helps to notch the 2 x 4 in way of the upper chine bar to bring it flush with the upper edge of the bar, so the plate will automatically assume the correct position to come home. The upper edge of the plate is gapped $\frac{1}{16}$ inch from the sheer pipe, and all butts are also gapped $\frac{1}{16}$ inch. The same type of butt clips used on the bottom plates at each longitudinal are also used on the topsides. All plates are worked from forward aft when tacking. One should make a template of wood to determine correctly whether the side plating is at the proper position (in or out) on the pipe. Side bracing to squeeze the plates tight to the framing is impractical; a movable prize bar, with a fixed hook on the lower end to catch the inside of the chine bar, will be easier and faster. Use a 2 x 4 on edge, about 4 feet long, as the prize, and then use a short 2 x 4 that can be slipped up or down the plating for the wedge. Pressure applied to the upper end of the prize is enough to hold the plate in place while the tack is being made to a longitudinal. Plate edges can be clamped in the normal manner. Figure 84 shows the prize as one would use it.

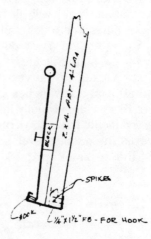

Figure 84. *A movable prize bar with which to snug a topsides plate to a longitudinal while a tack weld is made.*

PLATING THE DECK

The deck plating is next. The aft plating is laid first, starting with the centerline plate, then adding other plates from the centerline plate outboard to the deck edge pipe. Continue allowing a ¹⁄₁₆-inch gap (one-half the thickness of the plating) between plates and along the pipe, which also forms a seam. The bulwark stanchions will have to be removed to make the patterns and fit the plates (which explains why they were only tacked in place on the deck beam when the frame was on the platen); however, as soon as possible after fitting and tacking a plate, the stanchions should be replaced, trued, and welded.

Unlike the centerline plate, the outer plates cannot be worked with a rolling clamp. A lone worker will find that a couple of lead pigs will hold an outer plate down to the framing, provided they are set atop a scrap of wood that bears on the longitudinal or frame so as to concentrate their weight at that point; a helper standing on a block of wood could do the same thing. If 100 pounds or so is insufficient to bring the plate to bear, then the longitudinal has an unfair bend, and it is quite proper to shore this up a bit and apply some heat to the flange of the Tee so that it moves up to meet the plate. Before removing the shore, weld the Tee to the plating and let it cool. The cabin sides are not added at this time. Since they are straight lines, one need only allow for the thickness of their sides plus a gap.

The centerline plate on the foredeck is 7.65-pound plate, but not much thicker than the 10-gauge used for the remainder of the foredeck. This heavier plating eliminates the need for doublers in way of the bitts and windlass. The foredeck plating does not land on the pipe but on the bulwark plating. The bulwarks need not be in place, however, to lay the plates. After all foredeck plating is laid, transfer the frame marks to the upper side of the plate. Then with a long, square batten touching each of the marks, spring the batten into a fair curve. The deck edge is then scribed, cut, and ground smooth while in place. This is another instance where patterns need not be made. Note that none of the plating of the foredeck can begin until the fo'c's'le hatch has been cut, since there is no longer any access to this area. The Construction Drawing shows an oval hatch; however, the builder could elect to use some other shape.

THE BULWARKS AND TRANSOM

The bulwarks are plated next. Starting at the bow, work aft, paying attention to the scupper cutouts and the freeing ports. The foredeck edge is a floating one and will weld directly to the bulwark plates without a pipe, so the edge will need to be faired into a smooth sheer, since the cutting will cause some humps and hollows. It will be necessary to spring a batten around the deck, close to the bulwark, noting that all frame landings are correct. The humps are forced downward by clamping vertical stakes to the bulwark and driving them downward against the deck until the batten lies fair, and tacking at those spots. Hollows are driven upward by blocking against the topside longitudinal until the plate meets the batten. When the foredeck edge is fair, tack it to the bulwark plates at not more than 6-inch intervals, with very small tacks.

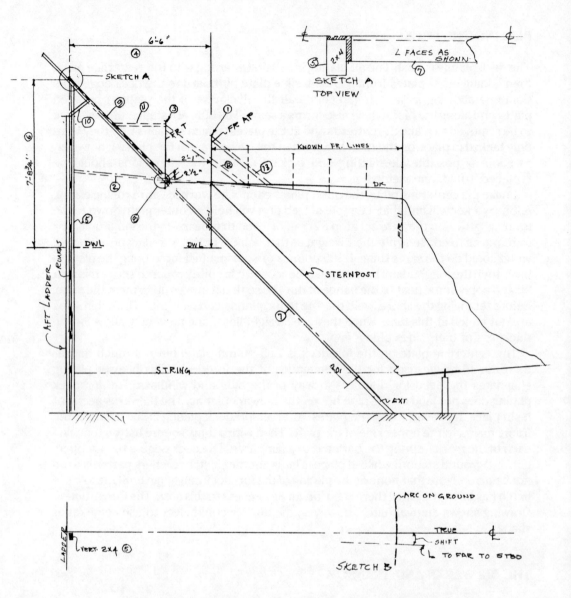

Figure 85. *A method for setting up the transom on the Pinky.*

The bulwarks present no particular problem until just aft of frame 11, where the bottom edge of the bulwark rolls outboard off the top of the pipe; up to that point its bottom edge coincides with the center of the top of the pipe. In itself this is not a difficult cut, but unfortunately, until now there has been nothing upon which to finish framing the hull, since the hull proper ends at the after perpendicular (AP), and the bulwarks overhang the base of the transom (T). Also, the transom still has to be fitted.

The transom is set up now, as shown in Figure 85. (The numbers in parentheses in the description that follows refer to numbers in the drawing.) The first step is to center and plumb the partial frame on the AP (1). When this frame was lifted from the platen, temporary bars were put in at the top and bottom to maintain the correct flare. The partial frame, AP, must be square to the only reference point above the deck that is accurate, which is the end of the cabin trunk at frame 11 (shown). It is tack welded to the top end of the sternpost, and since it is an after frame, its after edge is flush with the sternpost. The deck edge pipe was altered in the lofting, so this bottom piece will have to reflect that alteration where it will rest on the pipe. Tack two pieces of angle or T-bar (2) to the underside of the bottom of the temporary frame, one to port and one to starboard, running them aft to the after ladder. The T-bars or angles will be elevated on the ladder so that their top edges will provide a base for frame T when that frame is set in place. From the Lines Plan, it is noted that the offset height for the deck edge at the after end of the sternpost is exactly 3-0-1 (indicated), and its height at frame T is 3-2-5. Frame T (3) will be located 2 feet 1 inch aft of AP; therefore, in 2 feet 1 inch the T-bar or angle must rise 2½ inches (indicated). Again from the Lines Plan, it is determined that the end of the transom is 6 feet 6 inches aft of the AP (4). On the aft ladder, add a vertical 2 x 4 (5) on the flat with its inner edge clearing the centerline stick by the thickness of the leg of an angle (Sketch A) and having the prescribed distance from the sternpost at the deck. At a point 7 feet 8¾ inches up from the DWL mark (6) and 6 feet 6 inches aft of the AP, put the end of a length of angle (7) (it will have to be over 20 feet in length) with one leg pointing toward the aft ladder and the other leg pointing away from the centerline (Sketch A). The outer face of the leg pointing toward the aft ladder marks the true centerline of the vessel. The angle will of course slope downward and forward. The lower end of the angle should be pulled around and aligned with the centerline of the vessel, which can be done by sight alignment with the keel (Sketch B). Then, with a string, drop a plumb at several different heights along the angle, and carefully mark where it touches the ground. These points will form a straight line, which would intersect and coincide with the keel and the aft ladder's centerline stick if both were projected to the ground. If the lower end of the angle is incorrectly placed, a line drawn between the points just dropped will miss the centerline stick of the aft ladder. Adjust until this is correct and then secure firmly, after being assured that the upper flange of the angle intersects T at the correct height as marked by the two angles or T-bars that run back aft to the ladder (8).

Set the transom in place (9), the upper edge being exactly at the intersection of the angle at the top, and clamp it to the angle. Temporary pieces of wood (10) will be needed at the top about 6 to 8 inches off centerline to prevent the transom from twisting. Now frame T can be put in place and temporarily tacked to the transom. The temporary bottom and top bars of frame T will be cut away after the bulwarks are in place. In the meantime, T must be braced to the transom (11) and also to the deck (12). AP must be braced to the deck (13), since there will be some pressure exerted when the bulwark plate is pulled into place.

Now make a pattern that will extend the bulwarks from just aft of frame 13 all the way to the transom in one piece. A flexible batten will be required at both top and bottom after the pattern material is in place to get the correct curvature, for it will be noted on the Lines Plan that there is a sweeping curve to the upper and lower edge of the bulwarks aft of frame 13. After the patterns are made for each side, they should be checked, one against the other, and adjusted as necessary, because the upper and lower edges must correspond exactly as they pass beyond the hull. Bear in mind, however, that from frame 13 forward there may be discrepancies in the hull from side to side that must be accounted for in each pattern in order to assure a proper fit. On either side, add on a clip of angle to the lower edge of frame 14, with one leg up, running in line with the bulwarks and protruding outboard approximately 1 inch more than the frames. Do the same at frames AP and T. This will allow the last pieces of bulwark plating to rest and be moved. Fit the plates in place, allowing the necessary gaps at their butts to the forward plates. Since the forward edge of each of these plates is clear of the hull, a clamp between it and the last plate will hold the joint well enough at the bottom for tack welding. Clamp the top in also and tack weld it. There will be a slight bulge in the plate, and before tacking the rest of the joint, the bulge should be removed by clamping a shim behind a 2 x 4 over the seam, bringing the seam flush; then tack weld at about 4-inch intervals. When the plates come aft to the transom, clamp in the upper edges at frames 14, AP, and T. All of this should be checked one more time to make sure that these aft frames are still on the centerline of the hull. Now clamp and tack weld the transom to the bulwarks. Going forward, on the forward side of frame 14 and the forward sides of frames AP and T, tack weld the side frames to the bulwarks. All temporary bracing can now be removed except that which maintains the correct shape of frames AP and T.

THE CHINES

The last plates needed to complete the plating are the chine plates, often referred to as the "bilge plates." In my yard, they were called the *taint* plates: "'tain't topsides; 'tain't bottom; and 'tain't easy to clamp." The question arises as to why these plates were not installed immediately after the bottom plates, since they would then have been easier to clamp in place. There are a number of reasons for plating the chines last. First, the supports holding the hull do not have to be disturbed; second, good light and ventilation are provided in all compartments; third, the electrode wire need only be led in from one side, and the same holds true for the cutting torch; fourth, there is easy access to the interior of the vessel without having always to enter through a deck opening. A lone worker especially appreciates easy access, but even with more people working, open chines afford excellent communication from the inside to the outside of the vessel.

Before the hull can be closed up, the wooden legs that were shoring up the vessel must be replaced with shores under the bottom plating only. As long as the vessel remains exactly upright, there will be little pressure on these supports, as the three vertical I-beams carry all the weight. Thus, three supports per side will be quite enough, made from 2 x 4s and sited near frames 5, 7, and 9. Set them as far outboard as possible, but landing on longitudinals. Also needed will be six pieces of deck beam angle, about 6 inches long apiece. Tack weld them to the bottom, with the toe of the long leg up and the flange down (*not* flat against the hull—see Figure 86). Using a

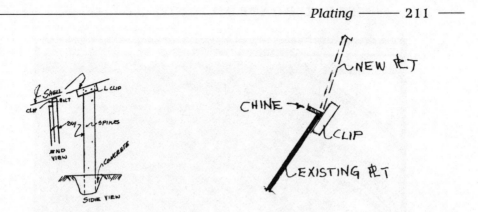

Left: Figure 86. *One method of placing supports beneath the vessel's bottom plating.* **Right: Figure 87.** *A flat-bar clip welded to the lower chine to provide support for the chine plate.*

temporary shore, determine the most normal line for welding each clip. At frame 7, the clips will be exactly square to the centerline, while at frame 5 the inboard edges will toe aft, and at frame 9 the inboard edges will toe a bit forward. When these have been tacked onto the bottom plates, dig holes immediately below, and cut the 2 x 4s to length, giving each one a top bevel matching the angle of the bottom. When each support is plumb in all directions, clamp it to the angle. When all six supports have been cut and clamped in place, fill the holes with cement, keeping in mind that some soils will require larger holes and sometimes also the addition of a bearer plate to resist any downward loads. Trowel the cement smooth on top. After it has hardened, cut six more 2 x 4s that will fit exactly between the concrete and the lower flanges of the angles. Drill two holes in the long leg of each angle and bolt the long shore to it; then spike the short shore to the long one as shown in Figure 86.

Remove all DWL 2 x 4s, all other shores, and all bracing; next, clear the interior of everything that does not belong there. Set the chine longitudinal in place, making the appropriate cut at each bulkhead, and tack weld it to each frame and bulkhead. Starting at the bow, make the pattern for the first plate and set it in place. At each frame, weld a short piece of flat bar onto the lower chine, with its outer edge protruding from the hull an inch or so, and angled upward a bit in order to support the plate in approximate position. At frame 1, an additional piece of flat bar projecting downward from the topside plate will be needed. Insert the plate at frame 1 and prize it forward until it meets the bearding at the stem. Clamp the plate to the longitudinal at its after end. Cut several clips, using scrap deck beam angle and cutting off the long leg of each clip to make it measure 1¼ inches deep (this gives a finished angle of 1¼ inches by 1½ inches). These clips will be used on the inside of the plate to snug it to the longitudinal as well as to position it correctly between the chines. Inside the vessel, weld the short leg of one clip to the plate at about the center of each frame bay, with its axis fore-and-aft, close to but not touching the longitudinal. Select a short length of 2 x 4 that will rest on the chine and the longitudinal, and clamp it to the elevated leg of the clip. A short piece of blocking may be needed at the chine to

Figure 88. *Sketch of a hull ready to be moved out of the shop for sandblasting and priming. All welds have been ground smooth. After blasting, the hull will be a uniform grey color. Blasting must be stopped at frequent intervals so that the surface may be primed before a rust bloom forms. Note that the DWL is struck, and this has been marked by centerpunching at frequent intervals so that the line can be reestablished prior to the finished color and antifouling coats. The narrow plates forming the forebody were required because of the hull's compound curvature.*

elevate the 2 x 4 enough to clear the clip. Snug up the clamps and, by sighting along the chines, try to get the plate positioned correctly. Once satisfied, snug up the clamps a bit more, then go outside and check to be sure that the plate is indeed correct. Tack weld the plate to the stem and then, alternating between the chines, tack the plate to the chines. Return inside and tack the plate to the longitudinals and to the after side only of the frames. Do the same on the other side.

Repeat this procedure with the next pair of plates, which will close up the vessel to just aft of frame 9. Then skip a plate and install the aftermost pair of plates, which will close up the stern; these are short plates, the forward edges of which are slightly aft of frame 12. This procedure is followed because the ends of the vessel are always the most difficult areas to plate. Once these plates have been tack welded in place, the last (closer) plates can be made and set in place. These are fitted between frames 9 and 12. This time, however, additional clips must be added at the longitudinal at each end of the opening on the already-positioned plates, because the plates prevent any clamping, and the closer plates will have to be dropped into place and held up by the lower clips.

With these plates tacked in place, the vessel is completely plated. The methods I have used in applying the plates to this hull would not necessarily be followed on a hull of a different design. I stress again that every hull is different—even sister ships—and what works on one does not always work on another. Nevertheless, what I have outlined is the method of applying plating to one of the more difficult hull forms. You will discover early on in the building of any vessel that when one thing does not work, something else will. It may try your patience at times, but let me assure you that there is always a solution.

13

▽

CABIN TRUNKS,
RAILCAP,
AND
WELDING

The remaining primary above-deck steelwork on the Pinky includes the cabin trunk sides, the railcaps, the cabintop boundary bars, the foremast partner plate, and the fo'c's'le hatch trunk. Once these are on, the finished welding can commence. In small shipyards with several welders working on the same hull, much of the finished welding would already have begun. Working alone, it is better to get everything out of the way and then do the finished welding all at one time. That way, one can take advantage of the weather, since a temporary tent or awning suspended above the deck makes it possible always to keep working somewhere on the vessel.

THE RAILCAP

The Scantling Plan shows that the railcap is a ⅜-inch by 3-inch flat bar, the top of which is parallel to the DWL, with its outboard edge welded to the bulwarks. This particular hull is not bluff-bowed; therefore, with a little patience, the bar can be bent directly on the hull. On fuller-bowed vessels, the first third of the hull would have to be bent on the ground to the approximate athwartship curve, then further bent on the vessel, taking into account the vessel's sheer. In large vessels, however, the railcap would have been another of the patterns picked up from the mold loft floor, expanded in both directions (sheer and half-breadth). The railcap takes a miter at the stem joint. To keep the bar elevated for this operation, clamp a 2 x 4 to the cabin trunk, resting atop the bulwark plate and extending far enough outboard of the bulwarks to hold the bar up; a second 2 x 4 clamps to frame 5 in like manner. The tack welds to the bulwark plate go on at about 6-inch intervals, with the twofold purchase hooked to the bar and to the hull well aft of the tack welder, to bring the bar gradually in. The tacks can be about 1 inch in length, since they have a double purpose—

namely, to attach the bar to the bulwarks, and to heat the edge so it will stretch. Keep some tension on the purchase at all times, but not too much; overtightening will capsize the bar, making it go edge-up or kink. If there is undue resistance in walking the railcap around, some additional heat will have to be applied on the outboard edge, evenly over about a 12-inch length, and with the heat gradually built up toward the inboard edge opposite where the next tack will be. A short pipe clamp hooked under the deck-edge pipe and onto the railcap will pull the cap downward. At times, the clamp will jump off, so a C-clamp is then used to hold the pipe clamp in place, with the screw end of the C-clamp always inside the bulwarks.

As the 2 x 4 supports are neared, remove them so the bar will not be restrained from resting on the bulwarks. With the forward bar tacked in place, start again at the stern, this time working forward. In the beginning, and until frame 11 is reached, the pull is outboard, which means the inboard edge of the railcap must be heated, rather than the outboard edge. Using a pipe clamp, pull the railcap downward from the bottom of the bulwark as required. Again, the tack welds will be closely spaced, each about an inch long. These welds constitute part of the finished welding, unlike the ones used in shell plating (which are truly not much more than spot welds). When this bar is in place, fit the required midsection piece to finish that side. This is another instance in the building of metal vessels where one may depart from the standard practice of working both sides at once. Repeat the procedure on the opposite side.

THE TRUNKS

The next focus of attention is the forepeak trunk. If built square or rectangular, it will be constructed similarly to the cargo hatch. One may either build it on the workbench and then set it in place as a finished subassembly (the easier method), or construct it on the vessel. Either way, the top inside edges of the trunk will be provided with an inward-facing lip to catch the flange of whatever type of hatch is used.

Next, the cabin trunks. Starting with the forward trunk, use patterns to make the sides, and then install them. At frame 4, port and starboard, cut a notch in the deck beam deep enough to allow the side plate to drop into position, for the plate's lower edge is 2 inches below the deck for its full length. When in place, tack weld the tops and bottoms of the sides to the cabin ends, and make several small tacks as required to fix the end joints in the correct position. Lay a batten along the sides of the trunk and check that the run of the deck in way of the trunk is a fair curve, elevating or depressing any area that offends, then tack weld the deck to the cabin trunk sides. At frame 4, add a diagonal brace on either side, from near the top of the trunk to the deck, to assure that the correct tumblehome is maintained.

The 19½-inch-wide foremast partner plate is added to the top by tacking the centerline of the plate to the centerline of the forward end of the cabin, then working the plate toward the edges of the trunk with closely spaced tacks. When close to the sides, scribe, cut, and grind the ends of the partner plate for a snug fit, and tack weld again at short intervals along the outboard edges of the plate.

The boundary bars are added next. Since the cabintop will be laminated marine plywood (four layers of ⅜-inch ply) bolted to the boundary bars, it will save time if, after all the bars have been cut to length, the bolt holes for the cabintop are drilled before tack welding the bars in place. The cabintop will be applied after sandblasting and prime painting (see Chapter 15). A drill press offers the easiest and fastest method of drilling the holes. In any case, do this job down on the bench to keep filings from dropping into the hold or onto the deck. The bolts are spaced on 4-inch centers at the half-width of the bar. Choose a bolt size (¼-inch or ⁵⁄₁₆-inch), and drill the holes slightly oversize so that neither the galvanizing on the bolt nor the paint in the holes will be harmed. Weld the boundary bars on the top edges only at this time, using an adjustable wrench as a clamp-on lever to elevate or lower the inboard edges in the way of the welds until they make the same angle with the sides of the cabin as they do at the cabin ends. This maintains the correct crown. The aft boundary bar takes the same slope as the fore-and-aft centerline of the cabin.

Following the same procedure described for the forward cabin, the aft cabin trunk sides are now added, with a boundary bar all around them. Diagonal braces will be required at frames 9 and 10 to maintain the correct tumblehome of the sides.

The 1¼-inch by 1¼-inch by ¼-inch angles around the top edge of the cargo hatch will be the last primary steel pieces to be measured and cut, but will not be fitted until the cargo hatch itself has been completely welded, inside and out. Before proceeding further, make three temporary ladders for access to the after cabin, cargo hold, and forward cabin. When needed, the forepeak ladder will be constructed of steel, and permanently installed at that time. Finally, cut the remaining ports in the cabin trunks and grind the edges smooth.

WELDING THE HULL INTERIOR

The finished welding of the inside of the hull may now begin. With the exception of butt joints, no welding is done outside unless that entire area has already been welded inside. Before doing any welding, take time out to review the types of weld called for, along with any notes on the plans that might prove useful for future reference.

Unless otherwise specified, tables 8 and 9 (Chapter 5) show the weld sizes and spacings to use. The Pinky is built like a battleship, and her transverse and longitudinal framing are such that in no area is there as much as 4 square feet of unsupported shell plating. Thus, for longitudinals, the weld will be modified to a ⅛-inch fillet, 1 inch long, at 12-inch intervals staggered from one side of the Tee to the other. Note that the 1-inch measurement means there is a full 1 inch of weld metal of the correct fillet size, and does not take into account the starting and stopping of the weld, which, if measured, would increase the length. In way of the floors, increase the increment length to ³⁄₁₆ inch by 1½ inch by 8 inches, staggered.

The never-ending difference of opinion as to which is better—building right side up or upside down—can be more or less resolved in favor of the former, since there is more welding on the inside than there is on the outside of the vessel. Right-side-up construction, needless to say, makes inside work easier—and all inside welding of an area must be finished before the opposing outside welds can be made.

The welding of the keel to the keel side plates can commence at any convenient place, the only stipulations being that no more than one-third of the length of a rod (electrode) should be deposited at a time, no weld segments should be spaced closer than a rod length apart, and both sides should be welded at the same time. Between bulkhead 3 and frame 4, the stem bar enters and rides on the main keel section. On this joint it is customary to use one-half a rod length at a time, making sure the opposite side is also welded in the same area to keep the stem bar from warping. Also at this time, weld the deep floors to the keel sides on both sides of the frames and bulkheads. A downhand pass is acceptable using ⅛-inch-diameter rods; however, if a vertical-up weld is used (which is preferable), switch to a ³⁄₃₂-inch-diameter rod.

It is customary to weld the longitudinals to the bottom plates first, port and starboard, then the chine longitudinal, port and starboard, followed by the topside longitudinal, port and starboard. The deck longitudinals are worked from the centerline outboard, alternating from side to side if the area is completely decked, or one side at a time elsewhere. Only one frame bay is worked at a time, always away from the midship section towards the ends, and outboard away from the centerline.

After all the longitudinals have been welded in place, start back through the hull. This time, make a finished weld on each frame to each longitudinal, and at the same time weld the frame to the shell. Weld on the aft side of the frame in the forebody, and on the forward side of the frame in the afterbody. When a bulkhead is reached, a series of short welds can be made, about 2 inches in length, on the midship side only. Frame welds should be 1 inch long at each notch, that is, at each terminal point of the

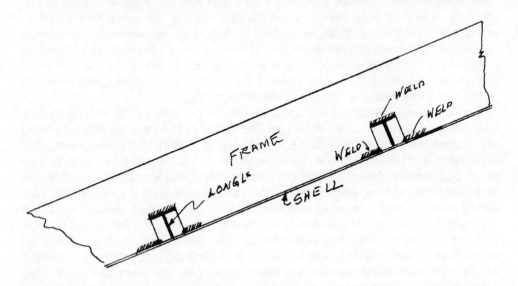

Figure 89. *Each longitudinal is welded to every frame it passes through, and at the same time the frame is welded to the shell plating on either side of the notch cut for the longitudinal. When this welding is completed, each frame segment between cuts will have two welds to the shell. The welds are 1 inch long.*

frame; thus, there will always be two welds for each segment of frame that touches the shell plating.

The continuous welds can now commence in the cargo hold. Starting from frame 7, weld the bearding to the shell plate, using one-third of a rod, skipping the length of a rod plus the weld increment, then laying down another one-third of a rod, and so forth, until bulkhead 8 is reached. Return to frame 7 and repeat on the opposite side of the vessel. Again return to frame 7 and do the same, working toward bulkhead 6. Then go up to the lower chine and repeat the sequence for the bottom plate only. Weld the chine plate to the top of the lower chine and the bottom of the upper chine, but stop one rod length from the butt weld 3 inches aft of bulkhead 6. Work alternately from side to side of the vessel. The top of the upper chine and the deck-edge pipe are now welded to the topside plate, following the same procedure as before, only this time stopping about one-half a rod length from the butt in the topside plating. Starting at the bearding, repeat the whole process, continuing the previous welds in that particular compartment, employing (as usual) a back-step method.

After the third series of welds, the welding will be complete, except in the way of the butt joints. Now weld the butt joints with a downhand pass, since the material is thin and the rod is of medium penetration. Do not use more than one-third of a rod at a time, making the same skips as in the unbutted seams, and skipping from one side of the hull to the other after each segment is deposited, allowing the plates to cool prior to additional welding. When each butt joint is completely finished and cooled, the same welds will be made on the outside.

The outside butt joints require cleaning-up in preparation for welding. Using the edge of the grinder, open the seams a bit, until they look more like a U than a V. The grooves should be deep enough to reach the roots of the inside welds and to guarantee sound metal throughout. Should slag, other inclusions, or a void be encountered, chip out and repair. Always wire brush the whole seam prior to making a weld. With such light plating, a downhand pass should always be used, in short increments, skipping from one butt joint to the opposite one. Skipping from one side of the hull to the other is laborious, but also essential.

The sequence of welding is important because of the potential for cracking in the weld joint itself due to metal shrinkage. The *length* of the weld shrinks very little; shrinkage occurs *across* the weld. Thus, if a butt joint meets a longitudinal seam after the longitudinal has been fully welded, the tendency will be to pull together the two plates that are being welded, causing a crack to start in the longitudinal weld, which in turn will propagate up into the plate. The reason for using short increments is that during welding, which is really a casting process, the molten metal causes the adjacent plates to expand and then to shrink upon cooling. The plate as cut and the plate as welded are always of two different dimensions. In other words, after an entire edge has been heated, the plate will be just a little bit larger than it was before. Keeping the heat-affected zone to a minimum lessens the swelling and shrinkage. As a general rule—and this applies to bulkheads and other members as well—where a continuous longitudinal weld is to be made, then any transverse welds intersecting the chines, bearding line, and deck-edge pipe should be made first, which is why the inside longitudinals were left unwelded in the way of the butt joints. These welds are completed at this time.

WELDING THE OVERHEAD

A builder usually refers to the underside of the deck as the "overhead" when he is down inside the vessel. The overhead is welded next. Start on the centerline and work outboard, welding the deck to the longitudinals, using the same sequence as on the bottom. The longitudinal seam is welded next. This seam could be considered partially restrained due to the proximity of the cargo hatch, but treat it as if it were unrestrained, and likely to go somewhere when heated. When one is making overhead welds, the weld position dictates that only one-fourth of a rod should be burned at any one time, in order to reduce the heat-affected zone. A seam weld will not cause as much distortion as a butt weld; however, all welding tends to shrink the vessel in all directions. I cannot stress enough the use of good judgment, as it is always preferable to eliminate or minimize distortion rather than have to correct it later.

With the completion of the longitudinal seam, the hatch ends and bulkheads may be welded. The hatch ends will, of course, be completed sooner than the bulkheads, so one can weld along the hatch sides at the same time he is completing the bulkheads. On bulkheads 6 and 8, once the increments have reached the pipe, one should weld the deck longitudinals between frame 5 and bulkhead 6, and bulkhead 8 and frame 9, to prevent any tendency for the plate to shrink on the bulkheads. Lastly, weld the underside of the deck to the deck-edge pipes.

I would advise welding the bearding line to completion before proceeding with the remainder of the shell welds. Avoid, however, welding the bearding in way of the butt joint just aft of frame 4, or, if working aft, the butt joints just forward of frames 9 and 12.

The welding now shifts to the next compartment either forward or aft, which will be completed in its entirety before the welder moves elsewhere. Remember that the welding always proceeds away from the midship section and toward the ends of the vessel. Work the plating toward the butts, and, as before, weld the butt joints on both sides prior to finishing the longitudinal welds that cross them. In large vessels that have numerous seams and butts, standard welding sequences are followed. In small vessels, however, builders normally use the largest plates available, since this reduces the labor and cost of plating the vessel. Welding procedures must be modified accordingly. By the time a builder is ready to weld up the shell, he has a feel for that particular vessel's behavior and how things need to be done in order to live with her. No two vessels are exactly alike, even sister ships, as any sailor or ship master will attest.

By this time the builder has crawled in and out of the forepeak enough to know the most convenient way, and has, in all probability, taken into account which way the hatch will open. Thus, he can now build the ladder. If the vessel will spend most of its time in the tropics, where crews customarily go barefoot, the ladder should be made of flat bar stock with either solid round bar rungs or, better yet, pipe rungs. In large ships, square bar is used instead of round bar, often set with one corner up rather than flat. In spite of the extra cost, consideration should be given to making the ladder of stainless steel, since this will eliminate painting. When designing a vessel, the designer suggests where the ladder might go and also what slope it might have, but should the builder perceive that another arrangement would work better, he should feel free to make that change. This might seem obvious, but some builders *do* just blindly follow the plans, regardless of the fact that with a bit of imagination they could modify the arrangement by a few inches here or there to make it more convenient or useful.

BULKHEADS AND CABIN CORNERS

The peripheries of all structural and water tank bulkheads facing *away* from the midship section now remain to be welded. These welds always cause some distortion to the shell plating and show up on the outside as "hard" spots, which are not usually objectionable in the underwater portion of the hull, but are unsightly on the topsides and deck. In a properly welded vessel, the distortion will be slight, amounting to perhaps $\frac{1}{1000}$ inch, which can be smoothed out later by sanding; however, sanding cannot cure gross distortion. This distortion occurs because the plating shrinks toward the weld, and on the far side of a bulkhead there is nothing to restrain this movement, since the hull diminishes continuously toward the ends; at the same time, on the midship side of the frame, the hull is increasing, and the plate shrinks tighter against the frame or bulkhead. Use downhand passes where possible, and keep the legs of the welds as close to size as possible, remembering that there is also a weld on the opposite side of the bulkhead. The water tank is the exception; since its material is 7.65-pound plate, the weld can have unequal legs, with the smaller leg to the shell plating. The tank top is not put on at this time.

The insides of the cabin trunks may be welded now, after which the builder will be welding only on the outside of the vessel. The boundary bars take an ordinary continuous weld. The cabin corners, however, take a special weld: the legs of the weld need to be about twice the thickness of the plate, because, after the outside weld is made, the corners will be ground to a small radius. This broad weld can be accomplished either downhand or vertical-up. In either case, when using E-7014 rods, one must make the weld in a single pass, using a weaving motion across the corner from one side to the other, dwelling a bit in the corner on each zig or zag. It is important to keep the weld zone fluid but not liquid. In the case of a downhand weld, the entire welding rod can be consumed at one time. A larger diameter rod ($\frac{1}{8}$ inch) could also be used.

WELDING THE HULL EXTERIOR

The outside welding may start either with the deck or the hull proper, since neither way has any special advantage. When building outside during the rainy season, finishing the decks first would make more sense because it would minimize contamination of the seams from rainwater. Starting with the decks, then, first complete all seams, working from side to side and forward and aft, doing a bit at a time on all seams rather than concentrating on one seam. Next work the transverse joints, and at frame 5, where the main deck joins the fo'c's'le deck, go ahead and work both at the same time. Upon reaching the bulwarks, weld the frame to them. The final welds on the deck are the longitudinal welds alongside the cabin trunks, to the deck-edge pipe on the main deck, and from the deck to the bulwarks on the foredeck. On the foredeck, make the weld segments at the same time to both the deck edges and the cabin trunk, working from aft to the stem and alternating from side to side. Although there is less danger of the vessel being pulled out of shape now, it is still good practice to keep going from side to side after completing each segment; in doing so, start the segments on the boundary bars.

On the main deck, the deck-edge pipe is welded to the deck bulwarks at the same time that the deck is welded to the pipe, but not in the same area. In way of the aft cabin trunk, weld all three seams at the same time—that is, the edge of the cabin, the edge of the deck, and the edge of the bulwark, and also the boundary bar as the opportunity arises. Before attending to the bulwarks, stanchions, and railcap, complete the outside cabin corner welds and grind them, first smooth and then with a radius. Weld the cargo hatch coaming corners inside and out, in the same manner as the cabin trunks. Weld the boundary angles continuously, top and bottom, to the coaming, rounding the corners as shown on the Construction Plan, and then grind them smooth. While the grinder is on deck, also grind smooth and slightly round the boundary bars on the cabin trunks, remove the support legs to the cabin sides, and grind their tack welds smooth, both on the cabin sides and also on the deck.

Ignoring deck seams and butts, inspect all other pieces welded on, and all other edges, rounding any edges that may have been missed. Sharp corners will not hold paint, and they endanger everyone who comes in contact with them, especially the crew with watersoaked skin.

Weld the underside of the railcap and the bulwark stanchions in their entirety. Cutouts in the stanchions (see Figure 76) relieve the builder from having to continuously weld the entire length of the stanchions on both sides, thus causing distortion. On exposed weather surfaces, intermittent welding is unacceptable, as any crevice will, in the long run, start to rust, and to keep these areas free of dirt, salt crystals, and rust is a never-ending task. Some builders resort to a filling compound of one sort or another, but this makes a poor substitute for proper welding, which will last the life of the vessel. Therefore, weld all around those portions of the stanchion that contact the deck, railcap, or bulwarks, including their sides and ends.

Nearing the after perpendicular, once again check the overhanging stern section for alignment with the vessel. At this time it helps to tack weld a series of bars from rail to rail to restrain any independent movement of the bulwarks while welding. The transom takes the same type of weaving corner treatment as the cabin corners. The cap that crosses the transom is best made from solid round, either ¾ or 1 inch diameter, since a flat bar in this area has a poor weld joint on the forward face, which will always give trouble. The center of the transom has a notch to accept the boom when the sail is lowered; thus, the transom also serves as the gallows frame. The cap bar will take a lot of banging and scraping, which will cause the paint to chip; therefore, it would be prudent to make this bar from stainless steel. Weld it in place, letting it extend to the bulwark sides and welding the railcap to it rather than to the transom. The outboard end wants to be well rounded. When the bulwarks are finished, all the outside welding to the hull can commence.

The best procedure now is to work one level at a time, thereby eliminating the need for having to move the scaffolding out of the way and reset it for the next segment of welding. On the Pinky Schooner, high scaffolding will be needed for the railcap and the upper side of the pipe, a lower level for the underside of the pipe and upper chine, and so on. The secret to good welds, aside from skill, is that the welder should always be in a comfortable position so that minimum fatigue is incurred. The arrangement of scaffolding necessary for working the steel into place seldom suits finished welding, which requires prolonged periods in one position.

Since the scaffolding is already in place for fitting the railcaps, it is in order to start high and weld the outside edges of the railcap, also welding the bulwarks to the deck-edge pipe. Working from amidships toward each end, use one-half a rod at a time, and skip two lengths of a rod before making the next weld. At the scuppers, make sure the outside weld wraps around the edges of the plate and connects to the inside weld, eliminating the end crevice. Both sides of the vessel should be worked at the same rate of weld metal deposit. It is possible, of course, to climb over the deck and pull the electrode cable from one side to the other, since the Pinky is a small vessel. A better procedure, however, would be to pull the cable under the hull and up the other side, stopping on the way to make the finished outside welds of the bearding and the keel to the keel side plates. Since the welding electrode for the keel is ⅛ inch diameter and that for the bearding is 3⁄32 inch, rather than change the amperage on the machine, finish the bearding weld first, then do the opposite side of the railcap and deck-edge pipe. On the way back, reset the amperage and do the keel, then reset the amperage for the smaller electrode and repeat the process. In this way, excessive heat to the keel side plates is avoided.

Using a welding rod for measurement of weld deposit and spacing rather than measuring these in inches or feet has a decided advantage, because it automatically takes into account the condition of the joint. A poorly fitted joint will consume a given length of rod in a very short space, and will limit the propagation of heat. A good fit, on the other hand, will allow the same amount of rod segment to go farther, with the same amount of heat input to the plate. A welding rod is the most convenient measuring device a welder has. Never forget that a welder should have a shield and gloves and, in all probability, a leather jacket to deflect the sparks, and also (when working on scaffolding) a bag of extra electrodes and a chipping hammer. Draped over his shoulder is the electrode cable with the electrically "hot" holder attached to its end. Reaching for a measuring tape can be quite awkward under these circumstances.

Numerous tack welds have been made on the outside of the vessel in the areas that must now be welded. These should be ground flush with the plating and then grooved to accept a continuous weld. Indeed, *all* joints must be opened by edge-grinding to assure that the new welds will be made to sound metal and not to slag entrapments or voids. Before making any weld, wire brush each joint to guarantee its cleanliness. If this is always done, it soon becomes second nature. Large yards employ quality-control groups, inspectors, foremen, and welding leaders, all trying to make sure that everything is done correctly. In the small yard, quality—like everything else—is an individual effort, and neglect and carelessness cheat only that individual.

Upon completion of the railcap welding, grind the whole joint smooth and round it over as required to finish it. Remove the temporary restraints welded aft of the after perpendicular, and grind that area smooth as well.

When welding the upper or lower chines, make the upper and lower welds of each at the same time, treating them as single joints. Skip in the welding from top to bottom on the bar, depositing about one-half rod per two rod lengths and always employing the back-step method. After completing all welding, grind smooth the exterior butt joints and the chines, rounding the latter slightly. For a yacht finish, it is desirable to finish sand and polish these areas. On many commercial vessels, these welds are neither ground nor sanded, since this beautifying means extra labor that improves only the vessel's appearance (to some eyes), and not its usefulness.

TESTING THE WELDS

The time has come to test the welds. The welding industry employs numerous methods—X-ray of all joints, penetrating dyes, and high-pressure water hoses, among others. In my yard we most often used light. This method requires two people and a dark night: one person inside the vessel with a light, and the other on the outside with a soapstone and a small hammer. The inside person systematically moves up and down each seam very slowly in an agreed-upon sequence; the person outside, having adjusted his eyes to the darkness, follows the seam from the outside looking for any pinholes of light. If one is found, a soapstone circle is drawn around the area where the light shows. The tapping of the hammer on the hull informs the inside person to move on. It takes several hours to check the hull completely. If there are any light spots showing through, the next day they are chipped back to find the cause. In most instances, it will be found that a weld was omitted or that two segments did not meet, or rarely, that there was a void.

Before the builder can rest assured that the hull is completely welded, he must go over each frame bay on the inside and inspect the welds to the frame and the plate, chipping off any slag that was overlooked and correcting any omission or fault. This process, once done, is repeated, as one looks for anything that might have been overlooked during the first inspection. The same is done on deck, especially under the railcap. Despite all care and diligence, it is always surprising how many small things will be found that need just a bit more work. Better now than later, so try to find them all.

The Pinky Schooner to this phase of her construction has encompassed, in one form or another, almost every situation, usual or unusual, that a builder will meet in the construction of a small steel vessel. The inward curving bulwarks and overhanging stern, free of the hull, are mainly peculiar to her type, but also occur in Chinese junks. The floating foredeck is sometimes used in trawlers and in larger vessels not employing a deck-edge pipe or fender. From this point on, the finish and construction of different vessels is all about the same but for detail and magnitude. At this stage of construction, 95 percent of the ordered material has been assembled and finished, but only 50 percent of the allotted time to work the metal has been consumed. The remainder of the time is spent making and installing the various parts that constitute a finished vessel.

I have presumed that the vessel is being built right side up. In adapting this chapter for upside-down building, you would have to readjust the sequence of building to suit. For example, all welding of the hull shell would have to be completed before it were turned over, and while it is possible to add bulwarks, deck plating, and cabin trunks before turning a hull right side up, to do so involves problems in fitting that most builders are reluctant to face. Some, however, will put the deck on upside down, even though it means the deck plating must be forced up to the beams.

After turning the vessel right side up, you would have to relevel it both fore and aft and athwartships, or failing that, you would have to resort to the use of a declivity board (as described in Chapter 8 of Volume 2 of this book). The apparent initial saving in labor when building upside down will be lost when the vessel is turned over and releveled for completion. I dislike building upside down, with the exception of a few hull types of very small size. A much greater number of things may be accomplished simultaneously when a vessel is built right side up.

I was once part of a crew that built a vessel in Mexico, upside down and with very limited facilities. When the time came to turn the vessel over, we elevated one side with the sheer legs until she balanced; then, with long poles, we propped up the elevated side until the falls could be released. With a bit of encouragement, the happy-go-lucky crew pushed until the vessel flopped over right side up! You may shudder at this procedure, but a steel hull tumbled about in this manner is in no danger of being deformed. I do concede, however, that there was a tremendous amount of noise involved.

14

▽

MISCELLANEOUS
STEEL PARTS
AND
DETAILS

In the preceding several chapters, I have endeavored to describe the construction of a particular design—the Pinky Schooner—since it typifies most of the usual as well as the unusual construction problems that a builder may encounter. I do not, however, assume that everyone would want to build a pinky schooner, and since the miscellaneous fittings and other fabricated parts for each vessel differ in detail, there is no reason to further limit myself to the building sequence of one particular design. In this chapter, therefore, I will digress to incorporate other details that you, as a builder, may need on other types of vessels. There is no proper order for completion of these details, since they are generally unrelated to each other and are more or less added at the convenience of other work in progress. These items are located at or above the deckline, and must be installed before sandblasting and priming.

TRUNK AND HATCH CORNERS

The Pinky Schooner makes use of a simplified cabin trunk corner, as detailed in the previous chapter. This style, with the square-cornered trunk inset into the deck opening, suits the structural and cosmetic requirements of many vessels up to about 60 feet, providing that the athwartship opening is not very large or that the weight (thickness) of the material is in proportion to the strength required. There comes a point, however, when a square corner is no longer acceptable, not so much because the corner itself would sacrifice strength, but because the surrounding material would be weakened by the notch effect that such a corner decrees. To eliminate the notch effect of these corners, one must use a radius in the deck plate at the corners and then weld the square-cornered trunk or hatch atop the deck, or better still, employ a trunk with fully radiused corners. In larger vessels, a plate would be rolled to the required radius; in smaller vessels, split pipe or tubing is the accepted substitute. The hatches and trunks on vessels less than 80 feet are usually so small that having the deck edge exposed inside could cause cargo damage or injury to crewmembers thrown against it in a seaway. In the cabins, however, such radii in deck plating could be used to advantage as shelves, and the square corner retained on the trunk for ease of joinerwork.

While the rounded corners do solve some problems, and, on sailing vessels, form a better edge should some of the running rigging become fouled and need to be surged, their presence can complicate interior joinerwork. In any case, avoid the use of constant radius corners. Instead the radii should vary with the transverse dimension of the opening; however, all radii should have the same proportions, to eliminate the visual grossness of one seeming too large and another too small when viewed at the same instant. Since there are two seams at each corner, these radiused corners require four welds rather than the two welds of the square corner.

MODIFYING DECK STRUCTURES

In the case of stock plans, where the vessel was designed for one purpose but may be used for another, modifications to the original deck structure must be made with caution. For example, in the Pinky Schooner, the 3-foot 3-inch by 4-foot 6-inch hatch is large enough to accept a standard 3-foot by 4-foot pallet where shoreside facilities are available for loading; however, small vessels such as this usually load case by case or a bag at a time, using the fore gaff for the heavier lifts. For a fishing vessel, this is also the minimum size, considering insulation requirements. If the vessel were to be converted for yachting, the hatch could be modified to incorporate a truncated skylight-type of top with its center section containing a sliding companionway or scuttle and its wings fitted to open, providing light and ventilation in this compartment. In this case, the mast would prevent greater length, while an increase in width would be redundant, since it would make little difference in usable headroom. Each hull has its own limitations. A yacht, on the other hand, when being converted for commercial purposes, will eliminate a portion of the cabin trunk, substituting a hatch in its place. The United States Coast Guard rules stipulate a 12-inch minimum height above the deck for weather deck hatch coamings. The best minimum is either 12 inches or 2 inches higher than the bulwarks adjacent to the hatch, whichever is greater. For sills, 9 inches above the deck in companionways that are 25 percent forward or aft of the lowest point of the sheer is the minimum; otherwise, they should be at least the height of the bulwarks.

WINDLASSES

The designer may suggest the windlass type and size, but it is not unusual for the builder or owner to substitute a different type or model than that indicated on the plans. The builder *must* have the actual item on hand, or at least have drawings indicating the bolt holes for attachment and the width between wildcats and warping heads, for these specifications determine where the spurling pipes (chain deck pipes) will be sited. The center of the hawsepipe is also located from this drawing, and the location, in turn, determines the final shape of the bolsters. A deciding factor in the final location of any chocks that must fairlead to the warping heads is the height of the warping heads, as well as their width from the centerline, for the line must not chafe in the chocks, and the permissible fleet angle must allow lines to pass through the proposed chock.

The windlass is mounted on its own foundation rather than just bolted to the deck. Some manufacturers provide drawings for these foundations. If they do not, then it is up to the builder to devise a foundation. The windlass experiences severe loads at times, since it not only must lift the scope of chain and the anchor, but also must simultaneously pull the vessel ahead. In any kind of a seaway, there will also be an added surge as the vessel lifts and sheers her chain. At anchor, the load on the foundation is a straight pull at an angle through the windlass axle that bisects the line of pull and the drop of the chain to the spurling pipe. The angles used to support the windlass should face outboard for ease of painting and bolting. Many builders tend to make these foundations, and indeed all foundations, not only too heavy but also too weld-intensive. Generally, 1 inch per 10 feet of hull length is a minimum height above deck for the foundation.

HAWSEPIPES

Hawsepipes, when used, must be built of heavier sections than would be needed elsewhere in the vessel. Schedule 80 pipe is always in order, and on larger vessels, Schedule 120 pipe would be minimum. Some designs call for pipes specially cast in steel, thicker on the bottom than on the top of the pipe; the bolster would then form part of the casting. The builder will have to send a pattern to the foundry, indicating the correct bevel angles of the deck and the outside shell. The foundry will then adjust the angle of the bolster and deck bevels to fit its standard pipe pattern. In smaller vessels, using stainless steel pipe eliminates some of the maintenance. The bolster takes all of the load of the anchor chain; therefore, the hull must be well reinforced in this area.

CHOCKS

Chocks should be of the closed type, because that way there is no limit to their use in tidal areas, where the lead to a pier or wharf may be upward from the deck a good part of the time. Chocks take a great deal of wear and tear from mooring lines and anchor rodes riding on their surfaces; either stainless steel solid round or pipe is the best solution for the long-term maintenance problems. The use of pipe returns (180-degree) or 90-degree ells, plus a short length of pipe nipple, is then required. The minimum height of a chock's inside opening is four times the diameter of the line it is to accommodate, and its length should be one and one-half times the height.

In addition to the normal chocks, it is desirable also to have a pair of oversized chocks forward, one and one-half to two times as large as the normal chocks, for use in case of towing. If feasible, another oversized chock, or perhaps a pair of them, is desirable aft, for pulling the vessel off sandbars and the like.

Prior to scribing and fitting in the bulwarks, one should, using a small line, determine if the proposed opening for each chock not only leads fair to the bitts, cleats, kevels, or warping heads, but will not allow lines to chafe on the stanchions or other structures.

BITTS

Bitts on the foredeck may have multiple functions, and are often incorporated into the bowsprit heelpost or the pawl post on certain types of windlasses. They may be either single or paired; either way, their crosspieces or pins always go athwartships. For anchoring and mooring, a pair is preferable to a single bitt. Larger vessels commonly have an additional pair, port and starboard, with their crosspieces parallel to the bulwarks. Aft on most sailing vessels, a single bitt, known as a quarter bitt, is placed port and starboard. The correct placement of quarter bitts is on a fair extension of the after deckhouse or cabin; the pin or crosspiece is always aligned with the trunk sides. Since these bitts are used for sheeting, they are located aft of the steering wheel. The best material for all bitts is pipe. In sailing vessels, the preferred installation is to run them through the deck and brace from below. A pawl post or heel bitt also needs knees or braces above deck on the forward side, due to the strains at anchor, so a doubler plate or heavier deck plating is needed here. The quarter bitts need only be braced from below. The crosspieces or pins are also made of pipe, and the ends plugged or capped. The minimum height above the deck to the bottom of the crosspiece should be 7 inches, with the crosspiece protruding on either side by the diameter of the post. If these conditions cannot be met, then a large cleat or kevel should be used. On the larger sailing vessels, mast bitts and fife rails are also fitted.

BOWSPRITS

Bowsprits are used on many sailing vessels; the most common type is round and can be made of pipe. On smaller vessels aluminum is preferable, since it usually weighs less than steel; wood may be used to maintain some semblance of tradition. With either aluminum or wood, the bulwarks forward must be pierced to receive a steel collar through which the bowsprit will slide. This can, in most instances, be made of a piece of pipe or tubing with an inside diameter slightly larger than the diameter of the bowsprit; the inboard end is left square but the outer lip is either flush with the bulwarks or protruding an inch. This sleeve replaces any gammoning that would be required with other materials. If the vessel will stand the weight, it is better to use a steel pipe or tube for the bowsprit, as it may then be welded directly to the outside of the bulwarks, leaving the foredeck clear. Some builders prefer to use square or rectangular tubing especially if, in accordance with the present fad, a swordfish plank, pulpit, and lifelines are fitted.

In any case, the bowsprit tapers toward its outboard end. Except for a few distinct types, either the top or the bottom of the bowsprit is usually left as a straight edge. To taper a plain pipe, cut out a segment in the form of a wedge, then squeeze the metal together and weld it up; with square or rectangular tubing, both sides would be cut to bring in the taper to the top, the bottom, or both. If there is to be a taper toward the centerline, the top and bottom must also be cut. (Details of this procedure are given in Volume 2, Chapter 3.) Care must be exercised on the athwartship taper to keep the bends uniform, so that the weld remains on the centerline. Any deviation will show. The round pipe bowsprit must be cut in a six-wedge configuration in order to achieve a uniform taper; if all sides but one are to be tapered, then cut only five segments. Drill a hole of at least ⅛ inch diameter at the apex of all cuts after tacking the sprit together, and terminate the welds in these holes to prevent cracking. Grind the welds smooth and add the eyes for all rigging. The round bowsprit may also require sail stop cleats; these should also be welded on at this time. Finally, weld in an end cap and grind it smooth.

Another bowsprit occasionally seen is triangular in section. Other than being lighter, however, it has no advantage over the others described previously, and requires three continuous welds for its entire length. The top is always the flat side.

BOW ROLLERS, CATHEADS, AND ANCHOR DAVITS

Fashion these days favors bow rollers for anchoring, and keeping the anchors in place over the bow at all times. In both sailing and power vessels, these bow rollers are fitted in a miniature bowsprit or plank extending just a couple of feet overboard, and in many instances the bowsprit is also fitted with railings. These stubs unquestionably require plenty of strength, but they do not need the heft of a regular bowsprit. In a steel vessel they are best made of pipe or rectangular tubing in the form of a U, fitted with a grating of expanded metal across the center. All-stainless construction will reduce their maintenance.

Catheads are the sailor's choice for anchoring because they keep the anchor well clear of the vessel's sides and allow easing out a generous amount of chain before the anchor is let go, to assure a good start and keep the anchor clear of the vessel's bottom. The catheads should be square with the bulwarks, forward of the windlass. They are best made of Schedule 80 pipe, welded to both the deck and the railcap. On their outboard ends, a bracket to house a single sheave is added, so that the sheave lines up with the cathead and the top of the sheave groove shows above the cathead.

Some vessels carry anchor davits; usually only one is made, then shifted from side to side. The davit should have both fore-and-aft braces to prevent its turning when in use.

CHAINPLATES, PAD EYES, AND TRAVELERS

Chainplates can be made in many ways; however, on any metal vessel they should be oriented in such a way that they line up correctly with the rigging turnbuckles, thus eliminating any need for toggles. This is done from the sail plan in sailing vessels, or the outboard profile plan in power vessels, by dropping a line perpendicular to the DWL from the shroud attachment point, noting the point of intersection, and referencing it to a deck structure. A string drawn taut from that point to the location of the chainplate eye is the correct lead. The most satisfactory chainplates are drop-forged welding pad eyes.

On most commercial and sailing vessels, additional pad eyes will be needed at various locations to set up running rigging and to hook in snatch blocks to fairlead lines to winches or belaying points. These are best made with drop-forged welding pad eyes or half-links of chain. The builder should locate these and weld them in place, taking extra care to assure perfect welds.

Stainless steel pipe or rod will give the best service for horses and travelers on sailing vessels. In making the traveler, check that the eye for the block shackle is correctly oriented. Also give some thought to the height above deck, as it is better to elevate the horse than to resort to thump mats.

TANK FILLS AND VENTS

The tank fills and vents should be sited, fitted, and tacked only enough to hold them in place until the tank tops are finished, with the exception that if the tank will be welded to the deck, the pipes may be welded in place right away. All fills should stand above the deck and not flush, as they would otherwise be impossible to fill in all but the fairest of weather without contaminating the tank. Fuel fill pipes should reach close to the bottoms of the tanks.

STEERING GEAR

In sailing vessels, the wheel and steering gear are usually on deck, with the gear enclosed in a box. If constructed of steel, the box is welded to the deck and scuppered on the forward corners by sniping both the forward and side plates. If constructed of wood, it is the usual practice to weld either a continuous flat bar coaming to the deck, or else angles at each corner to bolt on the wooden box. Generally the deck area within the box is watertight, and the rudderport is carried above and welded to the deck.

CARGO MASTS, MAST STEPS

Some power vessels have one or more masts used for cargo handling, general lifting, or to support the booms used in handling their fishing gear. These masts are seldom as long as those used in sailing vessels, although they may be as large or larger in diameter. If the vessel is being built near the water, the builder customarily installs these during construction. The loads imposed on them can be calculated; therefore, many designers and builders prefer to site them on a bulkhead, with a doubler plate on deck, and then bracket the heel of the mast fore and aft as well as athwartships. If, after construction, the vessel must be moved to a launching site via truck, the mast would not be installed, but a stump extending several feet above the deck might be used to permit performing all necessary welding to the deck before sandblasting. In this case, a sleeve should be added to the stump, having an outside diameter the same as the inside diameter of the mast; the remainder of the mast can then be set in place and bolted after launching. All drilling and tapping of the masts takes place while the vessel is under construction, with the masts in place. They are then taken apart for transport to avoid having to do any drilling after the vessel has been sandblasted and painted, thus eliminating any metal chips and filings on deck.

Mast tabernacles are common in Europe but seldom used in the United States except in yachts. If called for in the design, the tabernacles are made and welded in place at the same time as other deck fixtures. In multimasted vessels, they are best skewed to one side or the other so that both masts can be lowered without having to remove one of the masts from its tabernacle. On schooners and ketches, especially, the after mast will hinge so that it drops forward, clear of the forward mast.

Commercial sailing vessels normally have their masts stepped on the keel, or at least partway down a bulkhead, simulating a keel stepping. This requires penetration of the deck or cabintop to permit the mast to step. It is the strongest way to step a mast and also the least expensive, since, when wedged in place, the mast becomes a fixed-end column. A collar is made at the deck, its inside diameter at least 2 inches more than that of the mast to permit proper wedging. The collar should have the same rake as the mast, with its high point 3 inches above the deck and its low point at least 2 inches beneath the deck or cabin beams. The ends are left square.

The mast steps should be constructed as detailed on the plans. If the masts are metal, another collar 3 to 4 inches in height will be made to fit the inside diameter of each mast, so it can either be pinned with one throughbolt or drilled and tapped to accept several short bolts. Welding is done only on the inside of the collar, since an outside weld would prevent the mast from seating. Mast step collars for wooden spars are made to the outside of the spar, often square rather than round, to accept a very large tenon. Just as with metal spars, the mast step collar will be drilled for pinning with several lag bolts. Regardless of the material, several small holes should be drilled in the step below the spars to prevent a moisture buildup. The mast steps should always be square to the mast; otherwise, the bottom end of the mast will have to be beveled.

STANCHIONS, RAILINGS, AND GRABRAILS

Locate lifeline stanchions as indicated on the outboard profile or the sail plan. In steel vessels, they can be welded directly to the deck and to the inboard edge of the railcap if they are permanently mounted, or just to the railcap if they are short in length and merely an extension of high bulwarks. If they are to be portable, it is best to mount them several inches above the deck, on a plate welded to the bulwark and through another plate welded to the railcap. The lower ends of pipe stanchions may fit over studs welded to the lower plates, with a hole drilled in each stanchion for a pin under the upper plate, to prevent the stanchion from being pulled upward. Except for very small vessels, 27 to 30 inches is the shortest recommended height for stanchions, and nothing less than 1-inch Schedule 80 pipe should be used. The mid-wire may be threaded through a pad eye welded on the side of the pipe, or a hole may be drilled through the center of the pipe, then countersunk, and a copper tube inserted and flared. The upper wire always passes through an eye that seals off and plugs the end of the stanchion. The pad eyes for the terminal ends of the lifelines should be welded to the railcap. Yachts usually use polished stainless steel stanchions available from marine suppliers. Commercial sailing vessels seldom use stanchions, since permanent ones interfere with handling cargo, fishing, and getting the boats on deck.

Railings are used on many vessels, and quite extensively on some. A quarter rail or taffrail is fitted to many sailing vessels. The top rail and stanchions should never be less than 1¼-inch Schedule 80 pipe, not less than 27 inches in height from the deck, even on the smallest vessels. If the railings are welded to the deck, and the vessel lacks bulwarks or has only a toerail, the span from the deck to the top of the rail should be subdivided into three equal spaces and a pipe run between stanchions at each level. These pipes may be ¾-inch Schedule 40. Welding pipe ends to pipe is laborious at best, and in order to gain a better weld and appearance, the ends can be flattened to an oval by a bit of hammering. On motor vessels, 36-inch-high rails are possible in most instances, and can be even higher on larger vessels. These provide a safe barrier, but if located on a deck devoid of bulwarks, will need to be braced toward the centerline with pipe brackets. The lower rail in this instance should never be more than 9 inches above the deck.

Grabrails on cabintops are used on many of the smaller vessels, and may be of pipe or wood. The most common fault with them is that they have openings too small to permit a decent fingerhold, let alone a handhold. The opening must be 2¾ inches in the clear. There is no hard and fast rule for siting them, but 9 inches in from the edge of the cabin permits a good foothold when one must get up on the cabin deck without catching his toes.

Water catchment rails are used around the edges of the cabintops on many commercial schooners, especially those trading in dry areas where fresh water is exorbitantly expensive. During rain squalls, the vessel is able to supplement its water supply. The rain catchment is formed to eliminate the grabrails, and may be directed either via piping to the water tanks or to the low corners of the cabintops, which are scuppered to fit portable funnels, which in turn are attached to hoses led to a deck fill. The latter method is preferable, since it is easier to keep the water clean. The former method has a tendency to collect chips of paint and dirt, so the pipes must be well flushed before the rainwater will be usable.

Grabrails are fitted to deckhouses that are high enough to put the rails within reach of a person walking upright. They should not be made of less than ¾-inch pipe, and 1-inch provides a more comfortable gripping surface. They should stand off the house sides about 3 inches.

BILGE PUMPS

At least one manual bilge pump should be deck-mounted, with the suction pipes arranged in such a manner that the pump, with its suction fitted to a swiveling gooseneck, can connect to any other suction pipe within its radius. The bilge suction pipes may run through several compartments in the bilge before rising on a bulkhead and returning under the deck to the pump.

PIN RAILS, BOOM CROTCHES, AND DINGHY CHOCKS

When the bulwarks are high enough to permit using belaying pins, the railcap will be swelled out to accept them. Either a split pipe is welded to the underside of the railcap with one edge flush to the inboard edge of the cap, or a full pipe may be added, with its ends tapered and capped. The latter assembly is then welded directly to the edge of the railcap, which gives the effect of swelling. Belaying pins are made of solid round bar or pipe, fitting through holes drilled into the larger pipe. These pins must be proportioned to the size of line they will belay. After welding, everything is carefully ground smooth and round, so as not to chafe the lines.

Boom crotches are fitted for all cargo booms, typically in the form of gallows aft or forward of the hatch. Equally popular, however, is having the gallows on the fo'c's'le deck or house front. In smaller vessels, the boom or booms are often sited high enough on the mast that they do not interfere with visibility from the pilothouse, in which case they may then be secured to the top of the house. This is doubly advantageous in the tropics, as an awning may be used over them to shade the deck. Commercial vessels normally use portable scissors or crotches, whereas yachts more often use a regular gallows frame, so that any boom in the way of the helmsman can have three positions—one on the centerline and one on either side—which allows room to stand at the helm.

Boats carried on deck or on cabintops rest in chocks of one sort or another. These chocks are usually made of wood and then bolted to clips welded to the decks. The clips should be predrilled for bolting. Also, either eyes or ring eyes should be provided on deck for securing the gripes. Stern davits, if fitted, should be welded to the vessel. A dinghy or boat carried in stern davits requires, in addition to the sheaves for the falls, two ring eyes for the gripes and also for the frapping lines (which are always crisscrossed), and two fixed eyes near the boat's gunwale on which to affix an anti-sway brace.

VENTILATORS

Ventilation is essential not only in living quarters, but in all other compartments of the vessel. Nevertheless, designers often leave it to the judgment of the builder or the requirements of the owner. All too often it is either neglected or added as an afterthought, haphazardly thrown together. The deterioration of the interior is accelerated by stagnant moist air and dirt.

One of the most difficult compartments to ventilate is the forepeak, since it usually contains the chain and rope lockers. On smaller vessels it must also serve as a bosun's locker, spares locker, and paint locker, among other things. In some instances, what may be the forepeak would not necessarily meet with the approval of the regulatory bodies; however, the owners and masters always have an acute awareness that it is impossible to pour a quart into a pint, and thus, of necessity, they feel forced to adjust to their particular situation. On small vessels, mushroom ventilators mounted on the bitts offer a partial solution to chain and rope locker ventilation, provided the pipes measure 4 inches or larger. Vents on quarter bitts are seldom needed or used. The ventilation of the forepeak would ideally be accomplished with two vents—one for intake and one for exhaust—with a pipe extended all the way down into the bilge. This seldom proves satisfactory in practice, however, due to the small size of the pipes and the large amount of space they occupy. Mushroom vents are usually reserved for exhausting air, but they are the only type that can naturally fit on top of the bitts and still remain reasonably watertight in a seaway. A cowl vent fitted from the top of the railcap forward to a Dorade box would force enough air into the compartment, provided the box was sited well off the deck so as not to flood the vessel should she put her bows under.

Masts make natural ventilators in that they function as chimneys. The only modifications necessary involve inserting a pipe in the step and capping the top of the mast as a vent. For example, in the Pinky Schooner, the foremast serves as the outlet vent not only for the forepeak, but also for the forward cabin. The watertight collision bulkhead must remain intact; therefore, the piping will need to be welded to this bulkhead with a valve to shut the compartment off in the event of a collision. Otherwise, the forepeak vent pipe would need to be independent of the forward cabin, and extend well above the foredeck level. The mast ventilator can be made with 2-inch pipe by welding a 45-degree street ell to the bulkhead, and threading a close nipple to the ell and to a seacock. From there, one would thread another close nipple to a 3-inch Y and fit a reducer and a long nipple that would reach to the underside of the forward cabin sole. The seacock was selected because it has a lever, which is faster to shut than a screw stem valve; however, the seacock must still be in an easily accessible location. The upper end of the Y has a 3-inch nipple, and its end is inserted into the bottom of the step.

Cargo hold ventilation on small sailing vessels poses numerous problems, since there is seldom any place on deck to put the ventilators out of the way or free of potential fouling. The larger sailing vessels usually have one cowl ventilator at each end of the hold, and maybe also one in the middle. If increased ventilation is needed, then in fair weather the hatch covers are removed. Power vessels, on the other hand, can utilize cowl vents most efficiently; in some instances, the same vent may be used for both the intake and exhaust air by inserting a small trunk inside a larger one. It is rarely necessary to open the hatches while at sea, for cowl vents also have the advantage of being able to use forced draft.

On the Pinky Schooner, the ventilation of the cargo hold is done via the mainmast, for the outlet, and via a pair of 2-inch gooseneck vents incorporated as part of a fife rail at the mainmast, for the intakes. These vents have canvas sleeves to block them off in bad weather or when ventilation is not desirable. Were this vessel intended for fishing, hold ventilation would not be necessary.

Small vessels usually operate in a finite area, making ventilation of little concern, so long as there is some. Occasionally, problems do arise, as when receiving cargo from a cool warehouse and loading it into a warm hold. The ventilation then should be blocked off until such time as the cargo has had a chance to normalize, or the sweating of the hull and decks will cause damage. Also, even the small vessels that usually ply the tropics will occasionally voyage into colder waters, in which case their holds must be well ventilated or sweat will condense on the decks and beams of the hold. Note too, that wherever air temperatures outside the hold drop below the dew point, the hold will sweat inside as well. In general, if there is sweating in one place, there will be sweating in another; therefore, if you notice sweating *anywhere*, do something about it or the cargo could be ruined.

Engine rooms should rank among the best-ventilated areas, yet they seldom do. Internal combustion engines consume large quantities of air. The use of several ample-size cowl vents from the top of the cabin offers one solution; at least one of these should lead to the bilge of the vessel. When the diameter of the vents is large enough, a water shield with a drain should be added to deflect rain and spray. When passing through living spaces, ventilators can be made rectangular in shape, even though this reduces their efficiency. The exhaust vents can often be built into the fidley, or a conveniently sited mast could be utilized for venting; otherwise, separate exhaust ducts should be installed. If none of these options are open, then adjacent to the exhaust line of the engine another line of at least the same diameter should be run that will utilize a forced draft.

BINNACLES

Binnacle boxes are most often deck-mounted on sailing vessels and shelf-mounted on power vessels. The latter should be mounted high enough for the helmsman to see easily, and sited so that bearings can be taken over the compass. Sailing yachts commonly have their compasses mounted either on an aluminum pipe, with a suitable base plate for attachment to the steel deck, or in a wooden box attached to corner clips welded to the steel deck. In both cases, guards should be used to prevent lines and crewmembers from fouling the compass. These guards must be strong, as they are more often used for grabrails than is commonly supposed.

The Pinky Schooner uses a rectangular wooden box with a shelf upon which to affix the compass. The portion above the shelf is removable in its entirety for compass adjustment, but only the section over the compass is removable when underway. Below the shelf and well off the deck, louvers are fitted on the aft side to form the exhaust ventilator for the after cabin and the sail locker. This arrangement requires making a cutout in the deck, plus the installation of a 3-inch coaming above the deck and the same below, welded in place. The outside of the coaming has the same dimensions as the inside of the wooden box.

TRAILBOARDS

Trailboards, normally associated with clipper bows, may be made either of steel or

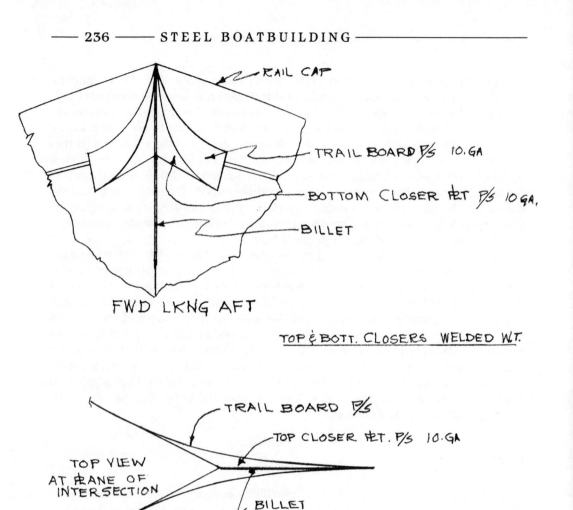

Figure 90. *A steel trailboard configuration, showing top and bottom closer plates.*

wood. If of steel, they will have the same shape and curve as if made of wood. Some builders leave them open top and bottom just like the wooden boards, but this is a bad practice, since it makes for a flimsy appearance and invites corrosion at the welded attachment points to the hull and billet. The proper way is to fit top and bottom plates to the trailboards (see Figure 90), thus boxing in the whole area behind the boards and making it airtight. The scrollwork and other ornamentation needed to finish the boards can then be welded on, using a 3/32-inch-diameter rod with the lowest heat possible for welding; lay on a bead about 1/8 inch proud of the surface. After sandblasting and painting the vessel, paint these welds in a contrasting color. Wooden trailboards should be fitted to the hull with clips to accept bolts. The ability to remove the wooden trailboards is essential to proper maintenance of the vessel.

RUDDERS

The rudder is fabricated and installed according to the plans. Some designers and builders feel that, once installed, the rudder need not be taken out, and they construct the heel bearing and rudder stock accordingly. Evidence from vessels 20 or more years old bears out this assumption, provided that the rudderport is always pumped full of waterproof grease at the beginning of each voyage. The only way to remove such rudders is to cut away the heel bearing, rewelding or replacing it upon reinstallation of the rudder.

There are two things to remember about rudders hung with gudgeons and pintles. First, if the gudgeon is attached to the aft side of the sternpost, and the pintles to the forward side of the rudderpost, a substantial gap will exist. The rudderpost will not have the same centerline as the pintles, and therefore, only a tiller will work. Second, steering gears require that the rudderpost and the pintles align with each other. If they do not align, the rudderpost must be bent forward near the top, to offset it enough to make its centerline coincide exactly with the centerline of the pintles. The alternate and better method is to form pintles from the rudderpost itself, with pipe gudgeons welded to the sternpost. While this method requires machining, it minimizes the gap and thus is more effective for steering, especially in sailing vessels. A block of hardwood can be driven below one of the pintles to prevent the rudder's coming unshipped. All rudders should have stops limiting their swing to not more than 45 degrees port or starboard. The generally accepted limit is 42 degrees.

When all the fittings described in this chapter have been taken care of, you, as the builder, will have completed almost all the deck fittings, fittings in the bulwarks, and fittings on the railcap for the time being. Of course, there will be more fittings as the remainder of the steel parts are made and installed. Engines using a dry exhaust, and all air-cooled auxiliary engines, not to mention the galley, water closets, and a host of other areas, have ducts, pipes, vents, and other items penetrating either the main deck or cabintops, which cannot be done until a good portion of the machinery installation and interior work has been finalized. The vessel remains a long way from the finished painting and launching, but the vexing details are now behind the builder. If the builder is constructing for a third party, the hull is now ready for delivery.

15

▽

INTERIOR
WELDING DETAILS
AND
PRIMING

The importance of completing as much as possible of the exterior welding on and above the deck cannot be stressed enough. Once the builder is satisfied that nothing further in this area may be done pending completion of other work, it is time to start work on the inside metal details. There is no easy, systematic procedure for interior details that will allow one at last to climb back out of the vessel and go on to other tasks, never having to look behind. The countless details that comprise the whole are interdependent, and each must wait its turn. The proper sequence involves compartmentalization, which permits the finish work to proceed rapidly in the less complicated compartments, while the more complicated areas can be worked at the pace dictated by material flow from the various vendors. The lone worker will experience some satisfaction in this method. There are times when finishing something—anything—provides the encouragement needed to press on.

THE FOREPEAK

In the Pinky Schooner, for example, the forepeak is dispatched first. Completing the forepeak requires installation of the following: clips to hold up the shelving for paint and miscellaneous gear; hangers for the mooring lines and warps; clips for bins; clips for the ceiling; and supports for the walkway. While installing these items, cut but do not yet install the transverse partial bulkhead on frame 2, which forms the ends of the chain and rope lockers, and a longitudinal bulkhead that further divides the chain as well as the rope lockers into port and starboard compartments. The best location for the deck rope pipes becomes obvious at this time, since one should be able to feed in the line without having to go below to coil it. The spurling pipe location, on the other hand, has already been dictated by the siting of the windlass. The bitter end of the anchor chains will be attached to a half-link or pad eye welded to the deck near the spurling pipe, in the event that the chain must be slipped. In large vessels, this pad eye is designed to part under a predetermined load; in smaller vessels, the use of a pelican hook will allow the bitter end of the chain to be released, should it have to be slipped. A bilge suction line must also be fitted; the best arrangement uses a single pipe to a sump that services both chain lockers. Actually, very little water enters the chain locker with the chain, and with proper ventilation this soon evaporates. The backup bracing for the foremast step in the Pinky is welded in place. The hatch leading to the forepeak should be temporarily fitted, and any holes needed to fasten it in place are drilled at this time. Then the whole compartment should be cleaned and vacuumed.

THE CABIN

Moving aft to the forward cabin, start with the cabin sole beams. Weld them in place if they are of steel; if they are of wood, cut them to size, drill bolt holes, and temporarily pin them in place. There are advantages to using a combination steel and wood sole beam, space permitting. This could be done in the Pinky, as is discussed in detail in Volume 2. This arrangement would use a sleeper bolted to the flange of the steel beam, of sufficient molding and siding to accept all cabin sole fastenings. This method eliminates having to drill and bolt to the steel each piece of wood used in the sole, with all of the chips and potential for rust. If the cabin sole is not excessively wide, and in the Pinky it is not, a 2 x 4 or a 2 x 6 could be substituted for the steel beam in its entirety, and this single piece would occupy about the same space as the steel beam plus a sleeper. Given a large span, however, using wood alone will require welding one or more vertical supports per beam to the frames, so as to prevent sag. Any joinerwork fastened to the cabin sole, such as bunk fronts, settee fronts, lockers, and the like, helps stiffen the cabin sole, but should not be considered a solution to stiffening the beams.

Water tanks generally go below the sole, forming an integral part of the hull. If they are part of the framing, as they are on the Pinky, they will already have been fitted and welded. If they are not, fit them now, but do not weld them in place until the cabin sole beams are properly sited. The piping to all tanks includes a fill pipe, a draw-off pipe, and a vent pipe. In fuel tanks a bleeder pipe is also needed. Using hose, PVC pipe, or both for water tanks has its advantages: hose, because it is easy to run and fair into the fittings; and PVC pipe, because it can be cut and glued with a minimum of effort. Metal fittings are, however, needed for welding at the deck and tank top.

Locating vent pipes is one of the most vexing problems a builder faces, since they must occupy a nonvulnerable position, being quite small in comparison to everything else on board. The vent pipe must always rise higher than the fill pipe. Furthermore, the vent must rise directly from the tank to its outlet with no loops. In some water tanks, however, it is possible to use one larger vent on deck, leading underneath to a manifold that accepts the smaller vents from the individual water tanks.

It is desirable to have cleanout plates in all tanks; however, their location and size often makes this impractical, and too much emphasis has been placed on this feature. Suffice it to say that if it is feasible to install them, one should do so; if not, rest assured there are ways to cope with any contamination that might occur in the future.

The forward cabin of the Pinky is bounded by watertight bulkheads, and the bilge suction will be fitted to its sump just forward of the water tanks in the keel. The suction pipe leads under the water tank, parallel to the forepeak suction pipe, and into the cargo hold, thence up bulkhead 8 to the bilge pump. The Pinky's plans call for permanent ballasting under the water tanks, with a closing end plate.

In vessels with steel cabintops, the deck irons for any heaters, stoves, and vents that penetrate them should be welded in place. As always, the siting depends on existing deck structures. All ports in the steel trunks should be fitted and drilled, but the ports themselves should be held in place by only two bolts at this time. Finally the whole compartment should be cleaned of debris and vacuumed, and the ballast worked into place under the water tanks.

THE CARGO HOLD

The work associated with cargo hold finishing consists mainly of installing clips for the cargo battens, as well as the means of holding down the ceiling. The cargo batten clips can be made either of flat bars having a 90-degree twist where they leave the frames to which they are welded, or of solid round bars welded to the frames. In either case, their free ends are turned up to accept the cargo battens, slipped in from the top. The former style works better, since the flat bars do virtually no damage to any cargo with which they come in contact; the round bars require dunnaging to prevent cargo damage. Figure 91 shows these clips. Where necessary, pad eyes should also be installed. The bilge suction is then connected to the cargo hold sump and its pipe run up bulkhead 8 (in the Pinky), or whatever location is suitable in another vessel. If hose or PVC pipe is used, it need not be run at this time; only the welded metal connections are necessary now. All sumps should have strainer plates. The mast step is finish welded, and a 4-inch nipple is fitted through the step as a vent. A ladder is needed for access to the hold and may be welded to bulkhead 6 or sited a couple of inches aft of frame 7, keeping the hatchway clear of any obstructions. When the hold is finished, clean and vacuum.

The aft cabin can be fitted with either steel or wooden sole beams, like the forward cabin. Construct a bilge suction sump, and pipe it to the cargo hold. Fit and drill the ports, then clean and vacuum.

WIREWAYS

There remains but one task to complete, in the Pinky Schooner at least: installing wireways for the electrics. But for the cargo hold and its watertight bulkheads, this could be postponed until a later date; however, nipples welded to bulkheads 6 and 8

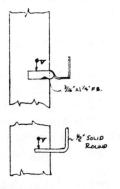

Figure 91. *Alternative constructions for cargo batten clips. The top style, a flat bar twisted 90 degrees where it clears the frame to which it is welded, works better.*

will finish the welding at or near deck level. The final decision as to wiring arrangement can wait, the only requirement being that the course of the wire through the cargo causes the least possible interference and is least likely to sustain damage from the cargo. The areas least exposed to damage are on the port and starboard sides, as close under the deck as possible and as far outboard as practicable. I would anticipate that on a vessel like the Pinky, a single 1½-inch pipe would hold all the necessary wires. In case 110-volt AC should be required in the future, it is nevertheless safer to install fittings both port and starboard (a total of four nipples, then). For the Pinky, the piping will be PVC, this being a nonconducting, noncorroding material.

SURFACE PREPARATION

One can substantially improve the life of a vessel by properly preparing the interior of the hull for finish coatings. It has been recognized for many years that a vessel is more likely to deteriorate from the inside out than vice versa, as much of the interior is unavailable for inspection after the vessel is constructed, due to insulation, tankage, joinerwork and ceilings. A thorough inspection of a completed vessel would necessitate some dismantling and subsequent reconstruction. Therefore, it rests within the province of the builder and first owner to decide the useful life of the vessel. In many ways this is unfortunate, for a vessel built for, say, a 20-year life will often continue in service long after that time, the owners always hoping to squeeze another voyage or so out of her before she sinks. Doing a proper job costs only a fraction of a percent more than doing a slipshod one, so cutting corners on the interior preparation is false economy.

A vessel not built under cover will have large areas of rust, loose scale, and dirt on her frames and plating. This, of course, could be cleaned by power wire-brushing and chipping; however, this is not only time-consuming, but is apt to cause further cracking in the scale, which in turn will cause accelerated corrosion if penetrated by water through the coatings. The scale on the plate when it arrives from the mill makes excellent protection for the plate, as long as it is not breached—which does occur, of course, in welding and cutting operations. Once breached, corrosion seeps back, destroying the coating and at the same time rusting the exposed steel. Therefore, it is prudent to abrasive (sand) blast the interior and then coat the entire surface with a primer that will not need overcoating for several weeks or months, with consideration for the fact that potable water and fuel tanks may demand a different and special primer.

Depending on the manufacturer of the primer, the following degrees of surface preparation are required: brush blast (surface free of all loose scale, paint, oils, and dirt); near-white blast (surface free of all patches of scale, but allowing for a mottled appearance); and white-metal blast (free of all scale and other foreign matter). Manufacturers have developed coating systems that usually do not require white-metal blasting of interior surfaces. Exterior surfaces demand blasting to white condition on new construction.

Vessels built under cover, with their material more or less free of rust, dirt, and loose scale, may dispense entirely with blasting the interior of the hull. After a thorough cleaning and vacuuming, prime the interior with a paint that does not demand blasting. There is a difference in longevity favoring a blasted interior, but another consideration is the amount of exposure to the elements that these surfaces will undergo, as well as the subsequent number of protective paint coats applied over the primer on the unblasted surface.

Painting and paint systems are covered in detail in another chapter. The Pinky, since it was not built under cover, will have the interior of her hull blasted and primed. Blasting the metal is not a fast process, and one never enjoys doing the inside of a vessel under the best of circumstances. The only rules to follow are that the person doing the blasting on the interior should not only wear the standard protective clothing and hood, but have a supply of fresh air pumped to his face mask (respirator) at all times, in order to prevent silicosis and other respiratory problems. Also, as much exhaust air as possible should be forced out, to rid the compartment of dust and thus improve visibility. Remember that, in blasting, 125 cubic feet of air per minute is being forced into the compartment along with the sand. Never blast more area than can be primed the same day.

The overhead is always blasted first, thence working down the hull toward the keel. As the sand accumulates underfoot, one will have to stop and shovel it out. The sand is not reusable, so it can be just dumped over the side. Before priming, the areas to be painted are swept, dusted, and vacuumed as required to provide a clean surface. Under no circumstances should the metal be touched with bare skin, as the normal body oils will contaminate the surface; many primers will not tolerate this.

With the interior blasted and primed, one may then blast to white metal the exterior of the cabin sides, hatchways, decks, bulwarks, and railcap, plus the outside of the bulwarks. Additional through hulls will be welded into the hull as the work progresses, and the remainder of the hull should not be sandblasted until after all this work is done, at which time the supporting clips to the hull and the keel supports are removed so that this may be accomplished all at one time.

FINISHING TANKS

The welding-in of the tank tops and the addition of the through hulls on the inside will not require further blasting; the areas affected can be mechanically treated. In the

Pinky Schooner, the tanks are too shallow to physically permit welding the interiors of the tank tops, but with handholes (access holes) cut and fitted there is at least sufficient room to clean up the interiors after completing the exterior welding, and they should be cleaned carefully, since, in all probability, some of the primer will have been burned away. Then touch up the primer, using a mirror to see that the coating is without voids.

ENGINE BEDS

Vessels with engine rooms would, in addition to the above, require blasting of that area after the installation of the engine beds and other machinery foundations. While practice varies from builder to builder, unless the engine beds form an integral part of the hull, their installation is usually deferred until after completion of all the hull welding, as they are then much easier to align with the stern tube. This eliminates much of the shimming often made necessary by welding-induced distortion.

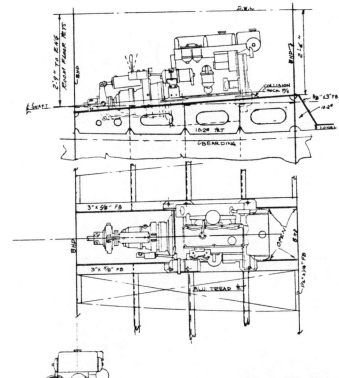

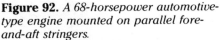

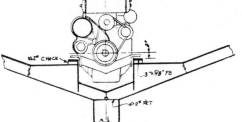

Figure 92. *A 68-horsepower automotive-type engine mounted on parallel fore-and-aft stringers.*

Sometimes, installation of the completely assembled engine would be impractical after the vessel reached the stage where the decks and deckhouses were already complete. In such cases, the engines are installed during the hull framing stage on preblasted, primed, and painted engine beds.

Engine beds take many forms and demand careful design and construction. Most small vessels use automotive-type engines—that is, those developed for land transportation or industrial applications but subsequently modified for marine use. These engines usually mount on beds having parallel stringers that run at least the length of the engine room, sometimes with bracketing that extends into the next compartments fore and aft. Their strength requirement is then a fore-and-aft main girder supported transversely. The engine mounts or brackets attach to the sides of the engine, extending outward the distance required to clear its block and any fixtures attached to the block in way of the beds. Figure 92 shows a 68-horsepower engine of this type, as installed in a 56-foot schooner, the engine weighing 1,056 pounds and turning 2,200 revolutions per minute (rpm).

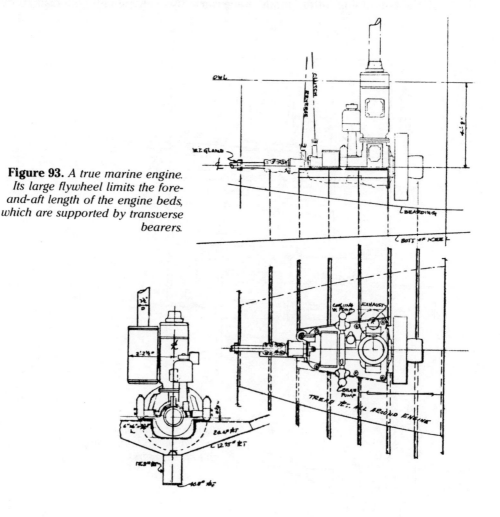

Figure 93. *A true marine engine. Its large flywheel limits the fore-and-aft length of the engine beds, which are supported by transverse bearers.*

True marine engines have their base plates extended outward from and integral with the block. The engine beds are short in the fore-and-aft direction, limited quite often by the diameter of the engine's flywheel. They depend, therefore, on the transverse system of bearers to support them. Figure 93 shows an 80-horsepower, single-cylinder semi-diesel, as installed on a 76-foot schooner. The engine weighs 8,500 pounds and turns 340 rpm.

All engines transmit vibrations to the hull, which are dampened in part by the construction of their beds. One cannot possibly eliminate every trace of vibration, but he *can* minimize it, aiming especially to keep the node of vibration out of the useful range of engine rpm as needed by the vessel. One often finds objectionable vibrations after launching, and modifications are frequently necessary after trial runs. Engines in ocean-voyaging vessels, especially auxiliary sailing vessels, must be firmly and rigidly bolted to the engine beds. Some automotive types, due to their higher rotating speeds, may benefit from vibration-absorbing—essentially rigid—mounts. Perhaps in very small engines, the popular flexible mounts are permissible; however, flexible mountings contradict not only logic but the physics of the ocean. The object in marine propulsion is not to encourage independent movement of several thousandths of an inch in a piece of machinery weighing several tons and having a momentum separate from that of the vessel, but to integrate the engine as a homogeneous part of the vessel and her propeller.

FUEL TANKS

In all vessels, the ideal fuel tank permits the builder physical access, not only for proper welding but also for sandblasting. The common assumption that fuel oil protects the steel is only correct up to a point, given fuel free of contaminants. Unfortunately, water is invariably present in the fuel tanks, due to condensation, even with the best of fuels, and tanks assembled with dirty, rusty steel will probably depend heavily on their filters to keep contaminants out of the engine. This begs the question of why a tank should be dirty, when it could, if nothing else, have been blasted prior to assembly, and its interior, if accessible, could also have been coated. The minimum opening for tank access is 18 inches in diameter, and if room permits, a 15- by 24-inch opening is easier to get in and out of. Figure 94 shows a typical manhole. The bolts are ⅜-inch stainless steel, their heads welded to the inside of the

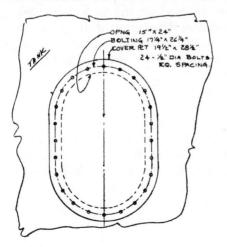

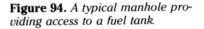

Figure 94. *A typical manhole providing access to a fuel tank.*

tank. Alternatively, the bolts could be stud-welded to the exterior of the tank. A gasket of neoprene sheet material, approximately ⅛ inch thick, is fitted over the bolts and between the tank and the face plate.

THROUGH HULLS

In the engine room, holes through the bottom shell of the hull are required for seawater intakes for engine cooling, exhaust cooling, fire pumps, and sometimes sanitary systems. Many of these holes can be eliminated by using single or dual standpipes. The tops of these standpipes are brought above the waterline and fitted with watertight covers, sometimes with a viewing glass. The hull in way of a standpipe is drilled with about ½-inch-diameter holes to form a coarse strainer. The individual pipes are then tapped into and welded to the standpipe, with their own valves and secondary strainers to collect small trash. The fewer through-hull openings below the waterline, the better and safer the vessel can be. The outlets on all but yachts can be located at or above the load waterline, which makes them accessible in the event of a line's bursting or becoming clogged; furthermore, they are not subject to ice damage. Waste pipes often exit into a chute made of split pipe welded to the side of the hull, which deflects the discharge downward, but only vessels with high freeboard need chutes under ordinary circumstances.

On the Pinky Schooner, the only through-hull pipe below the load waterline supplies the water closet aft. Galley water is supplied via a gravity saltwater tank on deck. The water closet and the sinks all discharge above the load waterline.

Tanks are tested by air pressure after completion, after which the final piping hookups can be made. The pressure required to test any tank equals the head of liquid formed by its fill or a 6-foot column, whichever is greater.

WATERTIGHT DOORS

Access from compartment to compartment is often done via watertight doors. The minimum usable door size is about 54 by 22 inches. Engine rooms should have doors of the quick-acting type, capable of being opened from either side. Piercing bulkheads with doors robs each compartment of valuable space, and in spite of the convenience of doors through bulkheads, access from the deck above through a watertight hatch has much to recommend it. In the event that the owner chooses vertical access to the engine compartment, the watertight hatches should be the quick-release spring type, so there will be no danger of entrapment below.

PORTS AND SCUPPERS

Vessels with high bulwarks need freeing ports to relieve the decks of excess water as fast as possible. The open-grill type is the most common, but has the disadvantage that it also allows water to pour through *from* the sea as well as *into* it. Five distinct

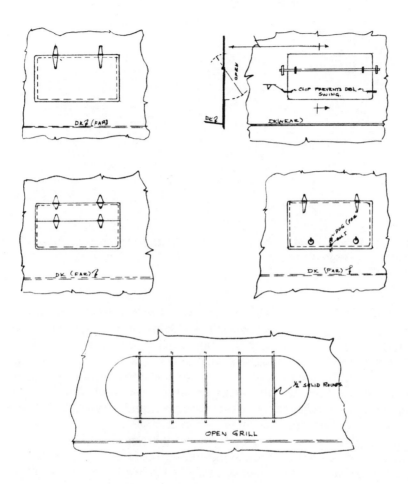

Figure 95. *Five varieties of closed-door freeing ports.*

types of the closed-door port variety are used: the single plate hinged at the top and unrestrained; the double-hinged double plate; the single plate dogged, with lifting ring; the single plate, longitudinally hinged across the upper third, with locking dogs; and the Freeman Marine type, hinged longitudinally in the upper quarter with an integral independent grate, which is available in several sizes as an off-the-shelf item. Figure 95 shows the first four of these types.

Scuppers should not be less than 2 by 4 inches (the ends describing complete

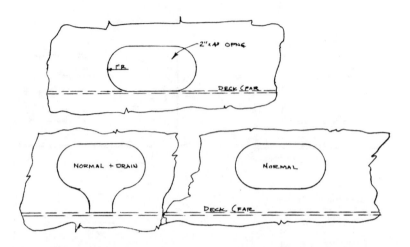

Figure 96. Top: *A scupper that doubles as a foothole.* Bottom: *Scuppers for drainage only can be elevated an inch or so above the deck, with those at the deck's low point being modified to ensure complete drainage.*

circles as per Figure 96) on vessels that have low enough freeboard to permit boarding from a dinghy or boat without resorting to a side ladder. This is the minimum space that a foot will fit into; if boots will be worn, as in cold climates, the openings need to be larger. Scuppers used only for draining the deck, and not as footholes, can be elevated about 1 inch with the ultimate drainage of the deck confined to two or three modified scuppers at the low point of the deckline. This prevents the many streaks that often mar the appearance of vessels with numerous scuppers allowing the water to dribble out over large areas.

After finishing with sandblasting and priming, it is possible to bed and bolt on all portlights and hatches. If there are no large items to be fitted belowdecks that cannot pass through the hatches, the cabintops may be made and bolted down to partially weatherproof the interior and make it conducive to finish painting, insulating, fabricating the joinerwork, and completing the machinery installation.

$\bigtriangledown$

EPILOGUE

There is never a good place in which to interrupt a sequence of building. It would be nice to be able to stop at a "halfway" mark and tell the builder that he may now take a break. In the days of yore, when there were no engines, refrigerators, showers, electrical items, and often nothing but a good bucket or "thunder mug" to take care of the sanitary needs of the ladies, completing the hull would have put the builder one-third to one-half the way through the construction of the entire vessel. Today, with all the modern amenities, the vessel is but one-sixth or, at best, one-fifth completed when her hull has been finished. A builder who is furnishing a bare hull to the owner is finished with his contractual portion of the vessel when the steelwork is done. Many builders prefer to stop at just that point, but I have always derived pleasure from finishing a vessel completely, including the making of the sails. Speaking from the viewpoint of a professional builder, the best way to do this is with an absentee owner, because experience and a great deal of thought without continuous interruptions are necessary in order to produce a satisfactory if not *almost* perfect finished vessel.

We have all been told that familiarity breeds contempt. I beg to differ. It is my feeling and my experience that familiarity breeds respect. Taking the time to understand the whys and wherefores of the material with which you, as a builder, are working is one of the most important things that you can do, because you, as an individual, will then have a total feeling for the subject. In constructing the vessel, you will then foresee any shortcomings that might be incorporated in the structure, and may then enhance such a shortcoming to make it an asset. Respect must be given to any individual, regardless of his field of endeavor, when he produces to the best of his ability. As an individual, I respect a competent fisherman, a competent farmer, or anyone else who exhibits competency in his own field, and as a boatbuilder, designer, and sailor, I expect you, as an individual builder, to do the best that you can possibly do, for I want you to succeed. I derive no pleasure whatsoever from thinking, "Oh, well, what can you expect from amateurs?" I honestly do not feel that such individuals exist. Almost without exception, the several thousand vessels built to my designs by "amateurs" have given me pride—pride not only in these people's ability to learn the art of boatbuilding, but also pride in what they have done to execute my designs.

It will be incumbent upon anyone, having built his own vessel to the stage of completion suggested in this volume, to continue on to Volume 2, which covers painting, launching, rigging, and other necessary details and considerations. There can never be any interest in something partially completed; the world is filled with incomplete articles that are foisted upon others as being complete. Therefore, I urge the builder and the individual to be diligent and never neglect the minuscule, because, at sea, the minuscule magnifies and predominates. Most disasters can be attributed to the failure of humans to do as perfect a job as they are capable of doing, and to their misjudgment of the situation as it then exists.

There is no feasible way in which a designer, builder, owner, or sailor may divorce himself from the prudence that must be exercised from the conception of the design to the actual sailing of the vessel on the high seas.

$\triangledown$

GLOSSARY

The following terms appear in the text of this volume or may appear on designers' plans.

Access Hole. Any hole cut into a bulkhead, tank, or shell to permit through-passage while the vessel is under construction.

Aft. Toward, at, or near the stern.

After. Nearer the stern.

Afterbody. That portion of the vessel that is aft of the maximum section.

After Peak. The space aft of the aftermost transverse watertight bulkhead and the stern frame. In many sailing vessels it consists of a deep floor that is watertight to the top of the box keel or DWL. It is often a watertight void in the event of damage to the stern frame. If carried several frame bays forward, it can form a useful water or fuel tank.

After Perpendicular (AP). A line perpendicular to the baseline, intersecting the after edge of the sternpost at the designed waterline (DWL). In small vessels it may be located at the intersection of the deck with the centerline of the transom to facilitate measurement by regulatory agencies that use measured deck length as a basis for their rules.

Amidships. In the vicinity of the middle portion of a vessel, as distinguished from her ends. This term is used to convey a general locality and not a specific point.

Anchor Rode. The line or rope attached to the anchor in lieu of chain.

Aperture. The area cut out of the keel or deadwood and rudder for the propeller.

Appendages. Items such as shaft struts, bilge keels, rudders, bossings, skegs, and fin keels. Used to denote fittings that are immersed.

Arc Blow. An occurrence associated with cellulose-coated electrodes, which generate large volumes of gases consisting of hydrogen, steam, carbon dioxide, and carbon monoxide. When the electrode arc becomes long (gap), a greater volume of gases is entrapped in the shielding envelope, thus generating greater heat which by itself (or when the arc is corrected) causes the molten pool to become liquid and blow through the base metal.

Athwartships. In a transverse direction; from side to side at right angles to the vessel's fore-and-aft centerline.

Auxiliary Machinery. Any pumps, motors, winches, etc. used on a vessel, apart from the propulsion machinery. In sailing vessels that have a propulsion engine, it is normal to refer to it as "the auxiliary engine," because it is assumed that the sails provide the main propulsion.

Baffle(s). A plate in a tank used to deflect the surge of liquids.

Ballast. Weight used to trim a vessel to a desired line of flotation, or to regulate stability.

Baseline. A horizontal line through the lowest point of a vessel's molded form. Some designers use the DWL as a base for all measurements, with notations of "+" for above and "−" for below, which results in smaller numbers in the measurements. This line is easily established in the plated hull as a ready reference.

Batten. A thin strip of wood used in laying down the lines on the mold loft and for drawing curved lines on the material. Also, planks of wood used in the cargo hold to keep the cargo away from the frames and shell of the vessel.

Beam. A transverse horizontal member supporting a deck or a flat. In a narrow vessel of unusual depth, it may be necessary to install *hold beams*, which support no plating or decking, usually at every fifth frame. In most instances, the use of deep web frames is a better solution to the problem of stiffening the sides of the vessel.

Beam, Great. *See* Great Beam.

Beam, Molded. The width over the widest portion of the hull, measured to the outside of the frame(s) and to the inside of the plating.

Bearding Line. The line of intersection of the keel, stem, and sternpost and the outer faces of the frames.

Bilge. That portion of the hull adjacent to the keel or keelson where bilge water can collect. It is the area below the floors, extending outward for the length of the floors. Any water due to leaks, condensation, cargo damage, etc., should drain to this area.

Bilge Keel. A metal plate fitted at the turn of the bilge to reduce the rolling of a vessel in a seaway. It is confined primarily to motor vessels.

Billet. A plate that extends outward from the face of the stem to form a clipper bow, onto which the outer ends of the trailboards are attached.

Booby Hatch. An access hatch from the weather deck to the interior of the vessel, protected by a hood in which a secondary companionway hatch may also be incorporated.

Bracket. A triangular plate or shape to connect two or more parts—a deck beam to a frame, a pillar to a girder, etc.

Breasthook. A plate joining the port and starboard stringers at the bow.

Bulwarks. That portion of the vessel's hull that extends above the main deck.

Butt. Any joint formed when two parts are placed edge to edge. In small steel vessels, this normally refers to the end joints of any two plates; longitudinal joints between plates are referred to as seams.

Buttock(s). The intersection with the hull (usually at the molded surface) of any vertical plane parallel to but not on the fore-and-aft centerline.

Camber. The rise or "roundup" of a vessel's deck beams, which traditionally form a segment of a circle or a portion of a parabola. Nowadays, there are designers and builders who utilize either a shallow angle with its apex at the centerline, or a truncated angle with a large section of flat along the center portion of the deck. While less expensive to construct, such decks need more camber to achieve the same strength than a deck with circular camber. Camber is indicated as a fraction of the vessel's beam amidships or as a stated rise per foot of half-beam.

Cant Frame. A frame that is not square to the keel. Such frames are needed in vessels with very full bows or round, counter sterns. The object is to swing them in such a manner as to have them lie normal (square) with the shell plating. The frames are always swung forward in the forebody and aft in the afterbody.

Cathead. An extension over the rail of the vessel on the foredeck, fitted with block(s) or sheaves enabling the anchor to be hoisted to its end. In other words, a fixed davit. The ring of the anchor is hoisted close up, after which the bill of the anchor is brought over the rail and secured. The chain from the hawse is also secured to the rail. On long ocean passages, the chain is detached and the whole anchor is swung aboard and secured, leaving the cathead free. The cathead also can serve as a sheet lead for squaresails.

Ceiling. The covering of an area with wood planking to isolate the interior of the vessel from the steel structure.

Center of Gravity. A point at which the combined weight of any item or group of items may be considered as concentrated. The *Vertical Center of Gravity (VCG)* and the *Longitudinal Center of Gravity (LCG)* are the vertical and longitudinal centers, respectively, of the combined weights of all materials in the vessel.

CFM. Cubic feet per minute, a measure of the velocity of air or liquids.

Chine. The intersection between the sides and the bottom of a hull, also known as a knuckle. A vessel may have one or more chines on either side of the hull. A single chine always denotes either a flat-bottom or V-bottom hull.

Chocks. Openings on or through the bulwarks through which a line, cable, or chain passes, thus achieving a fair lead from bitts, cleats, windlasses, etc. The chock is usually reinforced and may be open (the line can be dropped into the opening) or closed (the line is fed through the opening).

Coamings. Vertical plates bounding the edges of hatch openings to reinforce them. Coaming tops are fitted with angles, bars, etc., to retain the hatch covers.

Cofferdam. A space between two bulkheads or partial bulkheads that separates tanks of different liquids and is a safety measure in case one of the bulkheads ruptures.

Collision Bulkhead. The first watertight bulkhead in the vessel aft of the stem. On commercial vessels it must be not less than 5 percent nor more than 15 percent of the load waterline length aft of the intersection of the stem and the LWL.

Curtain Plate. A vertical fore-and-aft plate connecting the outboard ends of the beams of a deck that is supported at the vessel's sides by stanchions or an open framework.

Davit. A simplified crane used to handle lifeboats, anchors, stores, etc., which is usually made of pipe.

Deadrise. The athwartship rise of the bottom of the hull from the keel to the bilge, measured at amidships.

Deadwood. The area between the keel, the sternpost, and the bearding line.

Deep Floors. Floors that are deeper than ordinary floors. Usually located at every third frame in transversely framed vessels, and often used to reduce the gross tonnage of a vessel. In sailing vessels, deep floors are a continuation of regular floors into the box keel.

Diagonals. Straight lines on the Lines Plan running downward from the centerline at an angle to the waterlines and the buttock lines, thus intersecting the frames at an angle. Diagonals are used for additional measurements in laying down the body plan. When projected either in half-breadths or vertically, they are curved lines.

Displacement. The number of tons or pounds of water displaced by a vessel when it is afloat. It is expressed in long tons (2,240 pounds).

Double Bottom. A secondary, inner hull bottom that is water- or oiltight and is separated from the outer bottom by deep floors, webs, and intercostal stringers. It is primarily used in motor vessels as ballast or fuel tanks. A separation of at least 2 feet 6 inches is the absolute minimum, and 4 feet is normal.

Doubler. A plate fitted outside or inside, and faying against, another plate to give added stiffness or strength.

Drop Strake. A strake that is terminated before it reaches the bow or stern. This term is used in round-bottom construction only. Dropped strakes result from the difference in girth between the midship section and the ends. (*See also* Expanded Shell Drawing.)

Dunnage. Loose material placed under and around cargo to prevent any motion or chafing while a vessel is on a passage.

Dutchman. A piece of steel or wood inserted into a plate or plank to rebuild and replace a flaw in the material or to correct faulty workmanship.

DWL. *See* Waterline, Datum.

Expanded Shell Drawing. A drawing showing the hull flattened laterally as though compressed between two plates pushing from port and starboard. It will yield true girth measurements but leaves the length unchanged, and is thus distorted. It indicates the sight edges of plating in relation to frames and to the girth of the hull. It also shows through hulls, locations of appendages, and other details that may be difficult to show on other plans.

Falls. The rope used in a block to make up a tackle. The end that is secured to the block is called the standing end, and the opposite end is called the hauling end. At sea, the hauling end as it leaves the last sheave is referred to as "the fall."

Faying Surface. The surface between two adjoining parts.

Fidley. The casing from the engine room to the smokestack, and around the exhaust pipe on dry exhausts.

Flange. The part of a plate or shape that is at right angles to the remaining part.

Floor. The lower portion of a transverse frame, extending outward from the centerline to the bilge. In vessels with double bottoms, it is that portion of the frame that separates the inner and outer bottoms.

Fo'c's'le or **Forecastle.** A raised foredeck, or the living accommodations in the forward end of the vessel.

Forebody. That portion of the vessel forward of the maximum section.

Forefoot. That portion of the stem framing which connects the stem to the keel. It also denotes the forward, lower portion of the shell plating in that area.

Forward Perpendicular (FP). A line perpendicular to the baseline and intersecting the stem at the LWL. Some designers use the intersection of the stem at the deck for this line, to simplify measurement for some regulatory bodies.

Frame. A transverse member that makes up the skeleton of the vessel. Frames are stiffeners that hold the outside plating to a given shape and maintain the transverse shape of the hull.

Freeing Port. An opening in the bulwarks that allows the excess deck water to drain overboard at a faster rate than could be accommodated by scuppers.

Girder. A continuous fore-and-aft structural member supporting the deck beams.

Girth. The distance measured along any frame line from a given point of reference around the body of the vessel to the corresponding point on the opposite side.

Graving Piece. A shallow wood insert that corrects for a sap streak or an unsound knot in a plank.

Great Beam. A plate forming a rise in the deck from the main to the quarter deck, near the midlength of the hull. In sailing vessels, it is from 6 to 14 inches in height.

Gunwale. The intersection of the main deck and the shell plating.

Guy. A rope or cable used to steady an object in hoisting or lowering.

Gusset Plate. A triangular plate that connects members or braces.

Gypsy. A metal drum fitted outside the wildcats on a windlass or by itself, to exert a pull on rope. It may be fitted with "whelps," which are regularly spaced bands rising slightly above the drum. The inboard end of a gypsy is always larger than the outboard end, so that the rope cannot wind over itself at one end but is forced to slide outboard and free. Two to three turns are normally used. In spite of proper design, some surging is required.

Half-Breadths. The ordinates, perpendicular to both the vertical and longitudinal centerlines of the vessel, that divide the vessel into two symmetrical halves in plan view.

Hatch Beam. A portable beam across a hatch to support hatch boards (covers).

Hawsepipes. Cylindrical or elliptical pipes near the bow of a vessel, through which the anchor cable or chain runs. The lower edge is fitted with a heavy reinforcement called a "bolster." The diameter is never less than 10 times the nominal diameter of the chain.

Head Ledge. The forward and after thwartship plates that connect the side plates of the centerboard trunk. This term is used by older builders to denote the forward and after ends of a hatch coaming, but these are referred to as "end coamings" or just "coamings" by younger builders.

Heights. Ordinates that measure the outer form of a vessel vertically from a horizontal plane intersecting the baseline. The baseline may be a line at or below the lowest point of the hull, or it may be the DWL, in which case the heights are above or below that plane.

Hold Beams. Beams in the hold that have no plating or planking on them and are without camber. When present, they are usually located at each fifth frame.

Inboard. As a direction, toward the centerline. As a location, within the vessel's shell and below the weather deck.

Intercostal. The opposite of continuous; usually refers to framing members in separate parts that fit between frames, beams, etc.

Intermediate Frames. Frames that are between regular frames and are not fitted with floor plates. Also, frames that are added between regular frames in a sailing vessel when she is given an engine.

Joggle. To offset a plate or shape to avoid the use of backing strips or liners.

Keel. The principal fore-and-aft member of the vessel's frame. A *bar keel* is a vertical bar that also protrudes through the bottom. A *box keel* is an external keel, used mostly on sailing vessels, that is constructed with deep floors attached to a heavy bottom plate, the sides being plated with lighter material and the whole forming a watertight appendage to the hull. A *flat keel* is a plate or plates laid fore and aft along the centerline of the bottom, running from stem to stern and being reinforced on the inboard side by a vertical plate.

Keelson. A fore-and-aft member placed on either side of the centerline vertical keel plate, which it resembles.

Keel Blocks. Heavy blocks on which the keel rests during construction.

Knee. A plate that connects structural members; may be either horizontal (lodging), vertical (hanging), or diagonal (bracket). Knees are sometimes called gussets.

Knuckle. A sharp bend in a plate or shape.

Knuckled Plate. A plate bent to form a knuckle.

Lapped Plating. A plating joint wherein one part overlaps the other.

Laying Off. The development of the vessel's lines on the mold loft floor and the making of the templates therefrom. The marking of plates, shapes, and other parts for cutting, shearing, drilling, etc. Also known as "laying down."

Lightening Holes. Holes cut in floors, frames, web frames, longitudinals, etc. to reduce weight.

Limber Hole. A hole cut in a frame for the purpose of preventing water or oil from collecting, usually draining it to a central location known as a "sump."

Lines (Corrected). The Lines Plan of the vessel furnished by the designer, showing the lines as faired full-size on the mold loft floor using frame stations rather than mold stations; includes the corrected Table of Offsets. Designers who are also builders and loftsmen will usually design directly to frame stations to save time in lofting, and calculate the curves of form from a special office drawing. Unless a Lines Plan stipulates that the offsets have been corrected, it is assumed that each builder will lay them down on his loft floor.

Longitudinal. A continuous structural member running fore and aft, more or less parallel to the centerline of the vessel or to the sheer or baseline (when the longitudinal is located in the topside structure).

Margin Plate. The longitudinal plate that bounds a double bottom at the turn of the bilge. Its lower edge is always normal to the shell plating and its top edge is flanged to connect either to the hold ceiling or the double bottom plate.

Midship Section (Scantling Section). A drawing that indicates the general sizes and types of material used in the construction of the vessel.

Mold Loft. A floor used for laying down the full-sized lines of a vessel and for making the necessary templates for the vessel's structure.

Molds. Patterns made of thin boards that conform exactly to the shape of frames or other parts of the vessel, by the aid of which these structural items may be bent, cut, or fashioned to the required form.

Normal. Any perpendicular. Specifically, a line perpendicular to the line (or plane) that is tangent to a curve (or surface) at a given point.

Notch Effect. A phenomenon caused by square corners in a cut in any portion of a plate. If stressed enough, the plate will tear. This is not usually serious on vessels under 65 feet except in structures (such as foundations) subject to shock loading, and in engine beds, which are subject to torsion as well as vibration.

Offsets. The measurements used to determine accurately the molded form of the vessel. They are given in three tables: *heights*, which are referenced to a horizontal plane parallel to the DWL; *half-breadths*, which are parallel to the DWL; and *diagonals*, which are lines that intersect both the heights and half-breadths at an angle.

Oxter Plate. A bent shell plate that fits around the upper part of the sternpost; also called the tuck plate.

Panting. The flexing in and out of the shell plating as a vessel alternately rises and plunges into a sea.

Pinky. A New England type of fishing schooner that developed around 1800. It is a double-ended hull form with bulwarks extending aft into what is called a "pinked" stern. The actual transom is shaped much like that of a dory and is used as a crotch for the main boom. Within the pinked stern was usually fitted a "seat of ease." The lengths of the hulls ranged from about 30 to 60 feet, the more popular size being 40 to 50 feet. The common rig had three sails: jib, fore, and main. In the latter years of its development, a main gaff topsail and a fisherman staysail were sometimes used. Pinkies enjoyed an excellent reputation for seaworthiness and weatherliness. Some of the early vessels were still used commercially well into the beginning of the 20th century. The pinky has never ceased to be built for commercial use. In recent years it has also been built for yachting purposes.

Platen. A thick metal plate on which frames and metal parts are formed. The commercial type has round or square holes into which various fixtures such as clamps, dogs, billets, and squeezers are inserted to assist in the bending or holding down of metal parts. In small steel boatbuilding yards that are not engaged in the construction of round-bottom hulls, the platen may be temporarily made of several thicker plates that will later be used in the hull.

PSI. Pounds per square inch. This term is used when measuring pressure that may be exerted on a pipe or a structural member. It is also used in the calculation of strengths of materials.

Rabbet. The intersection of the outside of the planking and the side of the keel at the stem and sternpost. Its primary importance is in wooden shipbuilding.

Racking. Stretching or straining by force.

Rail (Railcap). The upper edge of the bulwarks.

Rat Hole. A half circle cut in a stiffener, beam, or frame in way of a seam or butt in plates to permit a continuous weld, drainage, or both.

Ribbands. Lengths of small timber (slats, battens) that are temporarily clamped to the frames to assist in alignment until a stringer, longitudinal, or other structural member of metal can be fitted.

Rider Plate. A flat horizontal plate attached to the centerline vertical keel.

RPM. Revolutions per minute.

Rudderpost (Rudder Stock). The vertical shaft or post through which the turning force of the steering gear is applied.

Scantlings. The dimensions of the various shapes, plates, girders, and other materials used in the construction of the vessel's structure.

Scantling Section. *See* Midship Section.

Scuppers. Small openings in the bulwarks at the deck edge or gunwale that carry off rainwater and small seas that may board.

Seam. A fore-and-aft joint in the shell plating.

Sheer. The longitudinal upward curvature of the deck, gunwale, and lines of a vessel when viewed from the side.

Shell Expansion Drawing. *See* Expanded Shell Drawing.

Snipe. A sharp bevel cut on the end of a stiffener or beam to provide the proper continuity of strength in the structure or to permit a continuous corner weld.

Soapstone. Steatite, a soft stone with a soapy feel. It is available in many sizes and shapes. Sticks of ⅛ inch by ½ inch by 6 inches are typical, and are used for marking steel. The marks are easily seen through protective goggles when cutting steel and can usually be seen through all but the darkest shades in welding helmets.

Sole. The bottom or lower surface of the accommodations, as in the cabin sole, which is in reality a partial deck. This term is used to avoid confusion with the word "deck."

Sole Beam. A beam that supports a cabin sole. May be of wood or metal.

Spanish Windlass. A simple device consisting of a loop of line into which is inserted a bar. When this bar is turned, it twists the slack out of the loop, thus constricting or squeezing whatever is placed within the loop.

Spurling Pipe. The pipe leading to the chain locker from the deck on which the anchor windlass is located. In small vessels, it leads from the main deck or, sometimes, from the fo'c's'le deck if one is fitted. The pipe is covered with a *spurling plate*, which is slotted to fit the chain link and prevents water from entering. Also known as the *chain pipe* and *cap plate*.

Stealer. A plate near the stem or stern that accepts the butts of a through and drop strake and continues these two on as one strake. Normally found only on round-bottom designs.

Sternpost (Stern Frame). The after end of the vessel's structure, supporting the rudder. The shell plating or deadwood ends here.

Stringer Plate. The plate(s) at the outboard edge of the deck, connected to the shell of the hull. It is used in small vessels when wooden decks are to be used, and is also known as the waterway plate.

Templates. Full-size wooden patterns that depict the shape of a plate, bulkhead, etc. and are used to lay out that shape on the metal prior to cutting.

Tons. A *short ton* is 2,000 pounds. A *long ton* is 2,240 pounds. A *metric ton* is 2,204.62 pounds. A *gross ton* is 100 cubic feet. A *net ton* is 100 cubic feet. A *British shipping ton* is 42 cubic feet. A *U.S. shipping ton* is 40 cubic feet. A *small vessels shipping ton* is 50 cubic feet. A *metric shipping ton* is 1 cubic meter, or 35.3145 cubic feet.

Tons, Deadweight. The total weight carried to the load waterline, over and above normal stores, crew weight, drinking water, permanent ballast, etc. It is not the difference between the light waterline and the load waterline, as temporary ballast is normally required to move a vessel in the light condition.

Trailboards. Ornamental boards on either side of the billet and extending aft to the bulwarks, sides of the vessel, or hawsepipes. When constructed of steel, they are an economical method of reinforcing the billet.

Transverse. At right angles to the fore-and-aft centerline.

Tuck Plate. *See* Oxter Plate.

Tumblehome. An upward, inboard slope of any structure, including the sides of the hull. Expressed as fractions of an inch per foot of height.

Warping Head. *See* Gypsy.

Wash Plate. A vertical fore-and-aft plate fitted in deep tanks, peaks, and bilges for lessening the movements of loose water in these compartments, which in turn decreases the free surface effect.

Waterline, Datum (DWL). That waterline from which a designer works for optimum performance of the vessel. In large vessels, it is customary to use the load waterline for the datum waterline.

Waterline, Light. Displacement in long tons of the vessel, complete with all equipment, outfit, and machinery aboard but excluding all cargo, fuel, water, stores, passengers, dunnage, and crew.

Waterline, Load (LWL). The displacement of a vessel loaded to her greatest allowable draft. In large vessels, this is determined by a regulatory body, which assigns a load line certificate. In small vessels, it is usually the maximum draft with which a master thinks he can make a safe passage.

Waterway. A gutter along the edge of the deck, used for drainage. This term is associated with vessels that have wooden decks.

Web Frame. A built-up frame that provides extra strength. It has an edge that is flanged or stiffened in another manner, and it is used in lieu of every third or fifth ordinary transverse frame.

Wildcat. A drum on the windlass, formed to fit the anchor chain.

INDEX